To Katy,

It was a pleasure♡ working with you and your Fellow ASTD'ers. I hope you can use this book in your professional development.

Dan White — Nov. '09

Coaching
Leaders

Guiding People
Who Guide Others

Daniel White

FOREWORD BY MARSHALL GOLDSMITH

JOSSEY-BASS
A Wiley Imprint
www.josseybass.com

Published by Jossey-Bass
A Wiley Imprint
989 Market Street, San Francisco, CA 94103-1741   www.josseybass.com

Jossey-Bass books and products are available through most bookstores. To contact
Jossey-Bass directly call our Customer Care Department within the U.S. at
800-956-7739, outside the U.S. at 317-572-3986, or fax 317-572-4002.

Jossey-Bass also publishes its books in a variety of electronic formats. Some content
that appears in print may not be available in electronic books.

Library of Congress Cataloging-in-Publication Data

White, Daniel, 1947-
Coaching leaders: guiding people who guide others / by Daniel White; foreword by
Marshall Goldsmith.—1st ed.
    p. cm.—(The Jossey-Bass business & management series)
  Includes bibliographical references and index.
  ISBN-13: 978-0-7879-7714-6
  ISBN-10: 0-7879-7714-4 (alk. paper)
  1. Employees—Coaching of. 2. Leadership. I. Title. II. Series.
  HF5549.5.C53W48 2006
  658.4'092—dc2   2005023902

Printed in the United States of America
FIRST EDITION
HB Printing   10 9 8 7 6 5 4 3 2 1

The Jossey-Bass
Business & Management Series

Contents

Foreword *by Marshall Goldsmith* vii

Preface xi

Acknowledgments xxi

The Author xxiii

Part One On Leaders and Leadership 1

Chapter 1 Why Coach Leaders? 3

Chapter 2 What Is Leadership? 11

Part Two The Practice of Coaching 59

Chapter 3 The Nature of Coaching 61

Chapter 4 The Process of Behavioral Change 75

Chapter 5 The Phases of Change 84

Chapter 6 Self-Knowledge 109

Chapter 7 Motives for Change 122

Chapter 8   Steps in the Coaching Process   130

Chapter 9   Coaching Skills and Techniques   154

Chapter 10 Coaching Perspectives   181

Chapter 11 Forces That Interfere with Growth   201

Chapter 12 The Timing of Learning and Change   217

Part Three Coaching Applications and Marketing   223

Chapter 13 Distinctive Approaches to Coaching   225

Chapter 14 Coaching Themes Familiar and Unique   240

Chapter 15 The Business of Coaching   281

               Bibliography   290

               Index of Cases   299

               Index   303

Foreword

A wise person learns from experience; a much wiser person learns from someone else's experience!

The profession of coaching leaders presents future coaches with a classic "Catch-22" dilemma: you can't get experience without a job and you can't get a job without experience.

When I was younger, I was fortunate enough to learn from some master teachers, such as Richard Beckhard, Peter Drucker, Paul Hersey, and Bob Tannenbaum. These teachers helped me by being kind enough to share their lifetimes of experience with a relative kid who knew very little and had a clear attitude problem!

Time passes—I am now considered a "pioneer" in the world of coaching leaders. What does "pioneer" mean? I am getting old! Another sure sign of getting old came when I recently received the Academy of Management's "Distinguished Speaker" award. At least I have not received the "Lifetime Achievement Award" (which means "near dead") or the dreaded "Memorial Award" (which means you are dead)!

The world of leadership coaching has been growing exponentially in the past few years. The huge majority of people who refer to themselves as "executive coaches" are relatively new to this field. It is hard to get a feel for coaching by reading textbooks. *Coaching Leaders* does a wonderful job of giving you, the reader, an ongoing series of real-world experiences through thoughtful case studies. Take your time to read—and hopefully, reread—these case studies. Imagine that you are the coach in each case. What are you feeling? What are you learning? How would you help this client?

Good advice needs to be based on sound theory. *Coaching Leaders* uses several well-established theoretical models as springboards that lead to application in cases. This approach helps make the translation between a *theory* of how behavioral change might happen—and a *practice* of coaching that can help behavioral change become a reality.

Coaching Leaders spends equal time on the two words of the title—"coaching" and "leaders." Some texts on coaching get so preoccupied with the *coaching* process that they seem to forget *why* the coaching is occurring—to help *leaders* become more effective! It is hard to help leaders become more effective without having a good grasp of what effective leadership is.

Ultimately coaching is about change. Over time leaders need to change and coaches need to change. We live in a world of rapidly increasing global competition. As Peter Drucker has said, "The leader of the past knew how to *tell*, the leader of the future will know how to *ask*." Leaders and coaches are going to have to continually ask, listen, and learn. Without continuous learning, both leaders and coaches can quickly become obsolete.

When Dan talks about the dangers of coaching—to the coach, he makes a profound point. He notes, "A risk for coaches is developing an inflated ego, thinking that *they* are too important." I could not agree more! The client I coached who had the greatest improvement—and made the greatest positive impact on others—was the client with whom I spent the *least* amount of time! After discussing his remarkable achievements, I laughed and asked, "You have gotten more out of my coaching process than anyone I have ever coached. Yet I spent the least amount of time with you. What should I learn from you?" He smiled and replied, "This process was never about your life. It was about my life and the lives of the great people on my team. It was not about the coach. It was about the people being coached!"

His next comment helped me understand why he is one of the greatest leaders that I have ever met. He modestly chuckled and said, "I have been given the honor of leading 40,000 people. Every day when I come to work I tell myself, 'This is not about *me*, it is all about *them*.'"

Coaching Leaders can do a great job of helping you learn to coach leaders. My final advice is simple. As you read the book, keep the focus on the clients—the leaders that you are serving—not on the coach, not on yourself.

September 2005

Marshall Goldsmith
Rancho Santa Fe, California

Preface

Coaching can be seen as a drama replete with possibility, danger, courage, success, and disappointment. In this drama, every client becomes a complex hero facing unique challenges. Every coach-client relationship presents real uncertainties and opportunities. Will clients be able to understand themselves and the situation well enough to accomplish real change? Will they be able to master new skills quickly enough to save the day? Will the coach be able to focus on the client's real needs rather than the coach's own assumptions?

WHY I WROTE THIS BOOK

As I've worked with clients on the interplay between their personalities and their leadership challenges, I have wanted to tell others (and not just my wife) about the interesting and moving things that my clients were doing. These stories need to be told.

To Share the Excitement

Initially, I wanted to share the human dramas that my clients and I were living. They were doing courageous and fascinating things in order to grow as leaders. They were challenging life-long habits and learning new ways of thinking and acting. To me these became more intriguing and exciting stories than those appearing on television.

To Tie the Cases to Theories

Another reason for writing was to explain how these clients changed by relating their developmental dramas to usable theories. Theories enable practitioners to read situations, label the forces at work, and consciously intervene. Interventions that are based on good theories are likely to be effective because they relate to the dynamics of the particular client and because they rely on approaches that have worked in hundreds of similar situations. Because the coaching profession is so new, little has been written to apply existing theories or generate new ones. This book attempts to give coaches the benefits of some good, pragmatic theories.

To Train Coaches

This book is meant to serve as a training tool for coaches. Most coaches I know followed a circuitous path into coaching. Unlike doctors, lawyers, and chemists, coaches cannot enter a postcollege program or embark on a predictable apprenticeship plan. My own path into coaching was fortuitous. My training, though relevant, was eclectic and haphazard. This book is intended to streamline the training for the next generation of coaches, as well as to share some of my insights and experiences with my peers.

Who Becomes a Coach?

Because coaching is growing rapidly, it is attracting many new and aspiring practitioners from several related professions. In particular, coaches tend to come from the ranks of four major fields, which include the following categories:

- Human resource (HR) and organization development (OD) professionals
- Career counselors
- Business executives
- Psychotherapists

Each professional group brings to the table both significant skills as well as knowledge gaps:

- HR and OD people often know about leadership, adult learning, organizational psychology, and organizational politics but may have limited experience with one-on-one counseling.
- Career counselors have counseling skills and understand organizational politics but may be missing a solid understanding of leadership.
- Executives know leadership and politics but may be light on counseling skills.
- Psychotherapists are strong at counseling but may lack an understanding of leadership and organizational life.

The goal of this book is to help all who come to coaching to round out their skill sets or at least provide a foundation for them to further pursue their development as leadership coaches.

How I Wrote the Book

By 1997, I was becoming a journeyman coach. I had worked successfully with more than twenty clients and was beginning to understand both what I did and didn't know about coaching leaders. I wanted to share what I was learning and create a forum for furthering this knowledge. Since there were no graduate courses in coaching at that time, I formed my own learning and teaching group, the Coaching Learning Group, through the New York Association of Career Management Professionals. This group met monthly, addressing one coaching topic at each session. In the first year, we explored such topics as coaching for emotional intelligence, coaching introverted leaders and narcissistic leaders, and delivering 360° feedback. In the program, I tried to combine theory with practice. Theories helped members label and make sense of what they observed, and cases enabled them practice their skills in a challenging yet safe setting. Over the years, the program grew in size and reputation. I suggested to Karen Metzger, my cofacilitator, that these theories and cases were so compelling that I wanted to write a book. She supported me in this idea and continued to act as an encouraging and guiding colleague throughout the writing process. Many of the chapters in the book are derived from my work with Karen and the Coaching Learning Group.

Theories and Research

Because of its newness, a comprehensive theoretical foundation for the profession has not fully evolved. Furthermore, little quantitative research has been conducted on coaching. To fill this gap, I looked to our more mature sister professions for relevant theories and research. One of the goals of this book is to bring some of this theoretical knowledge together in a single volume. These theories are first steps toward the creation of a body of knowledge about coaching. The theories and research in this book reflect my own interests and proclivities and document approaches that have worked for me. They are not intended to be comprehensive or to form or even approach a unified theory of coaching. They are meant as a start.

COACHING CASES

The book is built around cases. Cases are important because they demonstrate how each theory or concept can work in the real world. If a concept or theory holds any water, it should be able to be demonstrated and shown to be useful in practice. Cases contribute to learning by serving as vicarious experiences that readers can draw on when facing similar situations, like the cases used in law school and business school.

The cases are also meant to entertain and dramatize. I hope that as you read, you will develop some of the same fascination, respect, empathy, and even suspense that I felt while working with these clients. Each case is based on a real client. I tried to keep the details of the individuals and situations accurate while disguising their identity enough to protect their privacy.

MY BACKGROUND AND INFLUENCES

My path to coaching began in college, where as a curious and avid psychology student, I wanted to learn why people acted as they did. I was particularly fascinated with cognitive psychology because it explained how people developed the patterns of thinking, behavior, and emotion that form their unique personalities. (I later came to rely on cognitive psychology in my coaching approach because it provides a framework for learning about how clients organize and act on their experiences.) Another influence from my college years came from my involvement with the social movements and humanistic psychologies of the late 1960s. They fostered in me a sense of hope and possibility for creating a society that is fulfilling to its members. Facilitating fulfilling workplaces and helping people self-actualize remain among the motivators of my coaching work.

My early career plans of becoming a psychotherapist and psychology professor changed after two early experiences in the world of business. The first was a summer job in the HR department at Xerox Corporation, and the second was a job in the budding training and development consulting industry. In designing and teaching interpersonal skills training programs, I learned how to teach managers how to have conversations that led to success and at the same time became motivated by the mission of facilitating constructive behavioral and attitudinal change. Another influence came from the managers of my consulting firm. They were applied behavioral scientists who taught me the value and discipline of focusing on behaviors in the workplace. I gained an appreciation of the central importance of the impact of behavior at work, an orientation that has stayed with me throughout my career.

I eventually became first a director of training and later a director of organizational and executive development at Citibank, managing groups of up to forty people. I learned at first hand how to manage people and how to use interpersonal and political skills to operate in an organizational culture. I also learned the importance of contributing to business results, becoming a little less idealistic and a bit more realistic about what was possible in organizational life. I learned, mostly through trial and error, how to effect change in organizations.

In 1980, I experienced coaching for the first time while conducting follow-up sessions for participants in our management training programs. During one of these sessions, something interesting happened. A manager started explaining what he felt he could and could not do as a manager. At that moment, I recognized that leadership was tied more to the personality and self-concept of an individual than it was to any set of generic leadership skills. Leadership seemed more like marriage and less like changing spark plugs. Because I was still a training director, I filed that thought away and returned to my job of training a thousand people. But the thought stayed with me, and over the ensuing years, it guided my evolution into a leadership coach.

A few years later, I was offered an opportunity to provide career counseling to people about to be laid off by my company. Against the advice of my more ambitious friends, I took the assignment. The experience became one of the most important and fascinating stages in my career. For the next several years, I worked one on one, coaching outplaced managers. I studied career counseling and adult development in an innovative graduate program. I learned the art of individual coaching, including how to understand what made each client tick, when and how to ask questions, how to draw out the clients' hopes and fears, and how to help them take practical steps to fulfill their hopes and overcome their fears.

As a career counselor, I came to recognize the tremendous potential for change inherent in a coaching relationship. I imagined using this power not just to aid a single person's career but to help leaders build successful, fulfilling organizations. To prepare for this next challenge, I chose to learn more about the established theories of leadership, group behavior, and organizational change by completing a master's degree in organizational psychology. When it came time for my next challenge, the answer felt obvious. Executive coaching would combine the intensive and personal aspects of individual coaching with the skills and knowledge of developing leaders. I could help leaders become more effective and enable them to create organizations that were both successful and fulfilling places in which to work. I started telling people that I was an executive coach and within a year received my first paid coaching assignment.

Another influence on my coaching has been my experience as a psychotherapy client. Through my own therapy, I experienced several important changes in my thinking patterns, emotions, and behavior. Being a coach as well as a client, I observed and remembered the approaches that my therapist employed to help me change and grow. I also developed a grounded optimism in the ability of people to change. As I evolved as a coach, I came to recognize the practice and theories of psychotherapy as important sources of ideas for the nascent profession of coaching.

Coaching turned out to be as thrilling as I had expected. Along with the excitement of helping leaders change, coaching required every bit of skill, empathy, and insight I could muster. I recognized how very much one needed to know to become an excellent coach. I decided to pursue it for the rest of my working life.

My Own Growth as a Coach

Before I began coaching, I believed that my ideas and values were correct, and those of people who disagreed with me were incorrect. I would even argue with others in an attempt to prove that my way was right. Coaching taught me the futility and arrogance of that stance. I learned to respect and appreciate the people whose worldviews and mind-sets were radically different from my own.

Along with that relativistic view of my own ideas, I also learned the art of empathy. I tried to feel what clients might be feeling and to think what they might be thinking. Learning to empathize literally changed the way I related to everyone. It enabled me to understand clients more fully and for them to become more open to me. In the final analysis, empathic coaching has allowed me to become more connected to all people, not just my clients. My hope is that all who read this book may gain not only skills in coaching but also better relationships with everyone around them.

September 2005

Daniel White
New York, New York

Acknowledgments

This book was created with the help of others. First, there are several people who helped me learn the art and science of coaching. They include David Rottman of JPMorgan Chase, Sandy Bowers of Citibank, and the members of the Senior Coach Group: Steve Axelrod, Bruce Hammer, Peggy McMahon, Karen Metzger, Linda Smith, Bob Swanton, and Christine Wilson.

Next are the people who helped by believing in me and hiring me to coach leaders in their organizations or their client organizations. They are Amy Friedman and Yolanda Jackson of Partners in Human Resources International; Kym Goddu, Elizabeth Sorensen, Polly Kipp, Ellen Buller, and Sheila Cooper of Pfizer; Susan Preli of RR Donnelley; Gayle Irvin of the *New York Times;* Allison Weir of JetBlue Airways; Colleen Crooker of Columbia University; Gail Blanke of Lifedesigns; Bill Shulman of EmployeeROI; and Kay Monroe of Lundbeck.

I am especially grateful to Karen Metzger, my coleader in the New York Coaching Learning Group. Karen collaborated with me on developing the content for our learning group, much of which formed the foundation for the book. Karen also encouraged me to write the book as we observed the enthusiasm that the group members had toward the content.

A special acknowledgment goes to Neil Baldwin, who coached me through the proposal and book-writing process, allowing me to learn from his experience as a professional writer. Neil checked in every month or two to ask me about my progress, acting as a skilled mentor with a light yet persistent touch. Neil also introduced me to Deborah E. Wiley, who was very helpful in geting this book published.

Kathryn Kaplan and Lilian Abrams provided encouragement and suggestions for both the book and the proposal. Jane Hamingson, my private editor, helped me clean up the manuscript and keep it true to my intended message.

Neal Maillet, Mary Garrett, and Elizabeth Forsaith, editors at Jossey-Bass, helped move the book from idea to manuscript to finished product. Louise Sommers, my attorney, calmly and skillfully negotiated the contract with Jossey-Bass.

I am also grateful to my son, Ben White, who compiled the Bibliography and used his college study of self-psychology and philosophy to support some of the key ideas. And special thanks go to my wife, Maxine Davidowitz, who gave me space and emotional support and also put some of my ideas to the test in her leadership role in the publishing industry. She also helped keep my writing accessible.

The greatest thanks goes to the clients who let me into their professional lives and allowed me to work with them. Each worked hard on examining their leadership style and learning new skills. Their experiences enabled me to create the cases that are so vital to this book.

—D. W.

The Author

Daniel White began his career as a human resource intern at Xerox Corporation, where he learned about the importance of learning and leader-employee relationships. He next worked as a consultant at Praxis Corporation and then at his own firm, designing leadership and interpersonal skills training programs. In these roles, he deepened his knowledge of interpersonal behavior and became adept at teaching these skills in a way that resulted in behavior change. White then returned to the corporate world to serve first as a training director and later as director of executive and organization development at Citibank. In 1990, he founded his own consulting practice, Discovery Consulting, focusing on developing leaders through coaching and team learning. As a coach, he has worked with more than four hundred managers in a wide range of organizations in the financial, pharmaceutical, consulting, insurance, entertainment, education, and publishing industries.

White earned his bachelor of arts degree in psychology at the University of Rochester, his master of arts degree in organizational psychology at Columbia University, and a postgraduate certificate in adult career development at the City University of New York. He is co-chair of the New York Leadership Coaching Learning Group. His publications include

"Repairing Damaged Work Relationships," *Research-Technology Management*, May 2003; "Stimulating Innovative Thinking," *Research-Technology Management*, October 1996; and "Career Development of Scientists and Technologists," in *Special Challenges in Career Management: Counselor Perspectives*, ed. Alan J. Pickman (Erlbaum, 1997).

Part One

On Leaders and Leadership

Chapter 1

Why Coach Leaders?

Leaders have powerful impacts on their organizations. Their words and deeds affect all the people around them. The power implicit in their role causes people to look to them for direction. Everything they say becomes amplified as if spoken through a microphone. Their accomplishments as well as their missteps are exaggerated in the eyes of others.

Their actions affect people and the organization in a variety of ways. They provide vision and strategic direction, which can lead the organization down successful or ruinous paths. They maintain important relationships with members, which

To the Reader: Addressing the Personal Pronoun Problem
Since the 1970s, when our society embraced feminism, writers have grappled with the dilemma of the third-person pronoun. None of the choices are ideal. Using "he" is the old-fashioned, but sexist choice. Using "she" alone is progressive, but misleading and self-conscious. Using "he or she" or "he/she" is more gender neutral, but awkward. I have settled on "they" or "their" throughout the text to refer to individuals. This breaks the grammatical rule requiring consistency between singular and plural subjects. But it seems like the least of three evils. Although it may sound awkward at first, I expect the reader will become used to it.

can be inspiring, neutral, or demoralizing. They can stimulate learning and innovation or foster stagnant adherence to the status quo. They serve as moral exemplars who encourage either ethical or corrupt business practices. They serve as role models for many people who emulate their actions and attitudes, whatever they may be. Because of the tremendous impact inherent in leadership roles, investing in the development of leaders has a significant effect on an organization, its members, and the leaders themselves.

BENEFITS TO THE LEADER

Most leaders have risen to their position through some combination of managerial, interpersonal, and technical skills. As they moved up, they successfully adapted to each new role by studying their environment and applying their repertoire of skills. Yet there comes a point in the careers of most leaders when their repertoire and powers of observation don't quite fit their current challenge. Essentially, their old moves no longer work.

The old patterns don't work because the current challenge is significantly different from past challenges. Some typical situations calling for coaching include moving from a supervisory role to an executive role, specifically moving from managing doers to managing managers; moving into one's first management role; moving from a staff to a line position or vice versa; getting a new boss; needing to implement a new business strategy or a significant cultural change; managing during an organizational transition such as a merger or downsizing; and, more generally, whenever an old behavior pattern just isn't working in the current environment. Many leaders have tried to adapt to these new situations on their own, often with limited success, when they or their bosses recognize that they need additional help.

The goal of coaching is to accelerate the leader's development. In some situations, a leader may eventually develop appropriate new behaviors through a combination of self-observation and trial and error. However, that might take years, years that neither the leader nor the organization has to spare. Coaching speeds learning time, enabling leaders to make significant leaps in learning and behavior change in a matter of months rather than years.

Coaching also gives clients experience in self-development. As clients progress through the phases of change, they learn how to move from not recognizing the need for change (precontemplation)—to thinking about change (contemplation)—to preparation—to action—and to consolidation (see Chapter Five). They learn how to observe their behavior, recognize their impact, and reflect on and alter their underlying mental models. The self-development skills they learn through coaching become models for their continuing development throughout their careers.

Coaching brings hope and the possibility of change into people's lives. Clients recognize that significant change is possible. Engaging in personal change combats the routine and cynicism that can arise from working in a competitive, political workplace. It brings out the best in people by building a realistic optimism about what is possible.

Benefits to the Coach

Coaching can be a very rewarding profession. It appeals to people on at least four different fronts. First, it is a *people-oriented* profession that involves helping, teaching, and working closely with others. It is also an *investigative* profession, in which the coach learns, analyzes, and experiments. It is a *creative* profession that involves seeing new connections and inventing things to say and do that will facilitate change. And it is an *enterprising* profession, in which the coach leads, influences, and facilitates clients' success in the world of commerce.

In the people-oriented sphere, the coach helps individuals grow as human beings. Like other helping professions, coaching requires a close involvement with people. With each assignment, the coach embarks on an intimate adventure in which they explore their clients' outer and inner worlds related to work. The coach becomes immersed in the client's world, getting to know the client well enough to form opinions about how they might navigate their way through their present challenge. The coach becomes a close adviser and professional friend, at an appropriate professional distance. The coach helps clients make significant changes at important moments in their lives. For people who are energized by helping, coaching can be a thrilling profession.

Coaches also help make the world a better place in which to work. People spend almost half their waking hours working. If they work with a wise and skillful leader in a supportive environment, this time can be exciting and rewarding. If they work for a weak or abusive leader in a punishing environment, the workday can be frustrating and painful. A world full of competent leaders would make for both more fulfilling lives and a more flourishing economy.

Coaching *focuses on learning*. As a new profession, it has roots in several of the social sciences, including organizational, clinical, and cognitive-behavioral psychology; learning theory; organizational management; social anthropology; and even neuroscience. As an applied science, it offers opportunities to experiment, analyze, and learn. Coaches can draw on fitting theoretical foundations in developing their own approaches. Coaches also learn about their clients' business in order to form accurate impressions of the business drivers and organizational culture. Because coaching requires continual learning in a variety of disciplines, it is a very exciting profession for people who like to learn.

The goal of coaching as an enterprising profession is facilitating behavior change that leads to both the client's and the coach's success. The practice involves a good deal of influencing, both the coach influencing the client and the client influencing stakeholders. Coaching also focuses on results, both concrete behavioral change by the client and the client's discernible impact on stakeholders. Coaching can measure results to ascertain the client's degree of change. For people who are energized by influencing people and achieving visible results, coaching can be a very satisfying profession.

DANGERS OF COACHING—TO THE COACH

Facilitating change also has a dark side. Coaches dig into the problems that are challenging their clients, problems such as experiencing the frustration of misunderstandings with higher-ups or tensions with employees who are angry with them or the disappointment of not getting an expected promotion. The coach is close enough to empathize with the client's pain and removed enough to view it from a different perspective and to turn problems into opportunities. In many cases, the coach intensifies the client's pain but then helps the client use it to motivate change. The coach guides the client in working through the difficulty, and together they arrive at a new place. Crossing troubled waters can be both tense and interesting. Safely reaching the other shore can be exhilarating.

One risk for the coach is developing an inflated ego. The nature of the client's change can be so enormous that people may ascribe the success to the coach rather than the client. After all, the client acted one way before the coach arrived and is now acting very differently. Why, the coach must be a genius, right? Not at all—don't forget, it's the client who is doing the changing. Like an athletic coach, the leadership coach stays on the sidelines making observations and offering suggestions. The client is on the playing field, taking risks and managing the enterprise. If the coach develops a self-perception more as a savior than as a skillful facilitator, bad can things happen. The coach may become arrogant and focus less on the client or miss or undervalue the client's observations and ideas. Clients can be put off by the arrogance and withdraw or may begin to feel alone in their struggle. Worse, they can fall under the charismatic spell of the coach and continue working together out of a sense of obedience and admiration rather than out of their own belief in themselves. For these reasons, it is important for coaches to keep their egos in check and keep their engagements focused on their clients.

What Does It Take to Be a Good Coach?

First and foremost, good coaches are good listeners. They listen with a curiosity about how their clients operate. They are particularly skillful at tuning in to people—at understanding what they do well and what they avoid or do not do well. They also listen closely to understand their clients' thoughts, emotions, and values. They use this information to forge a collaborative partnership with clients, and to build on these characteristics to facilitate the clients' growth.

Coaches are both focused and flexible. They are able to create a working relationship that is both structured enough to maintain a focus on goals and flexible enough to invent new behaviors. They match their style and pace to their clients to achieve rapport. They explore seeming tangents that might hold clues to change. And they stay attuned to the goals, always ready to bring the conversation back to the objectives.

Coaches ask good questions, questions that explore the most salient topics. Their questions are rooted in an exploration of the client's psychology and a focus on the goals of the engagement. The resulting questions yield information that moves the client forward.

Coaches are also teachers, adult educators who expand the client's worldview by respectfully introducing new knowledge. They build a common language with the client by adapting

the psychology of leadership to this client and their environment. They can translate broad goals into specific behaviors and enlist the client in learning these behaviors. Like an actor, they can model new behaviors and rehearse until the client has mastered them.

Coaches know psychology. They use this knowledge to determine where and when to focus their efforts with each client—when to focus on behavior, when to focus on thinking, when to focus on emotion, and when to focus on impact. They can move smoothly from one aspect to another as they guide the client through behavior change.

Coaches are relationship builders. They earn trust and

credibility through their words and actions. They build rapport by tuning in to people and talking their language. They encourage opening up by modeling openness themselves. They inspire courage by addressing difficult topics with tact and sensitivity. They challenge just enough for clients to leave their comfort zone and enter the flow of self-development but not so much that they become overwhelmed or shut down. They use their relationship to foster their client's growth.

Coaches also understand leadership and organizational politics. They use this understanding to interpret the client's situation and to suggest development strategies. They are familiar with different approaches to managing people and leading organizations. They compare the client's actual practices to ideal ones in order to identify learning opportunities. They have mental models for team behavior and for managing up, and they use these models to seek to learning opportunities. They understand the cultural and political norms in the client's organization, especially the ways that people seek to influence and protect turf. They use this understanding to help clients become more effective leaders.

Chapter 2

What Is Leadership?

If they are to help leaders become more effective, coaches need to understand how leaders guide their organizations. Coaches formulate their own models of leadership and their own inventories of good leadership practices. At some point in this process, coaches compare what they learn about their clients to their own internalized leadership models. They use these models to assess their clients' talents, identify opportunities for improvement, and keep their coaching efforts focused on real organizational needs.

People have written and talked about leadership since the beginning of recorded history. Because of the central role that leaders play, researchers, business writers, consultants, and educators have invested a lot in understanding and teaching about

---

In this chapter, we introduce real case histories in which we use fictional character names to refer to the cases. Because these case names appear in numerous places throughout the book, we have numbered the instances of each case consecutively for the reader's reference and placed them in an Index of Cases at the back of the book for convenience.

leadership. In the 1970s, the "experts" defined *management* (a vogue word at that time) as "getting work done through others." Since then, the view of leadership has expanded in both scope and content. Researchers defined the broader role of leadership as something different from management. Abraham Zaleznik (1977) clarified the distinction by noting that managers focus on how things get done, while leaders give meaning to what is happening. Today's definition has evolved from a somewhat mechanical one to something more psychological: "the art of mobilizing others to want to struggle for shared aspirations" (Kouzes and Posner, 1995, p. 30).

If we subscribe to Kouzes and Posner's definition, the goal of leadership is to inspire and guide the efforts of others by creating an environment in which they can become motivated. From this perspective, the foundation of good leadership lies in understanding what motivates people and appealing to these motivators. Paul Lawrence and Nitin Nohria (2002), of the Harvard Business School, describe a unified theory of human motivation that has the potential to revolutionize the field of motivation and leadership. Their book, *Driven*, identifies four primary drives that motivate all human behavior:

1. The drive to *acquire*—to obtain objects and experiences, to successfully compete with others, to secure status
2. The drive to *bond*—to build trusting relationships, to belong to partnerships and groups
3. The drive to *learn*—to make sense of things, to satisfy our curiosity, to find consistent patterns that enable understanding of our environment and ourselves
4. The drive to *defend*—to protect our possessions, relationships, beliefs, and self-esteem

Lawrence and Nohria's four-drive theory uses knowledge and research in evolutionary biology, neuroscience, psychology, anthropology, linguistics, archaeology, sociology, and economics to demonstrate that most human activities are motivated by one or more of these drives, alone or in combination. Their theory is compelling because it unifies many other theories of human motivation and explains so much of human behavior. It will likely spawn much research and learning in the coming years.

The four-drive theory can be valuable to leaders because so much of their activity is focused on motivating and guiding others. For starters, the theory can explain common leadership practices. For example, when they set goals and set incentives for accomplishment, leaders are appealing to the acquisition drive. When they build teams or create an organizational identity, they are appealing to the bonding drive. When they sponsor research, training, and knowledge management, they are appealing to the learning drive. And when they justify their department's budget, get or give credit for an idea, protect market share, fight a hostile takeover, or invest in insurance, they are expressing the drive to defend.

Moreover, the four-drive theory can provide a framework that enables leaders to discover new practices. It can help them move beyond cookbook motivational approaches to develop practices that truly fit their style, values, and organizational context. Most traditional leadership training outlines a series of tasks that a leader needs to perform to be successful—skills such as creating a vision, setting goals, giving feedback, delegating, and empowerment. The more sophisticated models use research to identify the competencies critical to their job and then teach leaders to follow this set of success factors and to avoid the specified derailers. The trouble with these approaches is that the leadership activities they teach resemble "to do" lists and are not connected by any unifying theory. Therefore, leaders will be inclined to execute the list but have little guidance, besides their gut, to invent their own new practices.

When the best leaders do invent their own practices, they do so either by experimenting with new skills or by watching others. The four-drive theory can streamline this trial-and-error process by giving them a blueprint for a motivating environment. Using the theory, leaders can create structures, cultures, and conversations that enable people to fulfill their drives. They can help people maintain balance among their drives to prevent one drive from dominating the others. When facing challenging situations, leaders can examine the circumstances and ask and answer the two critical questions: "Which drive is most prominent here?" and "What action should I take to address the prominent drive?" Thus they can use the theory to become more creative and inspiring leaders.

DIMENSIONS OF LEADERSHIP

The following discussion is intended to serve two purposes. The first is to define a common language for what leaders do. The chart of leadership practices presented in Exhibit 2.1 can serve as a kind of checklist for leaders and coaches to use to identify strengths and development needs. (Many leadership assessment surveys ask people to rate leaders on practices such as these.) Indeed, almost all coaching clients choose to develop one or two of these practices. To help some of these concepts come alive, I describe how a client of mine went about developing a particular practice.

EXHIBIT 2.1 Leadership Practices

Leadership Practice	Drive It Fulfills
1. **Framing a vision, mission, and strategy.** Communicating a way of seeing the organization and its environment in a way that creates meaning for members; articulating them in a way that can be understood, believed in, and used to guide action; defining a pathway for achieving the vision that rallies support and guides action; regularly restating the mission to keep it in the forefront of everyone's mind.	Mission, vision, and strategy feed the acquisition drive by establishing superordinate goals. They also satisfy the bonding drive by articulating a common purpose for everyone in the organization.
2. **Developing and managing through systems.** Figuring out the necessary process to get things done; designing processes, workflows, procedures, and practices that allow managing at a distance; determining roles; defining timetables; coordinating activities; letting things manage themselves without intervening; seizing opportunities for synergy and integration; simplifying complex processes. Systems plan and organize activities by orchestrating multiple activities to accomplish a goal, breaking work down into process steps, developing schedules, anticipating and adjusting for problems and roadblocks, and arranging information in a useful manner.	Structures facilitate goal achievement and the acquisition drive. They also serve to organize communication and coordination among members, supporting the bonding drive.

(continued)

EXHIBIT 2.1   *(continued)*

Leadership Practice	Drive It Fulfills
3. Setting and agreeing on expectations, priorities, and direction. Setting and measuring performance against goals; enabling people to manage themselves to meet these expectations; establishing clear directions; measuring the right things; monitoring process, progress, and results; designing feedback loops into work.	Goals and priorities serve as the starting points and mile markers for acquisition, since they establish the targets on which material reward and status are based.
4. Delegating work and decisions. Distributing the workload appropriately; assigning work fairly in a well-planned and organized manner; matching tasks to the skills and interests of each person; trusting each person to apply his or her best efforts, skills, and judgment; letting people be responsible for and finish their work.	Delegating by matching people with tasks leads to high productivity and to task ownership, an aspect of the acquiring drive. It also satisfies the defending drive by providing a sense of security and of contribution, thereby enhancing self-esteem.
5. Communicating. Providing information that people need to do their jobs, make good decisions, and feel good about being a member of the team and the organization. Sharing information about activities and other knowledge. Serving as link between the department and the rest of the organization, sharing information about the larger environment, and passing information from the unit to the rest of the organization.	Communicating serves to bond members to the organization with information, enabling them to feel "in the loop." It also serves a learning function by providing new information.

Leadership Practice	Drive It Fulfills
6. **Influencing.** Gaining support for others' initiatives and ideas. Connecting with others and convincing them about the value of their ideas so that they can be acted on.	Influencing leads to power and therefore acquisition. It also builds mutually beneficial relationships and in that way feeds the bonding drive.
7. **Providing and seeking feedback.** Informing employees about how they are perceived so that they can start or continue doing things that are productive and well perceived and stop doing things that are ineffective or perceived negatively.	Knowing how their performance is perceived by others helps people learn and adapt. It also helps them succeed and therefore satisfy the acquisition drive.
8. **Recognizing and rewarding.** Observing and acknowledging people's performance; providing material and social rewards in relation to the value of their results.	Recognition and reward lie at the heart of the acquisition drive.
9. **Building teams.** Blending people into teams when needed; fostering open dialogue; creating strong morale and team spirit; creating a feeling of belonging on the team; defining success for the team.	Building teams creates the opportunity for people to bond and reinforce successful bonding.
10. **Developing people.** Using one's understanding of the abilities and interests of one's direct reports to provide opportunities for each of them to apply and expand these skills. Helping them further develop these skills and learn new ones. Providing challenging assignments; empowering people to make real decisions; holding frequent developmental discussions that include career goals; encouraging direct reports to accept developmental moves.	Developing people satisfies the learning drive.

(continued)

EXHIBIT 2.1 *(continued)*

Leadership Practice	Drive It Fulfills
11. **Building and maintaining relationships.** Understanding client and partner needs, negotiating expectations, jointly creating solutions and meeting needs.	Deepening work relationships is a bonding behavior that also facilitates goal achievement.
12. **Recruiting talent.** Finding and recognizing talent; hiring the best people from inside and outside the organization.	Bringing new talent into the organization is primarily a bonding behavior.
13. **Problem solving and decision making.** Making choices, finding new ways to accomplish goals, and deciding how and when to modify goals.	Solving problems facilitates goal achievement and acquisition.
14. **Using political savvy.** Maneuvering through complex political situations effectively and quietly. Anticipating where resistance may lie and planning accordingly. Being sensitive to how people and organizations function, viewing corporate politics as a necessary part of organizational life.	Political savvy satisfies both the bonding and acquisition drives.
15. **Creating meaning.** Helping people find relevance in their work by making connections between work and personal values.	Meaning helps people make sense of things, satisfying the learning need.

The second purpose of the chart is to link each leadership practice with the drive or drives that it satisfies. This fits the checklist into a unifying framework and describes the human purpose that each practice fulfills. By recognizing how each practice addresses its matching drives, we can better understand why the practice is important, as well as how each of the drives gets satisfied in the workplace. More important, we can see how an understanding of the drives can help leaders customize the practice or invent new ones to fit their unique situations.

1. Framing a Vision, Mission, and Strategy

One of the significant requirements of organizational life is that the members direct their individual actions toward organizational goals. In a sense, every member needs to lose some individuality, or at least channel their individuality in ways that benefit the organization. The role of the leader is to communicate the organization's goals and the behavioral requirements in a way that is both clear and compelling so that people want to channel their energies in the organizationally prescribed ways.

In most organizations, there is good deal of leeway for individuals to make many decisions about how to invest their energies. A role of the leader is to communicate a view of the organization and its environment that allows members to make wise investment decisions. Who are we? What is our purpose? Who are our customers? What do we do for them? What don't we do? What are our products or services? By answering these questions, the leader sets a direction for the organization that can be understood, believed in, and used to guide action.

Vision provides both direction and boundaries. A vision creates a framework within which people can act and make decisions. It describes the arenas in which the organization intends to participate. It also defines boundaries between parts of the organization to ensure that the actions and decisions of one group will be coordinated with the dozens of other decisions being made throughout the organization. Vision also determines the boundaries of where the organization doesn't want to go. Vision is usually stated broadly, leaving room for people to interpret it and innovate within its boundaries.

When leaders frame a vision, people can direct their efforts in useful and coordinated ways. When leaders neglect to frame a vision, people begin to act in noncoordinated ways. They may hold back on certain actions or decisions, not knowing what the organization wants. Without a vision, people perform their day-to-day work but yearn for long-term direction. They crave a framework within which they can feel connected and create something new.

A positive vision energizes the organization. It states a belief in a possible, desirable future that enables people to focus their efforts. It draws attention to that future. It encourages the best in the members and permits them to coordinate their efforts.

Vision Case: Ralph #1
Finding a Vision to Guide and Energize the Work

Leaders who express a positive vision can mobilize tremendous energy. When Ralph was promoted to director of production, he saw himself as a detail-oriented and tactical manager. His department and his company had just been through a difficult period of cost cutting and layoffs that had resulted in an every-man-for-himself climate. He recognized that his department needed a vision to reinvigorate and refocus itself, but he didn't know how to create this vision. He was skilled at identifying and solving problems and at finding flaws and fixing things but not at coming up with a big, strategic vision. He asked me for help in crafting and communicating a vision. I asked Ralph questions about the opportunities and challenges facing his department and about how he wanted to address them. Using his answers as a foundation, I helped Ralph formulate some statements about where he wanted the department to go and how he wanted its members to act. These statements formed the beginning of the department's vision. We then explored ways to communicate this initial vision to the members and involve them in fleshing it out and implementing it.

2. Developing and Managing Through Systems

Systems and structures enable organizations to assess progress and align activities. Structures like project plans, progress reviews, and budgets enable the coordination of work and the clarification of timetables and expectations. These structures often take the form of regular meetings and reports that permit departments to communicate progress, redefine priorities, and build a shared understanding of what is going on.

Structures provide two important benefits to an organization. First, they establish a path for follow-through so that the significant activities of organization can be synchronized. Second, they provide members with a predictable series of events that allow them to balance communication, production, and innovation. They reduce the number of emergencies by setting up pathways for organizational communication.

Every leader needs to determine how to use structure. In new organizations, leaders often need to create structures. In mature organizations, leaders often evaluate and revise the existing structures. Some managers love structures and live by them. Others eschew them and play by the seat of their pants. It can be particularly challenging when a leader who eschews structure is faced with an organization that needs to implement structures from scratch. This is the situation that Alice faced.

Managing Through Structures Case: Alice #1
Creating Structure

When Alice was promoted to senior executive of her biotechnology company, it had very few structures. The company had grown rapidly, from a start-up to a mid-sized firm. Because employees were so focused on the work, they never developed processes like goal setting or project reviews. The paucity of structure was causing misalignments among departments, project teams, and senior management. Although Alice liked the company's flexible, spontaneous culture, it was becoming evident that the lack of structure was hindering progress. Employees complained that there were too many last-minute demands to provide management with information, too much shifting of priorities, and too little coordination among project teams and functional departments.

It was clear to both Alice and me that creating structure should be part of her development plan. When we inventoried the existing structures, she first decided to redesign the senior management meetings to include project leaders. Her next choice was to revise the monthly and quarterly reports so that every department and project would communicate at similar levels of detail and would describe key events with similar language. At the same time, the parent company initiated new processes for goal setting and performance reviews. Though Alice appreciated the benefits of this new level of structure, she hesitated, not wanting to impose too much bureaucracy on her innovative, young company. After debating both sides for a while, she decided to initiate the new processes in a way that was as democratic as possible. She did this by fully explaining the rationale of each structure and involving employees in its design and implementation. Within a year, the company was operating smoothly and successfully; and everyone had come to accept and even appreciate the new structures.

3. Setting and Agreeing on Expectations, Priorities, and Direction

All jobs have expectations. Salespeople sell products, service people help customers, programmers write code, art directors design pages, and pharmaceutical scientists discover drugs. And every organization depends on people doing a certain amount of work, usually in a certain way. When people know what is expected of them, they can pretty much manage themselves to meet these expectations. Both the organization and the employees are happy. When expectations are unclear, people guess at the expectations and sometime guess incorrectly. When this happens, no one is happy.

Setting Expectations Case: Keith #1
Developing an Appropriate Writing Style
Keith was the director of creative services at an entertainment company. The performance of his staff ranged from excellent to mediocre. Two members of his team had a good understanding of the wishes of their clients and could create copy that appealed to their sensibilities.

Two other members did not get it. Their writing was too formal for the company's youth-oriented culture.

For months, Keith had been trying, with little success, to improve the writing of these two staff members. Most of his coaching efforts consisted of editing their copy, marking in red where they were off base, and then explaining how it could be better. In frustration, Keith asked me for help. He didn't want to fire the two writers, but they weren't improving fast enough to make real contributions. In discussing the situation, Keith realized that he wasn't sure if they were incapable of meeting the expectations or if they simply didn't understand the style that the company expected. It made sense for Keith to make a concerted effort to help them understand the expected style, for once they got it, it would become clear whether or not they could perform.

Setting expectations for creative jobs like copywriting is different from setting them for more measurable jobs like manufacturing or sales. Sales or manufacturing expectations are usually cast as measures of quality or quantity. Keith's challenge was to articulate the essence of a particular writing style. With me as his interviewer, Keith began to define what the expected style was and what it wasn't. He came up with descriptors like "irreverent," "sassy," "in-your-face," and "tongue-in-cheek" and showed the writers examples of the kind of copy he was looking for. He sat down with each writer, first explaining the style and then asking the writer to explain it back to him. Six weeks later, Keith reported that the expectations sessions had worked wonders. Both writers had improved significantly. They were taking up less of his time, and he no longer had to worry about putting them on a performance plan or terminating them.

Once upon a time, managers set priorities or methods for determining priorities. Employees used these priorities to guide their investment of time. In today's environment, priorities change frequently. Managers and employees need to reset priorities in response to rapidly changing conditions. The most skilled managers explain why the priorities have changed as well. This understanding enables employees eventually to notice conditions that require a change in priorities and bring them to the attention of their manager. In the most agile organizations, employees recognize these changes and adapt by resetting their own priorities. The manager's job involves training and coaching employees to notice changes and to support or alter recommendations about prioritization. They create two-way conversations about priorities so that everyone can be on the same page about what is most important.

4. Delegating Work and Decisions

All leaders delegate work to their staff. Some don't delegate enough, taking on too much for themselves and depriving their staff of meaningful developmental tasks. Delegating decisions represents an even higher form of delegation. Doing this takes a certain level of trust in the abilities and judgment of the staff member. This trust needs to be both bestowed and earned. A leader who delegates decision making needs to believe, usually from experience, that the staff member is capable and motivated to make good decisions.

For many years, management-training courses described two different leadership styles, which Douglas McGregor (1960) dubbed Theory X and Theory Y. Theory X management is based on the assumption that people have an inherent dislike for work and will avoid it if they can. They therefore avoid responsibility and must be controlled and threatened in order to do good work. Theory Y management is based on the assumption that work and responsibility are natural human functions. Under the right conditions, people will work hard, seek responsibility, use their ingenuity and become committed to the goals of the organization.

To most people, Theory Y is the more optimistic and more trusting approach and is more suitable for the current generation of employees.

The Theory Y leadership style is based on trust, trusting people to do good work and exercise good judgment. Good leaders express this belief by delegating tasks and decisions that are appropriate to each employee, then trusting them to "do the right thing." The manager's trust has several important benefits to the organization. It builds the self-confidence and decision-making skills of employees because they feel empowered to make and implement real decisions. It also increases motivation throughout the organization because employees feel more valued, respected, and important. And trust has the potential to improve the quality of decisions by expanding the number of people and perspectives contributing to the decision-making process.

Managing with trust is not as easy as it sounds. It involves several risks. One is the risk to the leader's ego, recognizing that employees may make decisions that differ from the ones the leader would make. Another is the risk to the organization, acknowledging that employees' decisions may have negative business impacts. A third is the political risk that senior management or other constituents will not agree with the employees' decisions.

Leaders, like most people, grant trust conditionally rather than universally. Trust needs to be earned. We need some evidence that we can trust a particular person with a particular task or decision. If the person has proved trustworthy in the past, we feel we can trust them in the present.

What makes it difficult for some leaders to trust their staff? One culprit is fear. Some people feel that the risk of trusting someone else is simply too great. They may feel the need to control what goes on in their department. A coach can help a fearful or control-oriented leader first by pointing out the pattern and labeling the fear or the desire for control. The coach can help the leader contemplate change by pointing out the negative consequences of the leader's behavior and working to develop an alternative. (I discuss alternative behaviors in Chapter Eight.)

Another reason for mistrust is egocentrism. Some people feel that only they are smart enough or experienced enough to make good decisions. Such leaders can seriously erode the self-esteem of their staff because they transmit the message that no one else is smart or talented enough to make good decisions. A coach can help these leaders become aware of their conceited attitudes and behaviors. Once leaders are aware of their pattern and its damaging effects, they can focus on learning to appreciate and respect the opinions of others.

A third cause of disempowerment may be rooted in the organization rather than the individual. Different organizational cultures engender different levels of trust. Some organizations have high-trust cultures in which employees at all levels are expected to use their knowledge and judgment to make many decisions. Other organizations have low-trust cultures in which managers make the decisions and few are delegated to employees. In low-trust cultures, managers learn to reflect the culture by delegating little authority. Or when they do delegate, they tend to second-guess or override employees' decisions.

Low-trust cultures present a special challenge to progressive leaders and their coaches. Although it might be beneficial for a leader to adopt a more trusting, empowering style, it can be dangerous for a leader to act counterculturally. The leader may need to walk a fine line between fitting in and leading in the most beneficial manner. It is also possible for the leader and coach to attempt to change the culture to be more empowering. This is, of course, a more ambitious project.

Delegating Case: Bill #1
Empowerment Through Delegation

Bill is an R&D director at a pharmaceutical company. He manages a department of scientists and clinical researchers, most with doctoral degrees. His organization is known for a top-down culture in which senior managers make the important decisions.

The R&D staff had become increasingly unhappy with their sense of powerlessness. One project manager stated, "We were hired for our competence and are now working at half that level." Many left the department because of this. Bill recognized the gravity of this situation and began working on delegating more decisions and increasing his trust in his staff.

Bill quickly recognized that in order to delegate more, he needed to trust his staff. He realized that his biggest challenge lay within himself. In theory, he believed that people should be challenged and responsible for their own decisions. But in practice, he was thwarting this wish by making most of the decisions. He began his change process by acknowledging his desire for things to be done his way and recognizing that fulfilling this wish was preventing the empowerment of his staff. By acknowledging his desire to control things, he was able to stay conscious of the tension between these two motives and allow the empowerment motive to prevail.

The second disempowering force was the corporate culture itself. Bill had learned his leadership style from his managers. Now he was trying to create a counterculture of high trust and empowerment within the larger organization. To protect himself and the department from an adverse reaction by the rest of the organization, he began working closely with his manager, looking for ways to buffer themselves from criticism and occasionally to stay under the radar of the larger organization.

5. Communicating

Communicating about the day-to-day events that affect the department is a small but important practice. In most organizations, there is a tremendous amount of activity and information, much of it having some impact on the department. The leader's job is to serve as link between the department and the rest of the organization, sharing information downward about the larger environment and passing up information from the unit to the rest of the organization. Each bit of information that a manager receives can seem trivial. But sharing it can enable employees to make more informed decisions and take more aligned action. Sharing information also makes employees feel more included. Communicating with one's team of peers is another important practice.

Communicating Case: Richard #1
You Gotta Keep 'Em in the Loop

Richard is the vice president of human resources for a large publishing company. When Richard was promoted into this role, he had little experience managing a department of this size. Initially, he focused most of his energies managing up by strengthening his relationships with the company's senior management team and by studying the company's HR data to formulate a strategy for his function. Only infrequently would he communicate the company's direction and his thinking to his staff. After several months of feeling out of the loop, his staff started grumbling to each other and complaining to him.

Richard recognized the effect of his tendency to work alone and keep things to himself. He decided to discipline himself to hold more frequent staff meetings, to copy his staff on most written communication, and to engage them in conversations about strategies and tactics. These efforts made a big difference in staff morale, to their joint decision making, and to their commitment to him.

6. Influencing

One of the biggest challenges that leaders face is influencing people. A leader's sphere of influence can include staff members, peers, senior executives, clients, and internal and external partners. Before they can influence anyone, leaders need to understand their own views and wishes. They can then articulate these views in messages that will be understood and believed. Since influence occurs in the context of relationships, they need to build relationships in which they understand the values and preferences of their colleagues. They can then tailor their messages to their audience. Because it takes time for people to change their views, leaders need to repeat their messages often enough so that others will remember them and act on them. As a human resource executive once said, "They become real leaders when they have followers."

Influence is a two-way street. Good leaders do not just exert influence but allow themselves to be influenced by others. When they embrace new ideas, not only does their thinking become more comprehensive, but they also become more successful influencers because people are more inclined to cooperate in an atmosphere of mutual influence and give-and-take. Leaders who shield themselves from outside ideas develop parochial views and dictatorial styles. They are viewed as autocrats and often find that they must resort to fear to get others to follow them. People need to trust their leader. The leader earns this trust by acting fairly and compassionately, by honoring commitments, and by telling the truth. Although these underpinnings of trust seem simple, they can be tricky to execute.

Influencing Case: Craig #1
Developing Influencing Skills

Craig is a research executive in a pharmaceutical company. He manages a department that identifies the company's future drug targets. As intuitive and creative scientists, Craig and his team generate new ideas that, they hope, the company will pursue. To make this happen, Craig needs to influence his peers, around the globe, about the soundness and promise of his ideas.

His former style of showing his excitement about new ideas with loud declarations and criticism of skeptical comments was not achieving the influence he needed. Through our coaching, Craig developed a new set of influence skills that made it easier for his peers to support him and to turn his ideas into realities.

7. Providing and Seeking Feedback

The term *feedback* gained popularity during the space race of the 1960s. NASA engineers would guide missiles by sending electronic messages to the missile's guidance system indicating whether it was on track toward its target or by how much it was off. The missile was programmed to use this feedback to correct its path. Feedback to people works in a similar manner. It tells them whether they are on or off track and what they need to do to reach their target.

Even though most leaders know about the value of feedback, useful feedback is still a scarce commodity in many organizations. Typically, managers will save the feedback conversation for the annual performance review, when tension is high and there is so much to communicate that a lot gets lost. The feedback often ends up being too little too late. As one might guess, giving more useful feedback is the developmental goal of many coaching clients.

When people don't get enough feedback, they become uncertain about how they are doing and about which path to follow. They make up their own assessments, which can be quite out of sync with what the organization expects of them and with what they need to do to succeed. Sometimes they work on developing new skills that are not needed by the organization.

One reason for the paucity of feedback is that it can be uncomfortable, for both the giver and the receiver. Giving negative feedback can be difficult because it involves talking about someone's mistakes or shortcomings and possibly hurting their feelings. The feedback giver may feel uncomfortable passing judgment on the other person's behavior and may be worried about the receiver's reaction. The receiver can feel criticized or even invalidated and can become defensive and angry or sad and depressed. Negative feedback can be so disturbing that it distracts or overwhelms the receiver, leaving them less motivated than before.

Positive feedback can also be uncomfortable. Compliments can be embarrassing to both giver and receiver, possibly because of the intimacy of the situation. Some people don't like being judged at all, even positively. And pats on the back may seem perfunctory, especially if the feedback is not specific, leaving the recipient in the dark about what to do to repeat or maintain successful performance. It is no wonder that some people dread both giving and receiving feedback.

People who are stingy with feedback fall into several patterns. First is the conflict avoider. Because the feedback contains some difficult information, the conflict avoider simply postpones the conversation or avoids it entirely. One client would postpone criticizing employees until it became pent-up inside of him. Then he would explode in anger and frustration.

In coaching feedback avoiders, it is helpful to focus on their emotion by acknowledging their discomfort with giving feedback. If their discomfort stays beneath their awareness, it can unconsciously prevent them from giving feedback. Asking them about the discomfort can bring it into consciousness and thus into the realm of self-management. Labeling the discomfort gives them the power to choose feedback over avoidance.

Some managers give only vague feedback. They might say "Great job" or "You really messed up" but provide no specifics.

These managers do take the time to notice and communicate about employee behavior. But because they do not give the specifics about the good or poor performance, receivers are left without knowing which behaviors to continue or which to change.

Vague feedback givers need to learn how to be specific. Practice in communicating specifics is an important part of their coaching. They need to learn how to observe the specific behaviors that enter into their evaluation. Then they need to describe these behaviors so that the employee can understand and act on the feedback. In coaching, we practice both of these steps until the client has mastered the skill of giving feedback.

As with all change, leaders need to become motivated to give better feedback before they will commit to addressing it. The motivation will need to be strong enough to counterbalance the potential discomfort of giving feedback. The compelling motivation can come from recognizing the benefits of feedback and difficulties that can result from lack of feedback. Once leaders understand how a shortage of feedback can harm others' performance and inadvertently encourage inappropriate behavior, they can take steps to alter their feedback behavior.

Feedback Case: Martha #1 Confronting Conflict

Martha is a smart, intuitive research manager who cares deeply about her staff and has built strong relationships with each of them. Yet some scientists had developed some bad habits, both in the lab and as team members. Martha was unwittingly permitting these counterproductive patterns by neglecting to confront them. She had a natural fear of causing discomfort.

When we talked about these habits in our coaching, Martha recognized that the only way her staff could change was for her to give specific feedback about their behavior and its consequences. Once she realized this, Martha's desire for a high-performing team overcame her fear of conflict. She began having these difficult conversations. Her staff responded quickly to the personal attention, the valuable information, and the challenge of changing their behavior. Each began changing with much less struggle than Martha had expected. They also became more committed to their work, respected Martha's insights, and grew to value these conversations with her.

Another form of feedback avoidance is the tendency to downplay the critical message. The manager will sugarcoat the feedback, keeping it vague enough that the recipient does not understand exactly which behaviors are at issue and their effect on others. The recipient may also miss the importance of changing the behavior. A coaching approach with vague feedback givers is to help them talk about specifics. Specific examples of the behavior and its impact are generally the most valuable. The coach can accelerate the client's learning through role playing to give them practice at providing specifics. In the role play, the client cites specific behavioral examples, and the coach listens to determine if the feedback is specific enough to take it to heart, recognize its importance, and initiate change. The coach then gives feedback on the feedback.

A third style of nonconstructive feedback giving is blurting it out. Some managers, in an attempt to get the difficult conversation over with, will bluntly state the criticism. It may come out as "Your presentation skills are terrible" or "You are disorganized" or "You don't think strategically." Feedback this blunt is often ineffective because it is seems so hostile. The receiver may feel sufficiently hurt or angry or unappreciated to become defensive rather than dealing constructively with the feedback.

Managers who deliver such blunt and painful feedback may lack emotional intelligence. A coach might help them craft more diplomatic messages without losing the specifics or sense of urgency. Helping these managers empathize with the receiver can enable them to deliver more effective feedback messages. Role-play practice is particularly valuable in helping them develop a more diplomatic and effective feedback style.

8. Recognizing and Rewarding

By most definitions, a manager "gets work done through others." This is why many managers wish, either publicly or silently, for a talented, highly motivated staff. But the law of averages implies that a majority of employees are averagely talented and averagely motivated. (Only in Garrison Keillor's Lake Wobegone are "all the children above average.") The challenge facing most managers is to get high performance from an essentially average group of people.

My clients, my staff, and my son have taught me a surprising lesson that runs counter to the popular wisdom on motivation. The lesson is that no one ever really motivates anyone else. People motivate themselves. Leaders can help people motivate themselves only by creating a potentially motivating environment, replete with a compelling mission, clear goals, regular feedback, fair rewards, ample information, and emotional support. However, it is the employees themselves who interpret the environment and determine their own level of motivation.

One way leaders help people motivate themselves is by recognizing and rewarding desired behavior. They can look for incidents where people performed well, such as a well-written report, a skillful handling of a customer, or a good decision. They can call attention to the behavior and cite how it contributes to the organization's success. People who are informed of the value of their contribution are apt to feel more important and appreciated and are likely to become more motivated. Soon they will internalize these recognition messages and engage in high-performing behaviors more frequently. Even autonomous, high-functioning people value authentic recognition for a job well done. Leaders who use the opposite approach and eschew recognition, contending that "no news is good news," are abdicating their responsibility and neglecting to satisfy an important human need.

There are two challenges in recognizing and rewarding. First, the leader needs to notice the good performance. Second, the leader needs to select the words or rewards that will appeal to each recipient. Because people's values differ, what is rewarding to one may be punishing to another. For example, one person might be thrilled being singled out for praise at a staff meeting, whereas another might be embarrassed by that kind of attention. Leaders need to learn each person's motivators and appeal to them at appropriate times.

Leaders also manage the reward and recognition system on an organizational scale. In distributing rewards across an organization, fairness and equity are the guiding principles. When people feel fairly compensated, they are free from the distraction of resentment and can focus on their work. Frederick Herzberg (1966) calls fair pay a "hygiene factor" because when such factors exist, people are motivated to a point, then take them for granted, like good lighting or clean bathrooms.

It is important to keep rewards in their place. Too much emphasis on financial rewards takes attention away from the more personal, values-based aspects of leadership and from people's intrinsic motivation coming from the work itself. Too much focus on financial rewards can turn the management-employee relationship into a purely economic enterprise. It can breed nickel-and-diming on both sides; it can cause people to leave for a few more dollars from a competitor and can actually reduce intrinsic motivation.

> **Rewarding and Recognizing Case: Dean #1**
> **Using Positive Motivation**
>
> Dean managed a large department in a union-based insurance organization. His staff performed largely repetitive work enrolling new members and updating their records. The supervisors in his department were concerned about the motivation level and turnover within the department. Dean and I recognized that the staff was probably feeling underrecognized and under-rewarded. He coached the supervisors to figure out what would be rewarding for each employee, then to talk with each employee about what they could do to earn these rewards. (Most were nonmonetary rewards such as special assignments or public recognition.) Within a few months, productivity and morale went up and turnover went down.

9. Building Teams

Most economic endeavors nowadays involve collaboration. Whether people work on a factory floor, at a bank, or in a research lab, successful results come from working together. Skillful leaders can form teams and keep them operating at high levels. They can facilitate communication, collaboration, and trust among the team's members and challenge the team when any of these begins to erode.

Team Work Case: Victor #1 Strategic Collaboration

Victor managed a large, profitable division of an information management company. The group was composed of three essentially separate business units. Victor recognized that the key to the division's future success lay in greater collaboration among these businesses. Together we addressed two team-building approaches. First, we worked on strengthening relationships and trust among the members of the leadership team and between Victor and the members. Second, we searched for and identified a new business strategy that called for significant collaboration between the business units and their leaders.

10. Developing People

Developing people is central to the long-term success of any organization, for two reasons. First, today's employees evolve into tomorrow's leaders, experts, and innovators. They are also aware of the history of the enterprise and use it to build the future. Without a group of talented, growing insiders, the organization will have to recruit many people from outside, who will need time to understand and work within the organization's culture.

Second, professional development is motivating and exciting to people. Most people like learning and trying new things. They like themselves better when they learn. Their confidence grows, along with their motivation. When employees recognize their leaders as vehicles for their own development, they give their best efforts, increase their satisfaction and self-confidence, and take full ownership of their jobs. They even develop loyalty and stay with organizations that create learning opportunities for them.

Developing people does have a cost. It takes time and competes with the day-to-day completion of tasks. In most organizations, there is real pressure to complete the day-to-day tasks. A majority of the conversations deal with the how, what, and when of critical tasks, because they are the source of a short-term payoff. Developing people is a longer-term deal. It takes both personal and organizational discipline to invest energy in the endeavor. In their early research on leadership, Robert Blake and Jane Mouton (1976) found that the most successful leaders balanced their efforts between concern for tasks and concern for people.

Developing People Case: Paul #1
Concentrate on the People, Not the Task

Paul is a marketing manager in a rapidly growing service company. He joined the company when it was a start-up. As the company grew, he moved into a management role. He learned his leadership style from his manager in the crucible of a start-up, with its intense focus on completing tasks quickly. As the company grew, it expanded its emphasis on developing people as the foundation of the corporate culture. Although Paul was regarded as a smart, productive contributor, he was gaining a reputation as a poor people manager.

This reputation came from his intense focus on completing tasks to the exclusion of developing people. In his conversations with his staff, he talked primarily about deliverables and deadlines. He gave feedback only about whether the task was on or off target, rarely addressing the skills or career growth of his people.

He realized that he focused on tasks to the exclusion of people, but he thought that was okay. When he received his 360° feedback report, he was surprised at the intensity of dissatisfaction with his leadership style. We talked about his management style and how he would manage differently if he were to focus on developing people. This helped him understand what would be involved if he decided to change. Like many people in the contemplation phase, he recognized that he was capable of becoming a developer of people and that it would take considerable effort.

I watched as he pondered the decision about becoming a developer of people. To help him with his decision, we explored the alternatives to making this change. One option was for him stay in his job and hope he could survive. Another was to move into an individual contributor role. A third was to leave the company and look for a job in an organization with less emphasis on developing people. Paul recognized that he was both ambitious enough to want to continue growing as a manager and loyal enough to want to stay with his company. He decided to stay and change.

Now we could work on skill building. We began by identifying several ways in which managers develop people. These included setting goals, observing performance, providing feedback, identifying developmental needs, assessing strengths and interests, and having career development conversations. Paul had recently completed a leadership training program and had mastered these skills in the classroom. I believed that his challenge would be his commitment.

Because we had only a three-hour coaching contract, I would not be available for much reinforcement. At my suggestion, Paul enlisted his staff to help him with his behavior change. He contracted with each member about the nature and frequency of development that he would provide. He agreed to ask for monthly feedback about his efforts.

When Paul and I had our follow-up meeting, he seemed to be on track and making real progress. He was meeting regularly with each staff member to talk about performance and learning. He selected and distributed assignments based with their fit with each person, rather than by who was most available. His staff noticed and appreciated his efforts and told him so in their monthly feedback conversations. Paul was on his way to becoming a well-rounded leader.

11. Building and Maintaining Relationships

Every work unit has clients. Some have external clients, who pay money for the service. Others have internal clients who use the service to make money for the company. Either way, high-performing departments understand and satisfy client needs. Skilled leaders help people develop constructive relationships with clients, focus on their needs, and ensure that those needs are understood, articulated, and met. Through these relationships leaders connect the needs of clients with the organization and the needs of its members.

Building and Maintaining Relationships Case: Tom #1 Collaborating with Clients

Tom managed a software development department in an investment bank. His department designed systems that enabled traders to make profitable trading decisions. Although their programs were technically excellent, their internal clients complained that they were hard to use and did not meet all of their needs. Through our coaching, Tom took this feedback seriously and took steps to make his department more client-oriented. He trained the technologists to build relationships and to ask questions that would enable them to understand client needs more fully. He devised a series of customer education courses to help clients use their programs more easily. And he conveyed curiosity, rather than arrogance, in his dealings with clients. After a year, his department developed a reputation as the most collaborative and responsive technology department in the company.

12. Recruiting Talent

Most leaders recognize that talented, motivated people are critical to their success. The most successful leaders hire only the best possible candidates into their organization. They recognize that they need to lobby for and justify the creation of new positions, then source candidates with a broad and selective net, interview to identify the skills and attitudes of every candidate, sell the best candidates on the organization, and make hiring decisions that place talented people in each position.

Recruiting Talent Case: Barry #1
Find and Hire the Right People
Barry manages the human resources department at a university. Although everyone in his department worked hard at servicing their customers (faculty, students, and staff), their reputation was only average. Through the coaching process and a process reengineering study, Barry recognized that he needed both more staff and more talented staff. He lobbied for and justified and gained approval for seven additional employees, including two managers. Even though he needed these

people quickly, he took the time to determine exactly what characteristics were required for each job, then screened and interviewed candidates against these traits. At the end of three months, he had hired seven exceptional employees. He invested the time in training them properly. Now the restructured department is perceived as one of the highest performing in the university.

13. Problem Solving and Decision Making

Leaders need to use their thinking, emotions, and intuition to make important decisions. Good decision makers take their personal values and ego needs into account and attempt to limit their biasing effect on decisions. Poor decision makers remain unaware of these personal biases and make decisions unaware of the impact of their distorting effects. One of the goals of coaching is to expand leaders' awareness of their own ego needs and emotional biases, enabling them to minimize self-deception and make better decisions.

Decision-Making Case: Peter #1 Thinking, Emotions, and Intuition—It Takes All Three

Peter is an experienced R&D manager. Shortly after his company acquired a small biotech company, he moved to the United States and assumed one of the leadership positions in the acquired company. In his first year, he made many changes that enabled his department to make significant contributions to the drug discovery effort. Yet he was hesitant to make personnel changes for fear of generating fear or animosity toward the acquiring company. By the middle of year two, he was growing increasingly frustrated with the performance of two of his managers. He had wanted to move them out of their central roles shortly after he arrived, but had postponed these decisions. He brought up his concerns early in our coaching process, essentially asking for permission to make these decisions. He recognized that he was being extremely cautious because he had never been involved in an acquisition before. When we discussed his rationale, he had essentially convinced himself that it was almost too late to make a decision. However, when he acted on his decisions, he explained his reasoning carefully and diplomatically to those involved. Everyone, including the two managers, understood. And all accepted his decision. Productivity and morale improved further following the decisions.

14. Using Political Savvy

Sometimes leaders recognize that doing what is right for their department is counter to the organizational culture. They need to decide how much they should follow their own ideas and values and how much they should follow the accepted organizational culture. If they stay too pure and do not accommodate to the culture, they will become pariahs and lose power, credibility, and resources. If they strive only to fit in and ignore their own views about what is best for the company, they are abdicating leadership and possibly contributing to the company's downfall. This is one of the most ambiguous and risky challenges that leaders face. Heifetz and Linsky (2002) explain that real leadership—the kind that surfaces conflict, challenges long-held beliefs, and demands new ways of doing things—causes pain.

Managerial Courage/Political Savvy Case: Bill #2
Risking Standing in the Culture

You will remember that Bill learned from his 360° feedback that empowerment was the number one concern of his staff. He realized that lack of empowerment was a likely cause of the turnover, malaise, and limited motivation among his staff. He decided to make empowerment his primary developmental goal. But he also recognized that his company did not practice empowerment. Managers at every level made the key decisions and second-guessed or reversed those made by their staff. He knew he would be bucking the managerial culture if he practiced a more empowering leadership style. He also knew that performance and turnover would not improve if he didn't.

In practicing empowerment, he would face not only his own resistance but resistance from his senior management and peers as well. Bill and I decided it was best to keep most of his empowerment efforts within his department and not to broadcast the practice throughout the larger organization. He hoped that his department would become visibly high performing and that his peers and seniors would wonder how they got that way.

There were times when his empowerment efforts did become more public. One of these came when his department was to present a key project to a group of senior product development and manufacturing managers. The expectation was that Bill would present and that Art, the project manager, would support him. Art asked Bill if he could present. Bill not only agreed that Art should present but decided to not even attend, thus reinforcing Art's leadership role on the project.

Both Bill and Art knew that this was unusual, that senior managers always took the lead in situations like these. But this was an important shift in enabling Art to become more visibly powerful. Bill helped Art prepare for the meeting and shared some of his insights about the group but ensured that the responsibility for its success or failure was clearly with Art.

When Bill's boss learned of this decision, he criticized Bill for exercising poor judgment and taking too much risk. Bill had prepared himself for this reaction and explained to his boss that this was precisely the type of empowerment that would turn his department around. He was never sure how much his boss bought into this rationale, but at least he stayed confident in his approach. Art handled the presentation very well and shortly after the meeting, the product and manufacturing managers began to approach Art, rather than Bill, for answers and advice. Art's status, satisfaction, and confidence in the organization rose. And Bill felt that he had become a better leader.

15. Creating Meaning

As we learn more about human nature and motivation, it is becoming clear that people want their work to provide personal meaning. When they can see the connection between their efforts and a larger purpose, their work becomes more important. People who find meaning in their work see themselves as contributing something that is important to society or to a larger purpose. For example, a retail banker sees himself as helping customers accumulate savings and purchase homes. A pharmaceutical scientist sees herself as working to cure disease. A magazine editor is providing advice and information to her readers. They are all motivated by the meaning they ascribe to their work.

Meaning is one of many motivators of human effort. Along with pay, recognition, affiliation, feedback, and a sense of accomplishment, meaning can provide the drive to work and create. Since meaning is a motivator, one role of a leader is to help people find meaning in their work. Before leaders can help others find meaning, however, they need to feel their own sense of meaning about their work.

Different people have different values and interpret the work they do in their own unique ways. To facilitate others' quest for meaning, the leader might have one-on-one conversations with staff members to learn what is meaningful to each of them. In these conversations, the leader can explore what is important to each person and how work contributes to this. They can talk about what each employee could do to continue to make the work meaningful and reopen this conversation from time to time.

Meaning is a powerful motivator because it is so conceptual and overarching. Because it is conceptual, it can be obscured or supplanted by day-to-day concerns. The leader can counteract this by reminding people from time to time about the meaningfulness of their work.

The quest for meaning at work has been linked to initiatives such as customer service quality, as well as to a strengthening of business ethics.

Creating Meaning Case: Carolyn #1
Healing Discord/Renewing Commitment

Carolyn manages a department that helps union members gain U.S. citizenship. She asked me to help her heal the discord that had developed within the department. Our team-building strategy involved two activities, addressing the specific causes of the discord and reinforcing the shared sense of meaning that the members felt toward their work. In the first session, the team members bravely and successfully addressed their specific interpersonal issues. This removed the negative component of the problem. But they also needed positive reinforcement to help them move forward. Next, we turned the team's attention toward articulating their compelling, shared mission. To a person, every member felt deeply motivated by helping members obtain citizenship. When they reminded themselves of the mission, they realized that it was so much more important than their differences that they were willing to adapt to each other and let go of some of their judgments of each other. Reminding themselves of this meaning also caused them to renew their commitment to work hard and smart in helping their members achieve this important goal.

ARENAS OF LEADERSHIP

One way to summarize the leader's job is to examine the content of the work and the working partners in these efforts. For example, in the realm of relationships, leaders may communicate upward with senior managers, sideways with peers, or downward with direct reports and junior staff members. Similarly, in the content of their work, they may focus upward on organizational strategy, mission, and vision; sideways on supply chain and interdepartmental interfaces, and downward within their unit on work processes (see Exhibit 2.2).

Clients and coaches can use this model to map key areas of client activity and to diagnose the leader's priorities, strengths, style, and areas needing development. Similarly, they can overlay the model on the current business situation and can use it to pinpoint areas where the organization is strong and where it has needs.

EXHIBIT 2.2 Content Focus of Leadership

Organizational Direction of Leadership	Working Partners	Leadership Focus
Upward	Direct manager, senior executives	Vision, mission, strategy
Sideways	Peers, clients	Interdepartmental interfaces, external supply chain
Downward	Direct reports, junior staff	Work processes, quality, efficiency

GENERIC SKILLS OR INDIVIDUAL STYLE?

The seventeen leadership practices describe general patterns of leadership behavior. An emerging leader faces two tasks in using these skills effectively. The first is recognizing the nature and importance of each skill. The second is using each skill in a way that is congruent with the leader's unique personality style. Leaders will have their own ways of delegating or recognizing or giving feedback. A coach can help a leader to develop a style for applying each skill.

Even though the leadership practices form the core of the leader's job, simply following them like a recipe will not necessarily lead to success. Effective leadership combines these competencies (skills and know-how) with authenticity (the leader's personality, character, and attitude). Although each skill might include a series of defined steps that can be taught in training programs or books, the skills need to be integrated with the leader's personality if they are to be truly effective. Without such integration, the practices will feel rote to the leader and come across as inauthentic or uncompelling to constituents. Herein lies an opportunity for coaching. A coach can help the client integrate the skills and tailor them to fit the client's personality and values. By combining skills and personal style, leaders feel more genuine, and constituents see them as sincere and trustworthy.

This approach is especially true when people get stuck. In these situations, leaders tend to apply more energy to their demonstrated competencies in order to control the situation, even though, in many cases, this is what got them into trouble in the first place. They think, "If I apply my skills more energetically, we will get the results we need." Often part of the solution involves enhancing authenticity. Leaders can help their organization adapt to a difficult environment by defining what is most important and meaningful to the organization and its people. When leaders authentically communicate the feelings that accompany the situation, they can change people's mindsets and lead them into new, more connected places.

THE DIALECTICS OF LEADERSHIP: JUDGMENT, NOT FORMULAS

Leadership involves making regular decisions about people and the enterprise. What makes leadership challenging is that different situations call for different practices. Leadership training programs describe a set of "best practices" that are effective in many situations. But these practices are best used situationally, rather than universally. In some situations, one practice will work well, whereas in other situations, another practice is the wise course of action. Attempting to apply them as a simple formula often does more harm than good. Because some leadership practices appear to contradict others, leaders need to regularly choose the practice that best suits each situation.

Zen Buddhists believe that the ideal way of living is to follow the golden mean, not by making middle-of-the-road choices but by regularly alternating between two extremes. One example could be alternating between generosity and self-preservation. For a leader, negotiating between opposites means understanding each situation, knowing the options available, and choosing the most appropriate; for example, sometimes delegating a decision and sometimes making it themselves. Leaders need to negotiate between these seemingly contradictory practices. Exhibit 2.3 describes some of them.

To navigate these seeming discrepancies, the leader needs to take a strategic perspective, recognize the subtle differences between situations, exhibit courage, and understand how each practice will interact within the organizational system. When leaders choose the most effective strategy, observers will credit them with good judgment. A developing leader will initially make these choices consciously, but over time, they gradually become more instinctive. In making these choices, it can be helpful for leaders to discuss the situations and the behavioral options in order to make the best choice. They can refine these skills with a coach and anticipate situations when each would be most appropriate.

EXHIBIT 2.3 The Dialectics of Leadership

Leadership Practice	Opposite Leadership Practice
Keeping an open mind to the ideas of others. Learning and adapting to a changing environment and benefiting from new ideas require an open, curious mind.	**Keeping focused on one's own views.** Holding on to certain ideas and persuading others to follow them enables the organization to align behind a clear and consistent leader.
Appreciating performance. People need to feel that their work is valuable and appreciated. Too much appreciation can lead to complacency.	**Challenging for higher performance**. People also benefit when a leader challenges them to stretch for higher levels of performance. Too much challenge can lead to burnout and feelings of incompetence.
Giving honest, authentic, and direct feedback. People need information about how their actions affect the organization's performance and how they are perceived by others. Without it, they may continue down unproductive paths.	**Avoiding being overly critical.** Too much constructive feedback can lower people's self-esteem to a point where they feel defeated. People need to maintain a level of self-esteem that keeps them confident and energized.
Sharing information completely and honestly. Open communication keeps people informed and enables them to feel involved.	**Filtering.** Editing or holding back destructive or distracting information protects people from unnecessary anxiety and distraction.
Being patient. Time enables people to do more thorough work, make more thoughtful decisions, and evolve new ideas.	**Driving for speed.** Quickly moving projects forward gets them to customers sooner. It can also motivate people and focus their energies on important projects.

(continued)

EXHIBIT 2.3 *(continued)*

Leadership Practice	Opposite Leadership Practice
Expressing feelings. Showing authentic emotions such as joy, anger, fear, or frustration expresses the leader's humanness and shows people how their actions affect the leader.	**Concealing feelings.** Too much expression of the leader's feelings can overwhelm or intimidate others. Withholding emotions or postponing their expression for appropriate moments creates a safer, less volatile work environment.
Promoting one's own business and career. Self-promotion builds leaders' reputations and expands their sphere of influence, enabling them to get more accomplished.	**Remaining humble.** Keeping leaders' egos in check strengthens their credibility with staff members.

Psychological Polarities of Leadership

Through coaching, clients develop greater awareness of themselves. They use this awareness to discover new ways of looking at themselves and eventually new ways of thinking, feeling, and acting. Because self-awareness is so central to this type of growth, I have looked to the field of self-psychology for ideas about how people experience themselves.

Heinz Kohut, the father of self-psychology (see Siegel, 1996), describes the self as the generally consistent way that we experience ourselves. It is a superordinate mental model that is made up of our awareness of our most noticeable personal states, such as happiness or sadness, confidence or insecurity, optimism or pessimism, as well as our personal energy level. According to Kohut, the self is built around two different poles. Pole 1 embodies our need for confirmation, approval, and acceptance. Ambitions for power and success emanate from this pole. Pole 2 embodies our experience in idealizing the world. It seeks out the goodness of certain people and things and looks for role models. It defines our values and ideals. Pole 1 seeks approval and power, and pole 2 seeks to create an ideal environment, the way things "should be."

These two poles can pull people in opposite directions, toward different goals and in different time frames. The ambition pole seeks recognition and power in the social realm, in the present or near term. The ideals pole seeks to fulfill personal values in an envisioned realm in a future time frame. People may experience this tension between the poles when they face a choice between an action that increases their power and an action that expresses their belief in a world they want to create.

Leaders face this tension more frequently than others both because of the combined effects of personalities and their role. They are so visible that both their expressions of ambition and idealism are closely watched and copied by their constituents. So whatever internal conflict they have is amplified in the eyes and actions of their observers.

Pole 1 pulls leaders toward personal ambition. Most got to where they are through a lot of personal drive. Their desire to achieve and their attraction to power and recognition probably motivated them to push for increasingly more powerful roles. They likely entered and won many competitions on their way up. They developed the skills and self-discipline necessary to achieve success. They built relationships and won the approval of their stakeholders.

Pole 2 pulls leaders toward developing a vision for their organization. In their leadership role, they need to set the vision for an idealized organization and "walk the talk" of actualizing it. They develop the vision by understanding the dynamics of their business, marketplace, and technological trends. As they articulate their vision, they spell out the changes needed to make it come true. These changes are likely to disturb some of the people who will be required to change their habits and leave their comfort zones.

Herein lies the tension. In driving for acceptance and power, leaders are seeking approval from as many people as possible. In articulating a bold vision, they are setting the strategic and cultural compass but upsetting some people in the process. On the one hand, they want to set direction, which will disturb people. On the other hand, they want to connect with people for mutual understanding and support. It can be a delicate balance combining these two forces into a single leadership style.

There is an adage that instructs leaders to stay ahead of their followers—but not too far ahead. This acknowledges the tension between power or approval and vision. If you stay too close, you are liked but not leading. If you get too far ahead, you will lose your followers. A coach can help the leader find a balance by clarifying and integrating these poles.

Navigating the Poles Case: Richard #2
Staying Connected

You will remember Richard, the VP of human resources at a publishing company. His analytical intelligence enabled him to understand the HR disciplines, grasp the strategic direction of his company, and determine how HR would need to change to contribute to the company's continued success. His friendly, straightforward style initially won him many supporters. Being a natural visionary, he spent much of his first year seeking a direction for HR by reading HR statistics, studying the HR operations manuals, and interpreting the corporate business strategy. Once he decided on this direction, he began to challenge his staff to reengineer their functions and change the way they operated. They rebelled. All but one, a director whom he had recently hired, felt that he had gone too far. Some even went to senior management asking that he be removed.

What had happened to our golden boy? His leadership style had become unbalanced with too much vision and not enough approval by a power base. He had spent several months in his office analyzing activities and trends. In doing that, he left his constituents behind. When he emerged with his new vision, his staff saw only the threat. He had weakened his connection with them to the point that his thinking was way ahead of theirs. He had not stayed connected with them or even kept them informed while he was creating his vision. So when he announced it, they were both in shock and disconnected.

Through our coaching, Richard came to understand what had happened. Over the next few months, he sought to reconnect with his staff and regain a climate of mutual understanding. He talked individually with his managers to understand their challenges and successes and gradually began a process of involving them in his new strategy. He replicated this process in his staff meetings until everyone supported the department strategy. Once he had rebuilt his base of support, he was able to forge ahead with a vision because he had the approval of his constituents.

Part Two

The Practice of Coaching

Chapter 3

The Nature of Coaching

To facilitate the leader's development, the leader and coach need to develop a unique relationship, one that is truly different. Their relationship needs to be both comfortable enough for the client to trust and understand the coach and different enough to interrupt the client's normal thinking patterns. Ideally, it has some features of a friendly, supportive business relationship—aspects such as using familiar language, focusing on goals, and occasional humor. These familiar aspects create a sense of comfort that enables the client to relax and explore behavior and motivation. The different aspects of the relationship create the opportunity to engage with someone who has a unique view of the world. The discussion can include tracing behaviors and their antecedents, asking about the client's underlying thinking, and sharing the coach's own emotional reactions to the client. These conversations are different enough to enable the client to reconceptualize his or her role in life and the business world and to explore new ways of behaving.

At its core, the coaching relationship is a collaboration in which the coach and client work together to guide the clients' growth as a leader. The coach works hard to understand the client and their environment. The coach listens carefully to the client's description of themselves and their actions, noting where they seem confident and where they seem uncertain. The coach attends to the client's descriptions of the people they work with, paying attention to the characteristics they notice and the evaluations they make. The coach listens to the client's descriptions of their work, noting what comes easily and what challenges them. Bit by bit, the coach gathers information about their client that the coaches can use to identify the client's opportunities to grow.

The information that the coach collects is not isolated bits but integrated pieces of a whole person. The coach listens for clues about the client's stylistic characteristics, for example, how formally or informally the client acts in relationships, how creatively or traditionally they approach their work, and dozens of other characteristics. The coach tries to fit the characteristics together to form a unified yet complex view of the person. While this is the primary focus of the assessment phase, in practice, the coach is always learning about the client and using these observations to stay connected to and appropriately challenge the client.

To stay connected, coaches use their evolving understanding of the client's style to deepen rapport. They use language that reflects the client's own language, preferences, and values. They observe the client's body language for emotion and energy. Then they use these observations as clues to the client's preferences and priorities. They ask about recent happenings at work and link their coaching to these events. All in all, coaches work hard to stay connected to their clients.

Rapport builds trust, which paves the way for challenge. From a position of trust, the coach can ask questions that explore the clients' thinking and actions. Through this examination, they hope to help the client broaden their perspective on the world, alter their thinking, and expand their repertoire of behavior.

The coaches' questions enable the client to examine their thinking on a level that is rarely possible in normal life. The questions themselves give the client an opportunity to look at the factual, intellectual, and values-based foundations of their own thoughts. What is special is the way the coach combines elements of curiosity, challenge, and support in their questions. The coach is genuinely interested in how the client thinks about themselves and their world. The coach also wants the client to examine their thinking and actions in a rigorous way to set the stage for change. Moreover, the coach recognizes that this sort of questioning may be entirely new to their client, so they are patient, supportive, and nonjudgmental. The coach makes sure they are facilitating the client's exploration of their thinking, rather than overlaying their own interpretations or advice. One colleague describes it as being brutally but sensitively honest.

These skills aside, the real goal of the coaching relationship is to enable the client to think in a new way. The coach's questions and statements are merely vehicles for stimulating these new thoughts. The coach can focus the client's thinking, model a type of introspection, and provide time for the client to imagine new ways of thinking and acting. But lasting change happens when the clients themselves create their own change.

What Does a Coach Really Do? The Goals and Roles of a Coach

Coaches play a variety of roles with their clients. Each role helps the client address a different challenge in the change process. In each role, the coach wears a different hat and uses different skills. The coach moves easily between roles, sustaining the rapport while doing what the client needs to maintain momentum.

- When acting as a mirror, the coach observes and listens intently to the client. The two fit their observations together, and the coach reflects them back to help the client understand their style, their environment, and their impact on others. The coach provides informed and constructive feedback. The coach can also share observations on the client's environment, helping expand or alter the client's views of their interpersonal and political world.

- As a creative guide, the coach helps clients explore and invent new behaviors that will enable the client to be more effective.

- As a teacher, the coach seizes learning opportunities and explains and demonstrates new behaviors, helping clients become consciously competent in these skills.

- As a thought partner, the coach helps clients discover their ideas and strategies by talking through opinions and intentions and batting around ideas about leadership strategies and practices.

- As a practice partner, the coach role-plays with clients to provide practice with new behaviors in a realistic yet safe setting.

- As a political consultant, the coach helps clients interpret the power and relationship dynamics in their organizations and plan how to exert influence within them.

Darwin discovered that the success of all living things depends on how well they adapt to their environment. A similar principle applies to coaching. Since there is no absolute set of leadership practices that will succeed in every organizational environment, the key to a leader's success, and therefore the goal of coaching, is adaptation.

The overall goal of leadership coaching is to help clients adapt successfully to their environment so they can produce tangible results. This is broader than some of the commonly held assumptions about the goals of coaching. Narrower goals, such as becoming a more skillful manager or advancing one's career, are noble but can limit the focus of the engagement or lead to cookie-cutter approaches to coaching and leadership.

The goal of adaptation enables the coach and client to focus on what will make the client most successful in their unique environment. By focusing on adaptation, coaches and clients can attend fully to a broad range of topics, including the clients' actions, beliefs, and perceptions about their environment, and the reactions of their constituents.

Adaptation also requires that clients learn. They investigate themselves and their environments. Client and coach study the accepted concepts and practices of leadership and customize them to fit this leader in this environment. They examine this culture and its people, determining which practices will work best for the leader. A goal of adaptation also enables clients to focus on interactions and relationships. It encourages them to stay pragmatic.

The goal of adaptation also encourages the client and coach to focus on the present. Environments change and people change. Most of us develop habits that once worked in a particular environment but weren't updated to fit a changed environment. The behaviors that were successful at one point in time or in one environment aren't necessarily successful in another time and place. This concept of adapting to a changed environment is especially important in today's rapidly changing economy.

Adaptation Case: Greg #1
Extending the Borders of His Tent

Greg was a successful information technology executive in a financial services company. He had developed a very effective management style based on several strengths. He understood the dynamics of systems development and used this knowledge to make cost-effective decisions about what programs to develop and how to develop them. He successfully met the needs of his internal clients. He developed and retained talented people.

A few years before we began our coaching work, a new chief executive from another industry took the helm of his company. The new leader focused on organizationwide synergies as a strategy for building profitability and innovation. As the organization evolved, Greg and his department continued to be seen as very productive and effective, though somewhat insular. They were seen as focusing entirely on their clients, their staff, and their technologies, and neglecting to share their knowledge and resources with sister departments.

The idea of investing energy outside of his immediate world was foreign to Greg. He saw such an investment as a waste of resources, which did not directly help his clients, his goals, or his department. Through coaching, Greg learned how others perceived him. Greg struggled with this perception at first, holding on to the view of the world he had developed ten years earlier. Gradually, he began to consider that the culture might be changing. For several months, he searched for evidence of the change and found it. This recognition enabled him to make a commitment to help his peers and their departments become as effective as his own.

ALL TALK, ALL ACTION

Since the invention of language, people have used words to interpret their world. Language is the way humans communicate with each other and with themselves. People from every culture use nouns to describe people and things; verbs to describe action and states of being, and adjectives or adverbs to describe qualities. Once they learn to speak, they use words to communicate among themselves as well as with others. When people think, they talk silently to themselves. They use words to describe to themselves their observations, ideas, and emotions. It makes sense, then, that if people change their internal language, they can change the way they think and eventually the way they act.

Talking can begin the process of changing thinking. Talking about one's thoughts enables others to understand them more clearly. Through talk, clients can test the validity of their thinking against the current reality. When clients express ideas, they often take raw, unverbalized thoughts and translate them into words. Once these have been verbalized, they can be examined. And as clients express their thoughts, they often find inconsistencies or outmoded assumptions that invite revision. Clients come to recognize thoughts formed in the past that do not mesh with the current environment, thus creating opportunities for updating.

Along with changing thinking, talking also plays an important role in preparing for behavior change. By talking through the planned change, the client anticipates the actual changes in behavior, thought, and emotion, as well as the setting and possible reactions of others. Talking about the change engages the imagination and enables the client to mentally rehearse a new mode. This practice frees the client from their bonds to the old actions and thoughts and begins building a path for the new ones.

Talking about new thoughts or points of view is a surprisingly effective way to give them a test drive. Talking brings these new experiences into the conscious light of day, where they can be examined and tested. The act of verbalizing alternative points of view provides an opportunity to try out these new views. Talking enables people to put a new thought or behavior at center stage in their mind and give it an audition. Rather than simply jumping into action, talking about an idea or a behavior enables clients to clarify their thinking and bring out new details. By responding to the coach's questions, clients can formulate a story about the topic. Their story enables them to make new neural connections between this topic and other thoughts, memories, and experiences. Telling the story helps people dredge up details that were previously overlooked. It allows them to see if a new behavior will make sense and to see how it matches up with their goals, values, and beliefs. Talking also enables people to explore their feelings about the new behavior. Talking allows people to become familiar enough with the new behavior to transform it from a vague idea into a possible reality.

Talking influences as well as clarifies. Talking with friends or colleagues can shape attitudes by introducing new words and concepts. Listening can literally alter people's reality. When people talk, they influence themselves in the same way that others influence them. When they talk about their thoughts, experiences, wishes, or fears, these structures migrate from the unconscious corners of the mind into conscious awareness. The more they talk about a topic, the more likely they are to understand it, embrace it, and act on it. This transformative potential of conversation gives coaching its power.

Once people begin to change, talking reinforces their thoughts and actions. In the preparation phase, the new thoughts, feelings, and behaviors are weak in comparison to the old, habitual patterns. By talking about the new patterns, people begin to reprogram themselves. They start hearing the new perspective more loudly than the old. The more they talk about it, the more the new pattern starts to make sense, and the more comfortable and attractive it becomes.

Note that the technique of neurolinguistic programming uses the making of connections between images, thoughts, and spoken words to build new neural pathways that lead to new behaviors.

How Talking Stimulates Change

Talking enables new points of view to gain power in three ways. The first is through logic. The conversation can explore the reasons why the new point of view makes sense. Clients can try out the new point of view in a variety of different scenarios to see if it holds true. They can compare it to their other beliefs and values to see if it is congruent. They will run the new point of view through a series of logical tests. If it passes, they begin to convince themselves that it is a correct way to view the world.

The second way is through emotional appeal. People usually explore alternative points of view because their existing view begins to seem incongruent or causes pain. By talking about a new point of view and its accompanying behaviors, clients can examine the emotional impact. They can test-drive the new thoughts and behaviors to see how they feel and to imagine how they will affect others. If the results seem pleasing, clients will like the new point of view more and more and gradually adopt it.

The third way is through simple repetition. The more people talk about a thought, the more it seeps into their minds. Especially when they say the new ideas and words out loud, they begin to form stronger neural connections. If they say something enough, they begin to believe it, especially if it has passed the tests of logical and emotional appeal.

Repeated talking about a nascent idea can make it strong. Religions use repetitive talk in the form of chanting and prayer to transform weak thoughts into stronger ones. When people prepare for behavioral change, the new thoughts, feelings, and behaviors are weak in comparison to the habitual patterns. By talking about these new patterns, they begin to reprogram themselves. They begin to hear the new view more loudly than the old. The more they talk about it, the more the new idea starts to make sense, and the more comfortable and attractive it becomes.

The process can also work in reverse. If people begin by changing their behavior, their related thoughts and feelings will usually change as well.

The connection between talking and the thinking-feeling-behaving axis is well supported by brain research. Neuroscientists tell us that our thoughts, feelings, sensations, and behaviors all exist as connections between nerve cells, or neurons. When we have a thought, feeling, or sensation, a whole series of neurons send electrochemical messages to one another. When one neuron activates, it sends an electrochemical signal to an adjacent neuron, which activates and sends a signal to other neurons, and so on. By firing sequentially, these neurons begin to form pathways in our brain. Each of our habitual thought patterns, whether adding a column of figures, deciding which shoes to wear, or being afraid of snakes, is triggered by a different neural pathway. Similarly, habitual feelings are initiated by their own neural pathway. Even memories, wishes, and beliefs all are grounded in their own separate pathways.

Neural pathways are created by continued use, the same way that a path is shaped by people walking repeatedly across a lawn. The more the path is used, the more distinct it becomes and the easier it is to use. The pathways we use frequently become like mental highways, well paved and easy to navigate. These well-traveled pathways underlie our habitual actions, our core skills, and our familiar emotions.

The new neural pathway is initiated when the person imagines, or wishes for, a new way of acting. Talking about the wished-for behavior forges the next stage in the construction of the pathway. Each vocalization of the wish makes the pathway deeper and more accessible. Talking about the anticipated change frequently deepens the pathway, eventually making it comfortable enough to use in their daily life. The process is similar to rehearsing a speech or practicing an athletic skill. Put simply, talking about a new behavior makes us more apt to use it.

When people articulate a wish, they phrase it using words that are familiar to them. Because they are familiar, these words fit into the existing frame of reference and activate neurons that form new connections with other neurons to form a new pathway. As the wish and its accompanying neural pathway are repeated through talk and then through practice, it becomes stronger, deeper, and more permanently wired in the mental repertoire.

Neuroscientists have actually watched neurons grow as a child learns a new behavior. What they observed, however, is that the new pathways grow only after repeated use. This is the reason that behavior change takes time and continuing effort. If the person stops the new behavior and new thinking after only a few weeks, the new pathway will never form, and therefore the new behavior pattern will disappear.

Talking reinforces the new pathways, even before they are tried out as behavior. In the early phases of change, the new thoughts, feelings, and behaviors are weak in comparison to the habitual patterns. By talking about these new patterns, clients can begin to reprogram their mental software. They begin to see the new view more vividly than the old. The more they talk about it, the more the new idea starts to make sense, and the more comfortable and attractive it becomes.

This finding has two implications for coaching. First, the client and coach should continue addressing and practicing the new behavior for several months. Second, the coach and client should limit themselves to one or two target behaviors, rather than five or six. The reason harks back to the biology that demonstrates that new pathways will form only with repetition.

How Coaching Conversations Facilitate Change

Sometimes semiconscious memories prevent a person from taking constructive action. These unintegrated experiences often exist in parts of the brain that remain outside of our conscious decision-making process. They can exert a kind of confusing control over people without their even realizing it. Only when these memories become integrated with the topic through a story can people gain control and take the action they desire.

Talking also serves as the first stage of experimentation. The act of verbalizing alternative points of view gives the person an opportunity to "try out" these new views. Similarly, talking about new behaviors provides an opportunity to try them out through words before trying them out through action.

Talking Case: Keith #2
Uncovering Embedded Assumptions

Several times during his first year as a manager, Keith had been told by his boss and others that he should act more like a leader during meetings. He acknowledged that this was the right thing to do and wanted to be successful as a manager. But something kept holding him back. When he was in meetings, he would clam up or whisper sarcastic comments to a colleague. Midway through our coaching process, he tried speaking out in a meeting and immediately found himself overwhelmed by powerful and confusing emotions. In our next session, we talked about this experience. As we explored it, he remembered a message that had been repeated by his father: "Good Japanese men are reserved in groups." When Keith realized that he had this message stored in his brain, his experience made sense to him. He gained the ability to say to himself, "I love my father, but I am different from him, living in a different time. I'm a different kind of 'good Japanese man.'" Keith's story brought new information into his awareness and gave him conscious control over a situation that had been controlling him for years. Talking about his experience enabled him to become aware of the forces that were acting on him and helped him gain more control over his actions.

Chapter 4

The Process of
Behavioral Change

*If you've ever been a person who somebody else was trying to "fix,"
you know what that feels like as a living system. Nobody wants to
be "fixed." In fact, nobody wants to be changed. People, regardless of
their culture or profession, have an immediate resistance to change.
But people are interested in developing and in growing; if you ask
them if they want to learn or grow, they will say yes. It's a completely different question than wanting to change. Understanding
the world of the living-growing phenomenon is the entryway for
people who are intuitively in tune with real change processes.*

—Peter Senge in an interview with
Richard Di Giorgio, December 2004

*Men are not troubled by things themselves but by their thoughts
about them.*

—Epictetus

*The greatest discovery of our generation is that human beings can
alter their lives by altering their attitudes of mind. As you think,
so shall you be.*

—William James

Mental Models and How They Influence Us

As each of us develops as a human being, we form our own ways of thinking, feeling, and acting. We form these patterns to fit the way we perceive the world. Cognitive psychologists call these patterns *mental models*. Peter Senge, in *The Fifth Discipline* (1990, p. 174), defines mental models as "deeply held internal images of how the world works." Our mental models consist of our own representation of a situation and our normal response to it. Some people refer to mental models as structures of interpretation. They govern the way we think, feel, and act. If we perceive danger, we enlist our mental model of fighting or fleeing. If we perceive someone needing help, we enlist models of either helping or walking away. We have mental models for thousands of different situations. All of our actions, thoughts, and feelings arise from our mental models of the world around us.

People begin building mental models in childhood. For example, one mental model defines how to avoid touching a hot stove. Another one defines how to act with a friend. As we mature, these mental models multiply and differentiate. The "how to act with a friend" mental model could expand to define how to act with a variety of people; including parents, teachers, babies, people we like, and people that scare us.

As we mature, some of our mental models become intertwined and complex. We naturally interconnect them, forming a kind of hierarchy. The mental models that represent our beliefs and values sit at the top of these hierarchies, where they can guide a lot of behavior. It is significant to note that different people can form very different mental models. In the "how to act with people," one person may develop an overarching belief that people should respect authority. Another person may form the belief that people should challenge authority. The mental models people devise make sense to them—and possibly only to them. Their model guides their actions accordingly.

We grow to depend on our mental models to guide us through life. We use them to provide efficient clues about how to interpret and act in a variety of situations. We rely on our array of mental models as useful, reliable routines that direct our thinking, feelings, and actions. Our models are part of us.

Our mental models make us efficient. They enable us to navigate through life without having to rethink every situation as if it were new. For example, when we go to start our car, our mental model for "starting the car" instructs us to put the key in the ignition and turn it, almost without thinking. Similarly, we may have mental models about how to run meetings or how to share information with clients or how to manage projects or how to pack a suitcase. By relying on our mental models, we don't need to take time to figure out what to do. Sometimes we are aware of the models we are using. At other times, they guide us, unconsciously, without our awareness. Whether conscious or unconscious, our mental models act as our operating system, directing how we think and how we act.

Changing Mental Models

Albert Einstein is said to have pointed out that we cannot solve problems using the same thinking that created them. Successful change involves both learning new models and unlearning old ones. When people change, they do both. They learn a new pattern of thinking and behaving and unlearn a familiar, old one. Let's examine exactly what happens when people swap an old pattern for a new one.

When we face a challenge, most of us rely on our tried-and-true skills and their underlying mental models to get us through. But these patterns themselves could be the source of the problem. Often they enabled some level of success or survival in a former environment. But they may not be successful in our present circumstance. Now we need a new way. We need to build alternative mental models that lead to more adaptive behaviors and results. The first step in this change is to understand our current models and related behaviors. Because mental models are so central to our way of life, changing even one of them can be difficult. Changing involves abandoning long-held ties to a comfortable pattern of thinking and behavior and then replacing it with a substitute mental model and new behavior. Changing a mental model involves changing a part of ourselves. As you might guess, this process can feel like the psychological equivalent of surgery. It can be uncomfortable, even painful.

The discomfort can express itself in different ways. Abandoning an old mental model and behavior causes feelings of loss similar to those associated with losing a friend, a job, or a pet. People miss these psychological friends and may long for their return. To maintain the change, people need to stay conscious, even vigilant, to ward off the temptation to return to these comfortable habits. They need to discipline themselves to remember to use the new and often unfamiliar mental model.

Abandoning a familiar mental model and adopting a new one can also cause feelings of incompetence. Often people feel lost without the support of their familiar patterns of thinking and acting. Similarly, trying out a new pattern can bring on a feeling of uncertainty. People can feel awkward and frustrated as they try out an unfamiliar pattern.

The sense of loss and insecurity can inhibit the change process. As clients experience these feelings, they may think, "This is not worth it," meaning the change feels too uncomfortable or too hard. This stubbornness of the old models and the frailty of the new ones cause the change process to take time. Clients progress by repeatedly practicing the new and challenging the old until their sense of loss for the old diminishes and their sense of competence with the new grows. They can stay motivated throughout the process by reminding themselves of the goals that are motivating the change.

Mental Models Case: Bob #1
Understanding and Changing Mental Models

Bob entered coaching at the request of the vice-president of his division. He is an intelligent, well-educated business analyst and statistician whose intolerance toward others' ideas has disrupted meetings and made him enemies.

Bob has been aware of this pattern for several years. He had been criticized for it and had been trying to control it for the past year. On his own, he was able to repress his annoyance and impatience, but the repressed emotions caused him to become red in the face and ominously silent. To his colleagues, his body language signaled almost as much danger as his tirades. Bob had been less than successful in his attempts to control his behavior without addressing his underlying mental models.

He entered the coaching process with both curiosity and reticence. He was curious to see if anything could help him change his problematic behavior. And he was reticent because he had tried to change it on his own and had failed. Our relationship began with him treating me in the same judgmental manner that he treated his colleagues.

Because Bob was aware of his behavior, my plan was to work with him on examining and modifying his mental models. I chose this cognitive-behavioral approach because Bob's efforts at working only on his behaviors had been unsuccessful. We began coaching by identifying his behavior and exploring his underlying thoughts and feelings. Bob talked, almost proudly, about not suffering fools gladly. He knew he was smart, insightful, and intolerant of others who didn't grasp things as quickly or as comprehensively as he did. He believed that it would be most efficient if people either saw things the way he did or simply followed his advice. This was his existing mental model.

In this model, his ability to apply sophisticated analytical concepts to marketing problems was his highest value. He devalued anecdotal knowledge and experiential wisdom, seeing them as crude and unsophisticated. He regarded people who didn't or couldn't embrace his analytical approaches as resistant or stupid. It is not hard to see why people didn't want him on their team, no matter how smart he was.

As he described his mental model to me, I was careful not to directly criticize it so early in our relationship. Instead, I asked questions and listened in an effort to draw out his model and identify some of its characteristics. Since he was such a logical person, I tried to keep his interest by using his language and keeping our conversation on a very rational plane. We began to analyze his models as if they were published philosophies, looking at their assumptions and implications. One particularly useful observation was that his model viewed his work environment as a completely rational place, rather than as a social and relationship-based environment. This concept of the social environment and its team-oriented culture was new to Bob, but it rang true. He became curious about it because it made sense and it explained some of his disappointing experiences better than his old model. I built on this idea by suggesting that his old model presumed that there was only one way to view a situation and that his was the only true view. To support this relativist approach, I shared some cognitive psychology with him. Bob enjoyed learning about this relativistic view. As an intellectual, he was drawn to this new knowledge.

Over three sessions, we analyzed his old mental model and revised it with this new perspective. Bob evaluated the new model we were building and showed his interest in it by asking questions and using it to explain events. Because his old mental model was so ingrained and drove so much of his behavior, it seemed impractical to ask him to simply abandon it. Instead, I asked him to become more aware of his old model by noticing when it appeared and the nature of the thoughts and feelings that it evoked. He recognized the triggers that sent him into his judgmental state. Now it was time to practice shifting from the old judgmental model to a new model based on curiosity about different perspectives and acknowledgment of the social environment. When he sensed the old judgmental state appearing, he would counter it by thinking about his new model. He took notes on this process of cognitive awareness, refining it to a five-step process that he could follow, even in the heat of a meeting.

Our next challenge was to learn new behaviors that would express the content of his new mental model. In retrospect, these were easier than changing the model itself. When he faced disagreement, instead of becoming critical and angry, he would ask how the other person arrived at the idea. He would also take the time to explain how he reached his conclusion, positioning it as a hypothesis rather than the absolute truth. We were both excited about the possibilities of his new mental models and behaviors. Within two months, his human resource manager called me raving about how much Bob had changed and what a delight he was to work with.

STEPS IN MODIFYING MENTAL MODELS

1. Envision a new behavior with more desirable consequences. For example, if empowerment is the goal, speak and act in ways that empower each person and that enable others to make decisions by gathering relevant information and making informed and wise judgments. People feel that they are learning and growing professionally. They feel more competent, more accomplished, and less dependent. More of them stay in the department and contribute at a higher level.

2. Contemplate a new mental model to support the new behavior. For example, abandon the old model and the belief that decisions that differ from one's own are wrong or dangerous. Adopt a model that embraces decision making by employees.

3. Reinforce the new mental model by connecting it to congruent beliefs and values. For example, reinforce beliefs

that project managers should make the decisions regarding their projects, that they are capable of good decisions, and that making decisions and studying the consequences will improve their judgment over time.

4. Identify situations in which to employ the new behavior and mental model. For example, when reviewing projects with project managers, ask them about the decisions they will need to make. Or when project managers ask what they should do, coach them to make their own decisions.

5. Develop reminders to block the old model and employ the new one. For example, when you find yourself about to say, "I think you should do this," stop and instead ask the employee, "What do you think you should do?"

6. Build an awareness of the old mental models underlying key behaviors.

7. Model, experiment, and practice new behaviors. Strategize and then rehearse what to do when an employee asks for a decision.

8. Build and implement a real-world plan. Schedule opportunities and behavioral trials, identify common trigger events, and become acutely aware in these situations. Rehearse; keep a journal to remember the situation, thoughts, emotions, and behavior; debrief to fully understand behavior and its antecedents; and reinforce the desired changes.

Chapter 5

The Phases of Change

To the client, the process of change can feel like a journey into unknown territory. Most clients have never taken this trip before and would benefit from a guide who could point out the milestones and landmarks and let them know how far they have come and how far they still have to go. A coach who understands the experience of behavior change can provide this road map.

James Prochaska, John Norcross, and Carlo Di Clemente (1994) discovered just such a road map. Through their ground-breaking research, they defined the step-by-step process that people experience during behavior change. Prochaska and his colleagues studied more than one thousand people who successfully changed habits such as smoking, drug use, and weight control. They discovered that their subjects went through a series of distinct, sequential phases that served as signposts along the way. (For simplicity, I have shortened Prochaska's six phases to five.)

1. *Precontemplation.* In the precontemplation phase, people are largely unaware of the need for change and have no intention of changing their behavior. If they are aware of problems, they tend to blame them on others, wishing that other people would change. If they have entered coaching or counseling, it was probably in response to pressure from others.

2. *Contemplation.* People in the contemplation phase are aware of a problem or opportunity and of their contribution to it. They are seriously considering grappling with the behaviors that contribute to this problem. They have not yet made a commitment to take action, usually because the effort seems overwhelming or because they feel positively about some aspect of their contributory behavior.

3. *Preparation.* People in the preparation phase intend to take action soon. They are planning new behaviors and anticipating trigger situations. They may have already made attempts to modify their behavior, but these attempts might have been sporadic and only partially effective. Possibly, they do not understand the situation well enough to take effective action.

4. *Action.* People in the action phase are taking concrete steps to change their behavior. The action may inspire both excitement and anxiety in them. If they have prepared well, they are emotionally and behaviorally ready for action.` Because action can bring up feelings of uncertainty, over-confidence, or yearnings to resume the old behavior, people typically benefit from a lot of support during this period.

5. *Maintenance and termination.* During this phase, people work to consolidate their gains, reinforce the new behaviors and attitudes, and prevent a relapse into the old

patterns. Once the new behaviors have become habits, people become more comfortable with them and can turn them into new habits. People then leave the self-conscious change process and prepare to part company with their coach. (Note: I have combined Prochaska's phases 5 and 6 into a single phase.)

There are many similarities between coaching clients and Prochaska's subjects. In my own informal observations of clients over ten years, all have passed through each of these phases on their way to long-term change. Both types of clients took some time in each phase before progressing to the next. Knowing the phases has helped me and other coaches understand where a particular client is today and where that client needs to go next.

When people successfully change a behavior pattern, they move sequentially through all the phases. Each phase provides both the learning and the motivation to propel them into the next phase. In each phase, they encounter a new level of awareness, a different level of commitment, and a distinct type of activity. After they spend time in one phase, people become comfortable with it and even impatient with it. This combination of confidence and impatience motivates them to move to the next phase. For example, in the contemplation phase, people become familiar enough with the benefits of the change that they are ready to prepare for action. In the preparing phase, they plan exactly how they will modify their actions and rehearse the new approach until they are ready to act. Individuals who haven't completed all the work in one phase may have to cycle back to that phase again in order to achieve genuine, lasting change. Skipping a phase often leads to a failed effort because of the important learning that takes place in each phase.

Understanding the phases of change helps the coach and client determine the agenda and pace of the coaching process. By understanding the client's experience within and between each phase, the coach can select a strategy that helps the client progress. The coach can look for clues to define the client's current phase. The coach can use these observations to either reinforce the clients' awareness of the current phase or to help the client move on to the next phase. The phases act like a road map for the coach and client, reminding them of where they are, where they've been, and where they need to go next.

PHASE 1: PRECONTEMPLATION

People who are pressured into coaching usually begin in precontemplation. They may begin by saying, "I don't know why I'm here." They are being honest when they say this. Even though they may feel that things are not going well, they have probably attributed the cause solely to someone or something else. They cannot see how they have contributed to the situation—and they certainly cannot see how they can change the situation.

People in precontemplation do not see any reason to change because they are not aware of their situation or their role in creating it. If they are aware, they may blame any dissatisfaction on others and have little appreciation of their own impact on others. Yet it is this impact that causes dissatisfaction.

Their lack of awareness can induce a fear of becoming more cognizant of their own contribution to their situation. This fear can manifest itself in bravado, anger, defensiveness, or avoidance of the subject, all of which protect and prevent them from examining the situation from another perspective. It is the coach's role to help the client break this cycle.

The coach's first goal is to build sufficient trust that the client will want to engage with them. One of the best ways to build trust is to ask the client to describe their perspective on the situation and then to listen and understand their perspective. Even though it represents only part of the picture, at this stage, trust is more important than getting the whole story.

As trust grows, the client may become ready to seek information that will expand their perspective on the situation, information that could stimulate a desire to change. The information that will motivate the client to progress to contemplation generally comes from others. The coach can help clients get information about others' perspective on the current situation and the ways that the clients have contributed to it. When taken seriously, this information can lead to contemplation.

To get the most comprehensive view of the situation, coaches usually gather information from multiple perspectives; for example, 360° feedback includes input from people above, below, and at a peer level to the client. The feedback will include valuable information about these employees' views of the client's behaviors and how they are affected by these behaviors. The coach acts as an intermediary, gathering information from the constituents and sharing it with the client.

Feedback can be a surprise to a precontemplator. Often people are not aware of how they are affecting others. Since most of us think of ourselves as competent and well meaning, learning of our negative impacts on others can be eye opening. This recognition is often the catalyst that moves a client into contemplation.

Feedback can create a discrepancy between how people see themselves and how others see them. This discrepancy can become a powerful motivator of change. Most people strive to like themselves and to act in congruence with their values. If feedback indicates that they are acting counter to their values, a discrepancy results. The dissatisfaction from the discrepancy can motivate a desire to change.

Precontemplation Case: Bill #3
Getting Bad News

Bill knew that some people had resigned from his department over the past year. He and his manager, Ken, weren't happy about the turnover, but they weren't concerned because they believed that these employees had left for higher-paying jobs in a more profitable division of the company. Bill and Ken didn't perceive a problem until Nora, their human resource manager, shared two pieces of information with them. The eight people who resigned represented nearly 30 percent of the department, about triple the industry average. Their comments in their exit interviews revealed that mistrust and a resentment of micromanagement were their main reasons for leaving. These two bits of information moved Bill from the precontemplation stance of "everything is basically OK" to a contemplation posture that "something is wrong and I want to change it."

Precontemplation Case: Michael #1
Turning Up the Heat

In some situations, the coach needs to be the bearer of the motivating information because the organization has either not provided enough information to motivate contemplation or not expressed it in such a way that the client could absorb it.

Michael is a marketing executive in a consulting firm. His manager, the president, suggested that Michael work with a coach to help him develop as a manager. When I first met him, Michael was aware of some issues with junior consultants but attributed them to demanding clients and the last-minute nature of the consulting business. He expected that we would work on polishing his "executive presence" to prepare him for more senior positions.

When I gathered feedback from his constituents, I learned that many consultants disliked working with Michael because of his last-minute work style and disrespectful relating style. Even when I shared this feedback with Michael, he persisted in blaming the consultants, the clients, and the industry culture. I worried that he would stay stuck in precontemplation and never move to contemplation.

Since Michael wasn't motivated to change, I decided to share some information that would turn up the heat on him. I explained that senior management thought that his behavior was so disruptive that if he didn't change, he would certainly not get promoted and perhaps even be demoted or let go. These words caught his attention. He was shaken and quickly began asking me how he could go about changing his behavior. He began to move from precontemplation to contemplating his change.

Defenses Against Contemplation

Accepting that some of our behaviors are maladaptive is a difficult process. Most people have some way to filter out challenges. Some people's filters are so strong that they let nothing through. Even when faced with compelling, realistic information, people can resist contemplation. When people become aware of a problematic situation, there are three common defenses they may use to avoid the hard work of contemplating change: denial, blame, and shame.

Denial. The easiest way to remove the discomfort of difficult information is to deny its truth. People can decide that the sources of the information are biased, irrelevant, or simply wrong. Technically trained people may deny the information by claiming that the statistical sample is not large enough to be valid.

Blame. Some clients blind themselves to their own contribution by blaming others. They can believe that the source people are immature, overly sensitive, inappreciative, or ignorant of the business realities. Others may protect themselves by believing that people are conspiring against them. People invent many clever ways to protect themselves from taking responsibility and therefore from the possibility of change.

Shame. Feeling ashamed is another way people avoid examining their own behavior. Shame is a type of self-blame. It is a big, broad, blurry emotion that obfuscates a realistic perspective about interactions between people. Shame prevents examination of one's behavior and its impacts by attributing the blame to one's whole character or being. It causes a crisis that assumes there is something seriously wrong with one's entire character and does not look for finer distinctions between adaptive and nonadaptive behaviors. It is so global, so demoralizing, and so obfuscating that it prohibits change. Shame is just as strong a defense as blame.

Acceptance. The coaches' goal is to help clients move beyond shame and blame to detailed self-knowledge. One way to soften defenses is to make the information less threatening. If clients perceive the requests for change as an attack on their whole personality, they will resist intensely. Sometimes coaches can help clients accept the information by framing its focus on a few specific behaviors, so as to counteract a focus on their whole being. This understanding may enable the clients to move toward contemplation.

Another approach is to point out blame or shame as behaviors, things the clients are doing to protect themselves from threatening information. If the clients see their defenses as choices rather than absolute realities, they can enter the path to change. This is often a big leap that may take weeks or even months. But if the clients recognize their defense as a choice that is hurting them, they will become ready to examine real and current data about their actions and how these contribute or detract from their success.

Phase 2: Contemplation

When coaching is imposed on clients, they usually begin in pre-contemplation because the awareness has come from someone else. But coaching isn't always imposed on the client. Sometimes the client initiates it. Their motivator may be an unfulfilled wish or a business challenge, as well as a problem.

The change process actually begins in the contemplation phase. It starts when a person seriously considers the possibility of changing behaviors. When people make this decision, they undergo a significant shift in attitude, from "I want to stay the way I am" to "There is something I want to change that will improve my life." The movement to contemplation involves a personal decision to develop a new part of themselves and let go of an old one.

Some people begin contemplation by themselves. Clients who request coaching have usually been contemplating an issue for a while. They seek a coach because they are looking for help in making the change. They believe that their work life would improve if they acted differently, and they want guidance in focusing and implementing their efforts.

Other clients need coaching and feedback to arrive at contemplation. Clients who have been urged into coaching are generally precontemplators who need help moving to contemplation. Though they may not be happy with their situation, their view of the situation it is often rigid and somewhat blameful. They rarely see their own contribution to the situation.

For these people, feedback from others represents a way out of their bind. Information about how others see them can alter their view of their situation and their own role in shaping it. Clients may struggle with this feedback. But with patience and firm, supportive coaching, they come to recognize its message and the benefits of change.

This new perspective involves a new awareness. For the first time, they know they are doing something that is negatively affecting their work lives. This thought represents a significant shift in how they look at themselves and their world. The decision to change may come from an incongruence between their values and their behavior. For example, they value respect for others but recognize that they are treating others disrespectfully. Or their decision might come from the recognition that they are preventing themselves from achieving an important goal, as when individuals who hope to get promoted come to realize that they are doing things to hold themselves back.

Accompanying this sometimes-painful awareness is hope— the belief that there may be a path to greater satisfaction and success. People contemplating change begin to see the possibility of overcoming hurdles in order to create something different. Coaches can help by reinforcing this optimism. As people who are experienced in dealing with change, they can confirm the potential for improvement. This optimism will be important in countering the defeatism that also exists.

It is common for people contemplating change to feel the mixed emotions of both attraction and fear. They are attracted by the potential to grow and improve their life. Yet they are reluctant to make the requisite effort because they know that the old behaviors are deeply entrenched. These old behaviors, thoughts, and feelings have been part of them for a long time. This knowledge causes both hope and skepticism.

Before reaching this point, contemplators are not ready to change. Perhaps they were not aware of their behavior or the consequences were not as pronounced as they are now. They may have been less aware of the negative impacts or better able to tolerate them. Maybe they felt that change was too difficult and that it was simply not worth the effort. Most clients in contemplation have been aware of the behaviors and their consequences for some time. Now, for a variety of reasons, they have become frustrated with the old pattern. Contemplators often talk about finally being ready to address issues that have troubled them for a while.

The most meaningful changes shake clients deeply. Like spiritual revelations, clients recognize this point in time as an opportunity to make a meaningful transformation. The coaching process becomes their vision quest, inspiring their personal growth.

In the contemplation phase, clients deepen the awareness building begun in precontemplation. They begin to examine the target behavior in greater detail. For example, if inattentive listening is their target behavior, I will ask them to consider questions such as these:

"When do I listen, and when do I neglect to listen?"

"To whom do I listen, and whom do I tune out?"

"What happens immediately before I tune out?"

"What I do instead of listening?"

"What is difficult about listening? Or what is rewarding about not listening?"

"What do I believe about listening?"

"What would be my reward for listening more?"

The goal of this examination is to understand when, where, how, and why the client uses the target behavior. Clients will commonly admit that instead of listening, they were "half-listening," "thinking about other things," or "preparing what to say next." They will understand the motivations behind their old behavior and the ways in which it rewards them. Increasing their consciousness of the behavior helps them prepare to change it. The more they can learn about themselves and their target behavior, the more tools they will have to help them with the actual change.

Contemplation Case: Keith #3 Looking Inside Himself

Keith had just completed his first year as a manager of an in-house advertising department. An excellent copywriter himself, he had assembled a competent staff and produced some very good work. During this year, he had gotten feedback that he didn't act much like a manager in meetings. His sarcastic and introverted style was causing others to lose respect for him, in spite of his creative skill and people management talents.

In the contemplation phase, Keith decided he wanted to act more leaderlike in meetings. The new behaviors he wanted to develop were voicing his opinion on all key topics and explaining to clients the rationale for his department's creative approach. His goal was to increase his influence with clients and their respect for him.

We began by examining his thinking, or self-talk, in these meetings. We realized that as long as Keith's thinking was preventing leaderlike behavior, no amount of practice would make the new behaviors stick. Keith described his typical thinking in meetings in words such as these:

"Since somebody already said that, the group will be bored if I simply repeated it and agreed with it."

"Why do they have to take so long? Can't they just make a decision and move on? This is boring."

"These clients don't get our creative approach. Boy, are they stupid."

It is easy to see how these thoughts would induce Keith to keep quiet and avoid adopting a leadership role.

I asked Keith if he could think of some alternative thoughts that might steer him toward more leaderlike behavior. With some coaching, he came up with these alternatives:

"I'm the leader. The group probably wants to know what I think about this."

"I guess these people are coming from a very different place than me. It may take them a while before we can arrive at a joint decision."

"The clients don't really grasp our rationale yet. I'll ask

them what they do understand and then describe our approach in their language."

Since these thoughts were still new and directly competitive with his old thoughts, Keith needed some time to get comfortable with them. As we talked about them, Keith realized that they were more useful than the old ones. He became committed to them. He said he could imagine thinking them in meetings. Now he was ready for preparation.

PHASE 3: PREPARATION

In the preparation stage, clients make plans for the actual change. During contemplation, their focus was expanding their awareness of the old behavior and the possibility for development. In the preparation phase, the focus is on new behavior. The clients explore, invent, and practice alternatives.

Once we have identified a developmental goal, clients begin working on incorporating new behaviors into their repertoire. Compared to the revelation and resolve experienced in contemplation, evolving new behaviors is more pragmatic and less conceptual. The guiding concepts in this phase are drawn primarily from behavioral psychology because the goal is for clients to invent, practice, and get used to new behavioral habits.

Clients have already decided, albeit tentatively, to change a particular behavior. They know which behavior and impact they don't want. Now they will determine exactly how to act differently. They will ask, "What words and actions will have the desired impact?" The task of preparation is to move from the conceptual to the concrete.

Identifying the Setting

In a sense, clients will be developing a new script for themselves. One way to start their creation is to define the setting. Where will the new behaviors occur? With which people? Around which topics? With what goal? Answering these setting questions helps the client focus on specific situations for the new behaviors. Thinking about actual settings may also provide details and clues about how to act. The more detailed their representation of the setting, the more fitting the new behavior.

Inventing and Rehearsing Behavior

Once clients have identified the situations in which they will be acting, they can invent alternative behaviors. Clients don't have to invent these behaviors from scratch; they have two guidelines that serve as boundaries: the new behavior should lead toward their goal, and it should be different from the old behavior.

Preparation Case: Bill #4 Making Progress

Bill had decided that he wanted to be more empowering toward his staff. He wanted them to make their own project decisions and to rely less on him for those decisions. One common setting occurred when a staff member asked Bill to make a decision for a project. Previously, Bill would have responded by giving advice and essentially making the decision for the project manager. Bill needed an alternative that helped the project managers make their own decisions but didn't make it for them. He had tried throwing the decision back to the project manager by asking, "What would you do?" But this was usually met with "I don't know. That's why I'm asking you."

When we began planning alternatives, Bill and I invented some responses that would help his project managers make their own decisions, such as the following:

"What possibilities are you considering?" (Ideally, the project manager would respond by describing two possibilities, A and B.)

"What is likely to happen if you chose possibility A?"

"How do you feel about possibility B? What is likely to happen if you chose possibility B?"

"Which possibility seems to promise the better outcome? Which do you prefer?"

Bill liked these questions because they helped the project managers clarify their own thinking and reasoning while breaking their dependence on him. In inventing these responses, Bill had first identified a setting that was explicit enough to plan specific, new actions. He invented these new actions and rehearsed them to the point of comfort. He was now ready to try them out in real settings.

Preparation Case: Keith #4
Explaining a Creative Approach

Keith entered coaching with the goal of acting more leaderlike in meetings. During the contemplation phase, he recognized the benefits of moving out of his comfort zone and speaking up in meetings. The key settings were meetings with clients when his staff would present their work or when his team and their clients would plan a campaign. His old behavior was to listen and remain silent, speaking only when he had something truly new to add.

He prepared things to say that would position him as a leader, enhance the quality of the meetings, and fit his style and values. The first new behavior, active listening, came fairly easy. As an astute listener and an introvert, all he needed to do was to vocalize his interpretation of the key ideas of the meeting. He was able to use his keen listening skill to determine the important messages and summarize them for the group.

The second behavior, voicing his opinion, proved to be a bit more difficult. It involved taking a stand in public and facing possible opposition. His goal was to weigh in on decisions so that both clients and his staff would have the benefit of knowing where he stood on the issue and use this stance to move toward a decision. I asked Keith to describe a conversation on which he might weigh in. He scripted and practiced some statements that would express his opinion without sounding redundant.

The third behavior, defending his staff's work, was difficult because it involved not only disagreeing with powerful clients but also seeking to win them over. We selected a project for him to practice explaining his department's creative approach. Then, he practiced what he would say in a real meeting.

Role Models

In the preparation phase, clients are inventing and rehearsing entirely new behaviors. To make these more familiar, it can be helpful to identify a role model. Observing the role model's actions, clients can use these as a starting point for developing their own new behaviors. The role model should be someone whom the clients respect and who acts successfully in the target situations. When the clients observe or imagine how the role model would act, they have a basis on which to base their new behavior.

Preparation Case: Keith #5 Selecting a Role Model

As his role model, Keith selected Linda, his boss's boss, because she was so skillful, poised, and intelligent when faced with the need to influence and disagree. He observed her attentively and even took notes on her demeanor to help him prepare. When we rehearsed later, Keith came across as smooth and confident, in part because he had absorbed some of Linda's skill and energy.

Preparation also involves anticipating. By predicting what might happen, clients can prepare for a variety of situations. If they anticipate someone disagreeing or getting angry or falling silent, they can plan their responses and ensure success in these situations.

Phase 4: Action

In the action phase, the new behaviors come to life. For clients, it can be a time of both excitement and anxiety. The excitement can come from trying out the contemplated change. If they have prepared well, they are emotionally and behaviorally ready for action.

The settings will feel familiar because the clients have practiced in them. The new behaviors will also feel familiar because they have been rehearsed. The clients should feel motivated and engaged because they have consciously acknowledged the payoffs for change.

When clients begin using the new behavior, they often feel proud of themselves for taking action. However, action can also bring up feelings of uncertainty, overconfidence, or yearnings to resume old behaviors. So in spite of their outward successes, clients typically need a lot of inner support during this period.

Action Case: Keith #6 On a Roller Coaster

Keith was a fast learner. In his first attempt at acting leaderlike in meetings, he succeeded mightily. He actively listened and summarized much of what was said at the meeting, speaking up nine or ten times. When a decision point arose, he expressed his opinion, explained his thinking, and ended up influencing the group. He even disagreed and prevailed when a vice-president criticized some copy written by his staff.

Keith came to our next meeting with good news and bad news. The good news was that he had been quite successful using the new behaviors in a client meeting. He had skillfully established a leadership presence, weighed in on decisions, and sold the rationale. The bad news was that he felt anxious at being so expressive in meetings. This style just didn't fit his image of himself and how he was raised to behave in public.

I first congratulated him on his external success. Then we started exploring his internal turmoil by asking about his thoughts and feelings. As we talked, Keith realized that he identified with a view of himself as a laid-back, creative, offbeat, wisecracking young man. His new posture was the opposite of this—expressive, organizationally committed, managerial, and politically skilled. As he contrasted these two roles, he seemed torn. I asked him which he wanted to be, the cool, independent young hipster or the responsible leader. (I'm not sure I selected my words that elegantly, but that was the gist of the question.) He pondered for quite a while. We sat in silence for several minutes as he considered his choice. (I sat anxiously awaiting his response. Naturally, I had a bias, but I knew that it was important for him to make this decision on his own, since he would need to act on it for years to come.) Finally, he announced that he wanted to be the manager. He felt he could leave his free-spirited self behind, at least some of the time, and fully assume his leadership role.

Once he turned the corner by making a full commitment to leadership, his development accelerated. He used the new behaviors regularly in meetings, becoming both skillful and comfortable with them. He used our meetings to fine-tune his skills at influence and leadership. He kept a journal and used it to maintain awareness of himself and his constituents. Journaling helped him recognize the few situations that continued to challenge him. He used our final sessions to ask my advice about these difficult situations. As we answered them, he became more and more proficient in his new role.

Self-Consciousness

Acting differently requires increased self-awareness, which can lead to the side effect of self-consciousness. Despite the negative consequences of old patterns, they still feel comfortable, and the new behavior feels awkward. Even in the action phase, people are used to entering situations and following their instincts. Now they are trying to act counter to their instincts.

Action Case: Martha #2 Back and Forth

Martha is a research manager who understands herself and her environment fairly well. She is intelligent and keeps strong relationships with her staff. These abilities helped her maintain a high-performing department through some very difficult times. However, Martha's taste for gossip, her competitive stance toward her peers, and her inability to say no to clients have hurt her reputation, as well the performance of her department.

Martha began the coaching process with pessimism toward both her career and the future of the department. As we progressed, she became more hopeful. She was succeeding in the action phase by reaching out to her peers to create a rapprochement and by making some unselfish staffing decisions. She curtailed gossiping, and she started positioning her department to fit the new business strategy.

Then she relapsed. She reread her unflattering six-month-old performance review and lost hope again. She decided that she could never change her boss's perceptions about her and that her career was over. She went back to blaming others for her predicament, sounding like the precontemplation Martha.

As I am writing this paragraph, I am preparing for our next conversation, in which I hope to talk with her about her current state and help her move back to a more constructive mind-set, back to preparation and action. I intend to begin as a mirror, reflecting her movement from optimism and action to pessimism and blaming. I will also ask her to describe her thinking and feelings in each of these states. I hope that by articulating her thoughts and feelings, she will gain some perspective on them and become able to exert some choice about her beliefs, rather than being unconsciously controlled by them.

Phase 5: Maintenance and Termination

During the maintenance stage, the client has three tasks: to habituate the new behavior, to avoid relapsing into the old pattern, and to see if they are having a better impact on others.

Once clients have used a new behavior a few times, it is tempting to claim victory and move on. But new behaviors are weak in comparison to established ones. Like alfalfa sprouts in a field of weeds, they need nurturing to survive and compete with the weedlike old habits. One thing both coaches and clients can do to strengthen new behaviors is to honor and celebrate success. When clients mention using a new behavior, reinforce it by talking about it and examining the successful experience. By examining the behavior, identifying the thoughts and feelings that accompanied it, and describing the settings in which it occurred, clients can relive the experience and strengthen their neural memory of it. Talking about the experience makes the process more conscious and therefore easier to repeat in the future.

There are several questions coaches can ask that encourage clients to relive experiences:

"What did you do?"

"What reminded you to do it?"

"What did you think about before doing it? While you were doing it? After doing it?"

"How did you feel?"

"How did people respond?"

"Would you do anything differently next time?"

Maintenance Case: Martha #3 Success

In a recent coaching session with Martha, I missed an opportunity to effectively reinforce a new behavior. She began the session by remarking about a situation in which she resisted the urge to gossip. I responded by congratulating her on her success. Martha thanked me and then moved on to another topic. My attempt to reinforce her new behavior by celebrating her success seemed to fall flat. I later realized that I was doing the celebrating, not her, violating one of the principles of effective coaching. I also recognized that for a thoughtful person like Martha, analyzing the experience would be more rewarding than a cheery congratulation. The next day, I e-mailed her asking a question that enabled her to analyze her success and thus reinforce it in a way that was meaningful for her.

Maintenance Case: Greg #2
A New Motivation Leads to Self-Maintenance

Sometimes progress is achieved by a coming to a new awareness, rather than developing a single new behavior. Greg began his coaching project with a desire to develop better relationships with senior managers. In the course of our coaching work, we focused on practical behaviors that would lead him to this goal. We worked on enhancing his clarity and succinctness in communicating. We also worked on broadening his horizons to collaborate with peers in other business units. And we worked on increasing his comfort making presentations in meetings. Greg was a quick study and made rapid progress in these areas.

Despite his steady progress, however, Greg continued to express ambivalence about being promoted. He worried that a promotion might lead him into a job he didn't want. He continued to learn and practice the new behaviors but held off on making a personal commitment to advancement.

One day, he recognized that he was engaged in this learning for himself rather than to get promoted by the organization. He proclaimed, "I can't stand still. I can either expand myself or stagnate." Once he shifted from an external to an internally motivated attitude, his learning accelerated. Moreover, he became self-generating. Rather than my asking him questions to elicit new learning opportunities, he began to identify them himself and tell me how he planned to act. He started talking about the things he wanted to do to continue his development. I became much more of a listener, endorser, and clarifier. I continued to ask him questions, but he was leading the process. I still felt a desire to reinforce his new mind-set, but I wasn't even sure he needed my reinforcing. I did explain my observations about his new self-reliance, and he affirmed how valuable our sessions were to him. It seemed like he would not need me much longer.

How Much Maintenance?

How much reinforcement do clients need to maintain a new behavior? On the one hand, people can be self-managing and change can be self-perpetuating. Once clients become self-aware and committed to the change, they will attend to it. If they have prepared well by developing a thorough understanding of their relevant behaviors and thoughts, they will use the new behaviors successfully. These early successes will reinforce the new pattern and lead to long-term success.

On the other hand, I have seen enough forgetting and backsliding to know that one success does not constitute permanent behavior change. Practice does make perfect. The behavior will become hard-wired if the client has many opportunities to experiment with it, to succeed, fail, and modify. Some clients need five trials, others ten, and others twenty before the new behaviors become habits.

Summary

Coaches can use their understanding of the phases to make sure their clients progress through them and don't skip a phase. One of the biggest mistakes made by new coaches is trying to move clients to action too quickly. I have observed inexperienced coaches trying to move precontemplation clients all the way to action in a single session. This often backfires, with the clients failing to take effective action or feeling manipulated and losing trust in the coach. Awareness of the phases helps coaches stay in sync with their clients while still nudging them through the change progress.

Chapter 6

Self-Knowledge

What lies behind us and what lies before us are tiny matters compared to what lies within us.

— RALPH WALDO EMERSON

Self-knowledge plays a significant role in a leader's effectiveness. Leaders who truly know their strengths can use them wisely and avoid their unconscious overuse. Leaders who understand their values and passions can look for opportunities to express them and make sure they are not applied inappropriately. Leaders who are aware of their shortcomings can concentrate more closely when they need to perform, delegate tasks in areas where they are weak to others, and learn new skills to transform soft spots into strengths. Leaders with low self-awareness are limited to their instinctual reactions and to habitual, often unconscious, and possibly ineffective patterns.

It is easy to view leaders as actors on the stage of organizational life. The members of the organization are their supporting actors, who interpret the leaders' behavior and act in response it. Since leaders play such a key role, they benefit from knowing their character well and deciding how to best play their part.

Leaders who know themselves not only observe their own behavior patterns but also recognize their underlying motivations, thoughts, and emotions. They know what they believe and the rationale for these beliefs. They understand the why as well as the what. By understanding the sources of their beliefs, they can more easily look at these beliefs in light of current information and decide if they still hold true.

Self-awareness precedes and accompanies growth. Increasing clients' self-awareness is both a component and a benefit of leadership coaching. Coaches use several approaches to build clients' self-awareness. Coaches gather and communicate 360° feedback, enabling clients to see themselves as others see them. Coaches share their reactions to clients in real time, calling attention to specific behaviors and aspects of behaviors and asking about related thoughts and emotions. Even setting aside the time for coaching sessions ensures that clients will invest time in self-reflection and questioning assumptions. Through coaching, clients receive regular, facilitated doses of self-knowledge that provide a deep and valuable understanding of their actions, motives, and impacts.

Self-Knowledge Case: Craig #2
Building New Influencing Skills

Craig is a vice-president for new drug research at a biotech company. He is highly valued as one of the most innovative leaders in the company. Before a large pharmaceutical company acquired the company, Craig had been successful at gaining support for his innovations because his peers knew him well and trusted his creative judgment. But now, following the acquisition, he needs to gain support for his initiatives by influencing his peers at the parent company.

In his first several months in this new role, Craig had been having trouble influencing his peers to support his promising research proposals. So his manager asked him to work with me on influencing skills. His initial awareness of how he exerted influence was fuzzy. He knew that people were not following him but blamed this on their conservatism and lack of creativity (a typical precontemplation reaction).

The 360° feedback pointed out several areas where Craig could develop influencing skills. One important area was paying attention to people. Whenever Craig talked about one of his innovative ideas, he became so involved in the idea that he seemed to forget about the other people present or see them as an audience rather than as participants. He would be thinking only about the idea, often barely looking at the others and rarely asking them questions or offering them a chance to speak. The first major step in Craig's change process was becoming aware of his tendency to withdraw from his colleagues into the more compelling world of his own ideas.

COACHING FOR SELF-AWARENESS

In humans, a behavior pattern is the product of an often-complex psychological "manufacturing" process coordinated by the mind and body. To change from an old to a new behavior, clients first need to become aware of all the components of the old behavior. They begin by identifying its sources, its triggers, and its impact, examining one component at a time.

One important component of the behavior is the setting that triggers its occurrence. The setting is a good place to start the process of analyzing the behavior because it is relatively easy to identify. Where, when, and with whom does the behavior occur? Does it show itself in team meetings or in one-on-one sessions? Is it most prevalent with direct reports, peers, senior managers, or clients? Does it occur when the leader is challenged or when they are under pressure or when they are trying to influence others? By pinning down the setting in which the behavior occurs and the people toward whom it is directed, the client gains self-knowledge critical to the change process.

Since behavior change is the trophy in the coaching process, enhancing the client's awareness of the target behavior is another critically important step. In building this awareness, the clients attend to exactly what they do and say in the target situations. For Keith, whom we met in Chapter Five, the settings were meetings with clients. The target behaviors were being silent and making snide side comments. For Craig, in Chapters Five and Six, the settings were both one-on-ones and meetings. The target behavior was ignoring and interrupting his peers.

A third component of behavior is the thinking that underlies it. Most behavior is preceded by thoughts that motivate and direct it. For example, if I am examining how I take credit for my work, one underlying thought might be, "My senior management doesn't know that I led this project, and I need them to know." Or I may be thinking, "If I don't get recognition for this, my career will suffer." By becoming more aware of these thoughts, I notice how they cause the target behavior. This recognition gives me a greater sense of control over the behavior. As awareness builds, the behavior becomes less automatic and less powerful. I feel less controlled by it because I realize that it is controlled by my thoughts. I begin to contemplate changing my thinking in order to change the behavior.

Beliefs are another component. Beliefs are a group of thoughts that fit together to form a higher-order mental process. They develop over time by interpreting experiences, making assumptions, and drawing conclusions from these experiences. For example, Tim believed that getting too close to people at work increases the risk of getting laid off. He had once observed all the members of a certain clique get laid off following an acquisition. From this one experience, he drew the conclusion that getting friendly with people at work and being part of a group was dangerous. His reclusive style at work had left him without a base of support and actually placed him in a less secure position. Another example is a manager who believed that giving people a lot of positive feedback would make them complacent and lazy. She was experiencing high turnover and a near rebellion by her staff in response to her apparently punitive management style. (I selected these two beliefs because they contradict two widely held and well-researched theories about successful leadership practices, the belief that networks increase rather than decrease one's influence and job security and the belief that feedback improves rather than worsens performance.)

In each case, the client became more conscious of their belief. They questioned it by tracing its origins to see where it came from. They examined current feedback to see if it was still valid in their current environment. In each case, the current data indicated that the behavior and its underlying belief were not working. And in each case, the client struggled as they gradually let go of their deeply rooted belief and considered alternatives.

Changing a belief can be a slow and painful process. Clients undergoing change are literally getting rid of a part of themselves and replacing it with something less familiar. It is like a cognitive version of transplant surgery. Coaches can play a particularly valuable role in the process. First, they can point out the behavior that is causing the problem and help the clients link that behavior to its underlying belief. Coaches can guide the clients in examining the belief, both by acknowledging how it came to be and by questioning its current validity.

Values are deeply rooted patterns of thought that also have a strong emotional component. Core values are important because they drive a lot of behavior. They vary from person to person. One person may value power and authority, while another might value helping customers, and a third might value creativity and aesthetics. Becoming more conscious of these values makes behavioral choices easier by highlighting behaviors that express these values. Because people's values are so central, they change very slowly, if at all. For this reason, I help clients clarify their values but do not attempt to change them.

Because values are so central to how a person thinks, feels, and acts, increasing awareness of them can be helpful in the coaching process. For example, Alice values knowledge and innovation. In her coaching work, she decided to focus much of her communication on encouraging learning and scientific innovation by her staff. She lobbied the parent company and won her group's designation as the focal point for new technologies and therapies. By becoming more conscious of her values, she could develop her leadership style in a way that expressed and sought to fulfill these values. Her awareness energized her and reminded her to focus on what was most important to her.

Emotions are another force that drives behavior. When people are aware of the emotions that underlie their actions, they can choose whether or not to express those emotions and how to express them. When they are less aware, their emotions can unconsciously drive them to do things that are harmful. For example, shortly after making a good start on improving his ability to influence, Neal became pessimistic about his future at the firm. He felt threatened by a new executive, believing that she wanted to take over his department. He felt that senior management undervalued his skills. He feared that his influencing efforts would fail. And he believed that the whole enterprise would fail due to the incompetence of the senior executive. His mood was overwhelmingly negative. This mood seemed so sudden and different, I asked him where it might be coming from. That question alone caused Neal to consider that he was experiencing a mood that had roots in himself rather than reflected some absolute truth. When he traced it back, he recognized that some two-year-old feelings from the acquisition had resurfaced and were causing his current pessimism. Acknowledging these feelings allowed his pessimism to wane and enabled him to address his leadership challenges with renewed vigor.

Knowing one's beliefs, values, and emotions is especially useful in the current, cost-conscious economic environment. Leaders have fewer external motivators at their disposal than in the past. Promotions, financial rewards, travel, and other perks have been cut back. What is left is the leaders' ability to create a stimulating, meaningful work environment for employees. To do this, they need to communicate their own sense of meaning and their own emotions even more. They need to expose what makes them tick. In doing this, they become role models, aware of their sense of purpose and using it to achieve their goals.

Self-knowledge enables leaders to consciously choose which aspects of themselves to express in any given situation. It also enables leaders to know their hot buttons, the situations and messages that stimulate powerful and sometimes defensive emotions. Self-knowledgeable leaders use their awareness to make conscious decisions about how to respond in these personally loaded situations.

The Hard Part of Self-Knowledge

People expand their self-knowledge by becoming aware of their behavior, its sources and its impact. This process is usually laden with emotion. Recognizing a strength, such as attentive listening, can be pleasurable and confirming experience, while recognizing a weakness, such as combativeness, can be painful. Becoming aware of a troublesome behavior can be so threatening that the mere mention of it can make people reject the information, even when it is pointed out in a caring way. Because most people perceive themselves as well meaning and competent, the contemplation of a negative aspect of themselves can be difficult. Constructive criticism makes them see red and causes them to reject the information. They try to protect themselves from the anxiety or shame of that accompanies accepting this part of themselves.

During a growth process, self-awareness increases, becoming a new theme in one's conscious life. It can be both a support and an annoyance. Like learning a new golf swing, self-awareness feels awkward and interferes with the fun and spontaneity of daily functioning. Clients can make growth easier by anticipating the awkwardness and viewing this increased self-awareness as a natural partner of learning. They can expect it and use it when it occurs and even will it to appear.

SELF-KNOWLEDGE AND INFLUENCE

Self-knowledge can strengthen the ability to influence others as well as to be influenced by them. Deciding when to influence and when to be influenced is based on comparing our beliefs with those of our colleague. Self-knowledge provides the flexibility to flow between holding fast and letting go of our beliefs. It enables leaders to be firm but not stubborn, to be open but not weak.

Knowing not just what we believe but also the source of each belief enables us to decide whether to influence or be influenced. The trick lies in reflecting on the source of our belief. By tracing back where the belief came from, we have a better chance of determining if it is valid in the current situation or not. Peter Senge (1990) describes this process as climbing down the ladder of inference. People experience things, make observations about these experiences, use these observations to form judgments, and use these judgments to form conclusions. Besides becoming aware of the source of our own ideas, understanding how people form conclusions can guide our inquiry into the sources of others' ideas. When people understand both their own ladders and the ladders of their colleagues, they can compare them fairly and make more informed decisions.

Reflection doesn't take anything away from decisiveness, from being a person of action. In fact, it generates the inner toughness needed to be an effective person of action—to be a leader. People who lack this flexibility to flow between holding fast and letting go of their beliefs are limited as leaders. Those who stubbornly resist being influenced are seen as authoritarian. Those who are too easily influenced are seen as weak. Skillful flexibility comes from the ability to know ourselves and use this knowledge when working with others

There are three additional benefits of this type of self-reflection. First is that we can apply our knowledge of the source of our thinking to other situations. Second is that it gets us in the habit of self-reflection and lessens our arrogant belief in the correctness of all our ideas. Third, it can enhance our ability to influence others. By describing the ladders of inference of our own ideas, we can help others understand our thinking and give them an opportunity to assess it and come to their own informed conclusions.

Self-Knowledge Case: David #1
Making New Inferences

David is the president of a twenty-person market research firm. He has a Ph.D. in statistics and an M.B.A. in marketing. The firm is known for performing high-quality research for consumer products and financial services companies. David called me to help with morale problems among his staff. Staff members were angry with each other and not speaking with each other. Many had retreated to doing the minimum and not assuming full ownership of their respective projects. When I interviewed the staff, they spoke with regret about their internecine wars and waning motivation. Surprisingly, their greatest concern was David. Every member indicated that David "always had to be right." They all felt that he believed that his ideas were superior to those of others and was very difficult to sway once he had formed an idea. Some team members were intimidated by him; others were frustrated and angry. And although they assumed responsibility for their own actions, most cited David's arrogance and bullying as the root cause of the firm's problems.

When I shared this feedback with David, he was both surprised and angered. As the firm's sole owner, he believed that he was the only one who felt truly responsible for its fate. As the strategic leader and father figure, he felt betrayed. David was accustomed to being right. His Ivy League education and his Fortune 100 pedigree reinforced his sense that his ideas were right. His mind seemed to have little capacity for reflecting on itself and questioning its own premises. David drew from his experience, his reading, and his apparently rigorous logic to conclude that his ideas were the right ideas. As his coach, I knew that this would not be an easy assignment.

The opening came from David's caring about the firm. He knew the importance of getting his team recommitted and realigned. He also valued social science data. And if my research said that his behavior was a cause of the problem, he believed it. The data and his caring led him into the contemplation phase, in which he could acknowledge that his behavior was having undesirable consequences. He was ready to consider altering his style but still a long way from recognizing that his ideas were not always the be-all and end-all. This was our next project.

I am a bit like David in this respect. As an educated firstborn male, I grew up believing that everything I thought was right. When I am in that state, I am so fixated on my own ideas, it feels like being in a trance. My certainty in my beliefs and my desire to prove to others that I am smart and right take over my consciousness. My logic and my experience become my weapons. Other people become pawns to win over. In my passion to prove that I'm right, my listening diminishes, my social graces recede, and my self-reflection disappears. I had no trouble empathizing with David.

Several years ago, when I was grappling with my own intellectual arrogance, I read the *Way of the Peaceful Warrior* by Dan Millman. He described how his own conversation with a guru helped him gain some humility toward his ideas. The guru began by asking him the simple question "Where are you?" to which Dan gave the confident answer, "In Berkeley." The guru followed with "And where is that?" Dan said, again in utter confidence, "California." They carried on in that manner with the guru continuing to ask, "And where is that?" Dan responded with "the United States," "the Western Hemisphere," "the Planet Earth," and "the solar system." When they got to "Where is the universe?" he knew he was in trouble because he could not answer it. From this somewhat trite lesson, Dan learned that he couldn't even be sure of something as simple as where he was, so maybe he shouldn't be so sure of other ideas as well. I admit that this anecdote is a bit simplistic, but it can begin the process of chipping away at people's certainty about their own ideas.

I wanted to find a way for David to develop a healthy perspective on his own ideas. The challenge was that David was so enmeshed in his own ladder of inference, he could not consider any other way of looking at the world. Even though David was not a very spiritual person, I needed a place to start, so I shared the *Peaceful Warrior* story with him. It humored him enough that he talked with me about where some of his firmly held conclusions came from. For example, we examined his belief that client reports should begin with a graphical summary of the data. As we walked down his ladder of inference, we hit a couple of interesting points. One was that the firm was doing well and pleasing clients using this report format. A second point was that he had learned to use this format twenty years ago, from his boss, a bank vice-president. As we traced his ladder, David began to understand how he came to believe in the "graphics first" conclusion. He saw that it came from his experiences and that he had generalized his experience into a hard-and-fast belief. He still believed firmly in his format but recognized that it came from the data he collected about his own experience, rather than being a divine truth. That day served as the first step in David's becoming more open to the ideas of others.

Chapter 7

Motives for Change

Motivation is necessary for change. Motivation provides the energy, commitment, and discipline necessary for change. People know that behavior change involves abandoning old ways and adopting new ways. They recognize that change will involve stress, discomfort, and awkwardness, as well as successes and disappointments. Because behavior change involves hard work and discomfort, their motivation to change needs to be strong enough to endure that discomfort. It needs to overcome the pull of their psychological and behavioral inertia.

When people are engaged in a change process, they grapple with the dual forces of motivation and discomfort. They regularly enact a drama that highlights the interplay of these two forces. When they succeed in using the new behaviors, they feel the satisfaction and pride of winning. When they slip back to their old patterns, they feel the disappointment of losing a round. The process takes time, effort, and often struggle. People need to be motivated to persevere. Their motivation to change provides the energy to carry them through the ups and downs of the change process.

Because motivation is so central, skilled coaches invest time in looking for it, highlighting it, and reinforcing it. They resist the temptation to skim over motivation and move right into the more alluring change work. Early in the process, coaches can explore motivation by simply asking clients about what would motivate them to make the desired change. Coaches listen for valid, compelling reasons. When they hear a meaningful motivation, they ask the clients to describe it further in order to lift it into consciousness. If coaches hear a motivation that seems weak or inauthentic, they share this perception with the clients and continue exploring until the clients identify a motivator that is powerful enough to fuel their upcoming journey. Then, at appropriate moments throughout the coaching process, the coach may refer to the motivation in order to remind the clients why they are working so hard. The coach treats the client's motivation as a very important component in the change process.

Perceiving Change as Challenging and Energizing

Coaches can help clients strengthen their motivation by harnessing the power of talk. They may begin by asking clients to talk about what might motivate their change. This exploration can begin with a question like "How will you benefit by making this change?" The purpose of this conversation is to enable clients to articulate and thus reinforce their motivation. In the ensuing dialogue, the clients can expand on and add detail to their motives.

Some clients will not be able to articulate a motivator. In these cases, the coach will slow the process down and help clients look for compelling reasons to invest in the change. Here the coach acts as a guide, stopping the process to allow the clients to pack their bags for the upcoming journey.

While the client's motivation is always a constructive topic, the timing of the motivation conversation can make a difference in the outcome. It is especially valuable to address motivation soon after the client identifies their developmental theme. By addressing it early, the client can establish a clearer sense of what it might take to adopt this particular behavior and what the rewards might be. Envisioning both the challenge and the reward can prepare them for the work that lies ahead.

MOTIVES AND GOALS

Identifying a personal goal for the coaching work can clarify and focus the client's motivation. Most people have a goal or two that they truly, even deeply desire. They have real purposes they want to achieve or real experiences they want to have. However, these goals are often so fuzzy or so long-term that people are not fully conscious of them. The purpose of the conversation is to bring to light the client's goals and motivators.

The coach can create an opportunity to articulate this goal by asking a question like "What do you really want in the next phase of your career?" Once this has been articulated, the client can begin to use it as a guiding light to direct their development. The benefit of articulating a personal goal is its power. It is something that the client truly wants, as opposed to something that others want for them. It is easy to remember because it is so important to them. Thinking about it reminds them to make choices that lead them to it. A conscious goal begins to free clients from the habits and inertia of daily functioning.

The goal can be referred to in subsequent coaching conversations. The coach can bring up the goal as a reminder of where the client is going. Both coach and client can use the goal to plan activities that will lead to its achievement and measure progress against it.

ALIGNING BEHAVIOR AND VALUES AND ELIMINATING CONTRADICTION

For decades, managers, human resource professionals, and psychologists have been trying to understand motivation. Literally hundreds of books and thousands of articles have been written on the best ways to motivate people. The theories of motivation claim that people become motivated when the benefits of expending energy on a task outweigh the benefits of not doing so.

These benefits are related to the person's values. And values differ from person to person. For some people, getting ahead or getting promoted is their driving value. For others, it is influence. Some are motivated by the opportunity to innovate. For others, it may be building efficient structures or solving complex problems. For some, the prime value is having many solid relationships. For others, it may be helping people. For others, it is security or stability. For still others, it is getting out of trouble. Some might be motivated by improving their organization's performance. And others might aspire to becoming more like their ideal leader. The list of possible human values is long and varied. Coaches can provide clients with the opportunity to find the motivators that are most meaningful to them.

Consciously connecting personal values and the desired change can become a powerful motivator for that change. Most of us face numerous opportunities to change but rarely follow them through. We tell ourselves that we'd like to do more of something or less of something or do something differently. Our lives are so full that many of these wishes are ignored because they are not connected to truly important personal missions. We need the motivator of knowing that the change will make a real and valued difference in how we feel about our work lives.

The coach can help the client find their motivators for change by listening for clues about what is important to them. When they hear a clue, the coach can confirm it with active listening questions such as "So innovation is very important to you?" They can also ask direct questions like "What would you most want to accomplish in the coming years?" Once the client has identified their core motivators, the coach can remind them, at appropriate moments in the process, of the connection between the motivator and their behavioral goal.

It can be helpful for coaches to use the four-drive theory to identify potential motivators for each client. Coaches can ask themselves, "Might this client be motivated most by career advancement and financial reward or by building better work relationships or by learning and mastering new skills or by protecting the present job or by power and resources?" Finding the drive that is most salient to each particular client at a given point in time can make a big difference in the client's motivation and success in behavior change.

Sometimes, the client's situation provides the motivation. Clients may find themselves in a new position or facing a new challenge in which their old leadership patterns are inappropriate. Or they may if they find themselves in a situation they don't like. They may be dealing with a mistake or a problem that won't go away. Or they may have successfully addressed several other challenges and are now ready to address this one. They may have reached a life stage that simply makes them ready. Or they may be moved by an external event such as a training program or a character in a book or movie. Whatever the reason, desiring something different becomes their motivating force. Finding a motivator and articulating it becomes a critical task in the coaching process.

Clients can come to this point of readiness to change in a number of ways. Sometimes they come to this recognition on their own by recognizing a situation they would like to change or by observing an undesirable effect. In other cases, they are led to it by a manager, peers, staff, or coach who point out this effect. Either way, they decide that now is the time to address this issue and that the change will be worth the effort.

Recognition of an undesired effect of one's behavior often comes through feedback. Feedback might help the client recognize that they are acting in ways that are inconsistent with who they want to be. For some, the feedback may communicate a new message that inspires them to action. For others, it might shed light on a message they have heard before that they are now ready to act on. But if they have heard the message before, why is it motivating them now? The message may be clearer and more compelling than before. Or they may have heard it often enough that they are now ready to deal with it. The coach can help the client seize this moment of contemplation of change and help them transform it into motivation for action.

Overall, people decide to change because they desire something better. They have come to believe that change will be more satisfying than the status quo. They recognize that changing their behavior will lead to a more successful, more fulfilling, less frustrating work life. They become motivated because the benefits of making the change outweigh the discomfort of trying something new.

Transformational Change

Sometimes coaching can stimulate a truly significant personal change. Conditions in the client's life can converge in such a way that an opportunity appears to make a deep and meaningful change in the way they lead. It can go beyond mere behavioral change to an expression of an important personal value that may have been latent for a long time. The arrival of the coach, the absorption of the feedback, the recognition of a changed work environment, the arrival at new life stage—all these can come together to signal that this is the time to make a substantial change.

Motivation Case: Bill #5 Commitment to Change

After our review of his 360° feedback, Bill said, "I've been thinking very seriously about the feedback. I have decided I can make a real difference here and like myself more by becoming a different kind of leader, by becoming more of a servant-leader and less like a military leader. Here is what I want to do . . ." He proceeded to outline some new management practices he could adopt.

He had studied the feedback report and now better understood the wishes and concerns of his constituents. Along with acknowledging the validity of their wishes, he recognized the situation as a long-awaited opportunity to change the culture of at least his part of the organization. He rose to the occasion by making a commitment to himself to make a change. For the first time, he led our coaching session. I supported him by creating opportunities to turn his insights into sustainable behavior change. In the rest of our session, we refined the specific changes he would make.

What was most important about this process was his dialogue with himself. He told me that one side of him wanted to defend himself and the current management culture of his organization. The other side recognized the information as a valid and important message. He knew that some of his management practices diminished people and hindered their performance. He connected with the part of himself that respected people and wanted to bring out the best in them. He knew he was capable of this change, and decided to start it today.

Chapter 8

Steps in the Coaching Process

Most coaches consciously follow a series of activities designed to move the client forward. Although coaches will skip around in response to the client's situation and statements, they do follow a basic process. This chapter will cover the steps in the coaching process. It looks at the change process from the perspective of the coach and what the coach does to facilitate change; this differs from the phases of change (presented in Chapter Five), which take the perspective of the client.

STEP 1: ENTERING THE ENVIRONMENT AND CONTRACTING (WEEK 1)

The coaching process begins with either the client or the manager looking to help the client grow as a leader. A member of management, often the human resource manager, contacts a coach and invites the coach to discuss the situation. In this initial meeting, the coach may meet with the HR manager, the client's manager, the client, or all three.

They talk about the desired change, what led to the decision to hire a coach, and their expectations of a successful coaching project. The coach asks questions to learn about the client and their situation. The managers ask questions of the coach to learn about their experience, style, and approach. Sometimes the management team interviews several coaches in order to select the one who best fits the situation.

In this initial meeting, the coach informs the management team about how they work and at the same time learns about the client, the organization, and the challenge. The coach listens carefully for clues about the organization's style and culture and about how the client is perceived. They assess the nature of the relationship between the client and the boss and try to discern the organization's motives for investing in the coaching process. If all goes well, the coach accepts and is accepted for the assignment.

Step 2: Building Rapport and Planning the Development Process (Week 2)

Next, the coach and the client begin meeting privately. As with any collaboration, they need to size each other up and get to know each other before digging into the work. The coach might begin by asking the client about the work they do and the challenges they face. Understanding the client's job and their approach to it will enable the coach to more easily appreciate the environment and how the client views it. Understanding the nature of the client's work will also enable the coach to relate it to their own personal and professional experience.

Most clients begin the coaching process with some trepidation. They may be anxious about sharing their inner life with a stranger hired by their company. They may also be concerned about feeling incompetent as they try to learn new behaviors. Asking about the client's job temporarily shifts the power from the coach to the client. It gives the client the opportunity to begin the partnership by taking control and being the expert. By starting the process with the client in the driver's seat, the client gains a sense of comfort that will carry through the project.

In the first meeting, it is helpful to define the structure for the engagement. The coach can lay out the steps in the process, set expectations for what will happen, and define the roles that each party will play. This includes agreeing on how often to meet and how long the meetings will last. The coach also describes what will be kept confidential, as well as what information will be shared with management and how it will be shared. Determining a structure for the project increases the client's comfort and enables them to begin to envision the steps in their own change process.

Asking the client about their goals is a good way to align expectations about the work. It serves multiple purposes. By articulating their wishes, the client starts to generate motivation for the behavior change. Talking about their wishes can move them from the precontemplation to the contemplation phase. Listening to the client's goals enables the coach to understand how the client sees themselves and their world. By listening to which behaviors the client chooses to describe and how they describe them, the coach gets a first peek into the client's mental models. Talking about goals also gives the coach an opportunity to compare the client's perspective to that of the company's management. Talking about the client's job, the coaching process, and the client's goals make for a full, productive first meeting.

STEP 3: ASSESSMENT (WEEKS 3–4)

People grow in response to new information about themselves. Until this point, the client has been operating with a particular set of information about themselves. This information, and the way they interpret it, serves as the foundation for their current mental models and behavior. To explore new behaviors and build new mental models, the client will need new information. The most useful new information will be about their behavior patterns and their psychological preferences and needs.

Feedback from Others

Most people rarely get to see themselves as others see them. Feedback from others can provide this valuable perspective. It can facilitate change by pinpointing a specific opportunity for change. Many coaching projects begin with some general wishes expressed by the client's management. These wishes are often expressed in honest but vague terms, such as "to act more leaderlike" or "to be more influential" or "to be more empowering." While these wishes make good starting points for a coaching project, they are not specific enough to begin real behavior change. The coach and client need more detailed information, such as examples of the client's current behaviors, when and where these behaviors occur, the impact of the behaviors, and effective alternatives. Interviewing or surveying the constituents can provide much of this detail.

The second purpose of constituent feedback is its motivational potential. Most nondepressed people are content with themselves. They believe that they are doing the right things and that others appreciate their actions. One source of this belief is an unconscious tendency of humans to like themselves and believe in themselves. As Martin Seligman (1990) points out, healthy, optimistic, successful people have a more positive, self-supporting bias than depressed, pessimistic people. This positive view is further reinforced by colleagues who diplomatically refrain from criticizing them. Together, these two forces conspire to make people believe they are more effective and more appreciated than they actually are. They may be truly unaware of their detrimental behavior patterns.

When a coach gathers anonymous feedback from the client's constituents and shares it with the client, the client gains a new perspective about how other people perceive them. The feedback can elucidate aspects of themselves that were unknown or glossed over. It can reveal previously hidden details about the behaviors that are most appreciated by others and about the behaviors that make others' lives difficult. The frank perceptions of colleagues can serve as a wake-up call. It can motivate change by helping the client recognize behaviors that are damaging to others and to the organization.

Feedback readies the client for change. It provides information about the impact of behavior. It helps them accurately determine which behaviors get them what they want and which are getting in the way. Feedback expands the client's self-knowledge and enables them to focus their growth efforts.

Gathering Feedback

Interviews and written surveys are the two most common ways of gathering feedback. Many coaches prefer interviews because they can provide detailed examples of the client's significant behaviors. Interviews also engage the constituents more directly in the client's development process.

Many coaches begin the 360° interview process by asking the client to select five to ten people most able to provide useful feedback. The coach asks the client to include a cross section of colleagues, both supporters and people with whom the client has had difficult relationships. The client then contacts the stakeholders, asking them if they will participate in the feedback process. Once they have agreed, the coach calls each stakeholder to introduce him- or herself, to position the interviews as an important part of the client's leadership development program, and to make an appointment for the interview.

The stakeholder interview is important because it will provide much of the basis for the coaching engagement. The coach wants to gather as much information as possible during a thirty- to forty-five-minute interview. Open-end questions work well because they give the stakeholder ample opportunity to describe the client's behaviors and their own reactions to these behaviors. These could include questions such as the following:

"How would you describe Diana as a person?"

"What are her strengths? How do these strengths affect you? How do they affect the organization?"

"What are her weaknesses? What would you like her to

do differently? How do these difficult behaviors affect you and the organization?"

"What advice would you like to give her?"

The coach may also ask more specific, closed-end questions about specific behaviors that were pointed out by the client or management, on such topics as how the client sets strategy, delegates, influences people, or handles herself in meetings.

As with any interview, the coach will follow the stakeholder's responses by probing for more detailed information. "Can you tell me more about how she does that?" or "What did she say when you told her the project would be delayed?" Obtaining actual behavioral examples will enable the coach to give specific and supportable feedback to the client.

During the interview, the coach listens carefully to the stakeholder's answers and takes as many verbatim notes as possible. The coach should focus as much on the positive behaviors as on the negative so as not to appear to be engaged in a witch hunt. It is important that the coach offers no opinions of their own and focuses primarily on drawing information and examples from the participant.

During my interviews, the only opinion I may give is to express optimism about the client's ability to change. This can be important because there are many people who believe that people can never change. Promoting a belief in the possibility of change serves two purposes. It encourages stakeholders to wish for, look for, and even expect changes in the client's behavior. And it may inspire stakeholders to consider changing their own behavior.

When all the interviews are complete, the coach analyzes the notes and writes them up in preparation for sharing them with the client. Sorting the notes into themes permits the most meaningful interpretation. The themes should summarize the most important messages from the interviews, so they will be different for each client. An effective strategy is to write exact quotes from the constituents. This reduces the coach's temptation to prematurely leap to interpretations and gives the client an opportunity to see the raw feedback and develop their own interpretations. Interpreting them personally can give the client a stronger sense of ownership of the feedback. Each theme should be treated on a page of its own.

Here is an example of the themes that might be used for one client:

Strengths	Project leadership style	Delegation
Recognition	Enthusiasm	Listening
Body language	Respect	Arguing
Trust	Advice, wishes	

The written feedback summary contains a great deal of data. It will be important for the client to understand and digest these data. But because the data are so personal and so voluminous, pacing the presentation is critical. Reviewing one topic at a time helps the client focus on that topic and gain a thorough understanding of it before moving on to the next topic. By dealing with only one topic per page, the client and coach can attend to that topic and avoid the temptation to read ahead to the next topic.

For most clients, the feedback will contain a balance of positive and negative comments; for example, several people appreciate the client's commitment and enthusiasm but are confused by this client's disorganized delegation style. For clients with balanced feedback, it is appropriate to go over the verbatim summary together. For some clients, however, the negative statements will outnumber the positive ones by a considerable margin. Reading a succession of negative comments can be painful, leading to defensive reactions or even immobilization. In such instances, therefore, it is wiser to deliver a written summary of the feedback without submitting the verbatims.

Feedback has both positive and negative effects. Learning that some behavior bothers others can shake people out of their self-satisfied complacency and give them a reason to be better leaders. This same information can also be painful. Learning that they are doing something damaging can jolt the calm of self-contentment and disrupt self-esteem. Because of this potentially powerful negative response, it is important for the coach to provide both challenge and support, to communicate the feedback in a way that will both gain the client's attention and minimize defensive reactions.

The coach has several goals in reviewing the feedback with the client. First, they want the client to understand their own significant behavior patterns cited in the feedback and relate them to their own perceptions of themselves. The coach wants to help the client use the feedback to expand or revise their mental models in a way that integrates both their strengths and their weaknesses into a broader, more comprehensive sense of themselves. The coach can facilitate this by asking if the feedback makes sense, if the client has heard similar messages before, and if they can imagine how others might respond to them in this way. If the client uses the feedback to enrich their mental models, they will be better able to invent new behaviors and manage the continual expansion of their leadership skills.

The coach's second hope is for the client to be moved emotionally by the feedback, to feel pleased by the recognition of their strengths and disturbed by the negative effects of their behaviors on others. These emotions will energize their motivation for change. They may also strengthen their ability to empathize with their stakeholders.

Third, the coach wants to home in on a few messages that will guide the coaching project. The coach wants the client to become more aware of their strengths so that they can use them more consciously and mindfully. And the coach wants the feedback to highlight one or two areas for learning, development, and change. All in all, the coach hopes the feedback will spark a spurt in the client's development.

The coach hopes that new information from the feedback will thrust the client into contemplation about the possibility of change. If the client takes the feedback seriously, they will actually modify their mental models with this new and often challenging information. They will recognize that others are not seeing them as they see themselves, or that their view of their work environment is out of sync with the views of others. Behavior patterns they believed to be effective or innocuous turn out to be ineffective or damaging. In order to become more effective and successful, they will begin to contemplate changing their behavior.

Feedback Case: Stan #1
The Positive Use of Negative Feedback

From his 360° feedback, Stan learned that his staff did not feel he listened to them, and because of this they believed he did not respect them. Stan was concerned because he did respect his staff but understood how his poor listening could create their perception of disrespect. He was disturbed because this is not how he saw himself or wanted to be seen. He decided to correct the situation by developing his listening skills.

Everyday work life does not usually provide focused feedback and the opportunity to reflect on it. Normally, executives move from one action to another, receiving only sporadic feedback and spending little time reflecting on their actions and comparing them to an ideal. The coach can help the client mine the feedback for a motivating purpose.

The coach can create an opportunity to focus on the disparity between the actual and the ideal. The coach can help the client use this tension between the actual and the ideal to motivate their change effort.

360° Feedback: Clues, Not Prescriptions

Feedback describes the other people's perceptions of the client's behavior. Their feedback depicts how they experience the client. The information they share is based on these perceptions. It is important for the coach and client to note that although these individual perceptions are not necessarily absolute facts, perceptions are as important as facts because they form the basis of one's reputation. For example, it may be a fact that a manager completed the project on time and on budget. But it is perception that determines whether he "bullied people into getting it done" or was simply "very focused on achieving results."

Because 360° feedback describes people's perceptions, it needs to be interpreted in context to be of value. It is rarely a good idea to interpret it literally and follow it unquestioningly. By asking the question "What do we think this means?" the client and coach can add their own knowledge to the feedback and come to a realistic interpretation of it.

Feedback Case: Carl #1 Using Feedback to Address Organizational Issues

Carl had moved into a management role in pharmaceutical research. In our 360° interviews, Carl's direct reports described his style as meddling and micromanaging. They said Carl did not trust them to make their own scientific decisions and did not "go to bat" with senior management on behalf of their projects. When I shared this information with Carl, he was not surprised. He went on to tell me about a yearlong struggle with this project team. He needed information about the project to properly sell it to management and get appropriate support. He would regularly ask the team for this information but found it difficult to obtain.

The project team members felt that his questions were intrusive attempts to make scientific decisions that were theirs to make. So they gave Carl only minimal information. This tense cycle continued. In our coaching work, Carl and I recognized the systemic nature of this struggle. Carl decided to meet with the team members and work out a solution in which he would get the information he needs to win the support of senior management while they would retain latitude to make scientific decisions. Carl interpreted the feedback to successfully resolve the issue.

Systems Thinking

Carl's case illustrates the systems of organizational life. Most phenomena, like the perception of micromanagement, are the result of the interactions of several different members of the system, with each responding to the behavior of the others. Looking to one person or group as the cause of the dynamic or as the sole source of change is fruitless. They are inexorably intertwined. The solution lies in all the members of the system recognizing the negative pattern and agreeing to change it.

Survey Instruments

Survey instruments are an efficient method for gathering 360° feedback about a client. The instrument is sent electronically to stakeholders, who rate the client usually on a five-point or seven-point Likert scale (multiple choice rating scale). When scored, they provide clear, quantitative measures of the stakeholders' perceptions, usually in the form of bar graphs. (Some coaches and some organizations prefer surveys because they are less costly to administer than interviews.)

Although survey feedback is concise and quantitative, it is also limiting. The questionnaire restricts the respondent's answers to a limited set of questions. So if the respondent wants to communicate a perception that is outside the questions, they will need to fit their perceptions into the question with closest meaning. Consequently, the coach and client often need to read meaning into the responses to find the most significant bits of feedback. (A sample of a portion of a leadership survey report appears in Exhibit 8.1.)

STEP 4: DETERMINING BEHAVIOR CHANGE GOALS (WEEK 5)

Even though the change process is not particularly linear, the coaching conversations do take place in a series of scheduled meetings that follow one another in calendar time. If we are following this time and activity sequence, up to this point the coach and client have built rapport, planned their project, discussed initial wishes, gathered and interpreted feedback from others, and identified key strengths and development needs. They are now ready to set behavior change goals.

The objective foundations of the goals come from interpreting the feedback, exploring the client's wishes, identifying the organizational challenges, and attending to political and cultural realities. The subjective foundations come from the client's psychological readiness and their decision to attempt a change. If these foundations are in place, the client should be able to identify a behavior change goal. This is usually not hard to do because the information from the client, stakeholders, and culture often converges on a few opportunities. The critical task at this point is to select one or two behaviors and to define them in a way that is specific and meaningful.

The ideal is to identify a new behavior that when regularly employed will make the biggest difference to the organization. Keith's goals were to express more opinions in meetings and to actively coach his staff. Michael's were to communicate plans more specifically and give longer lead times to the consultants. Bill's primary goal was to delegate more decisions to his project managers. For each of them, the goal was no surprise. It had been previously mentioned several times by their stakeholders

EXHIBIT 8.1 Leadership Development Survey

Interpersonal Skills	Positive Responses (%)			
	25	50	75	100
1. Builds relationships with people who can contribute to their results	+ + + + + + + + +			
2. Effectively influences others	+ + + + + + + + + + +			
3. Negotiates and seeks compromise	+ + + + + + + +			
4. Reconciles own needs with the needs of others	+ + + + + + + +			
5. Shows empathy in dealing with others	+ + + + + + + + + +			
6. Successfully manages resistance to new ideas and initiatives	+ + + + + + +			
7. Faces and resolves conflict	+ + + + + + + + +			
8. Seeks to understand and leverage the capabilities of people different from themselves, e.g., different race,gender, sexual orientation, style	+ + + + + + + + + + + +			
9. Politically savvy: uses the formal and informal system to get things done	+ + + + + + + + + + + +			
10. Collaborates actively and effectively	+ + + + + + + + +			
11. Manages relationships with clients (internal and/or external)	+ + + + + + + + + + + + + +			

and in most cases stated by their manager as the goal of the project. The feedback served to validate the organization's wishes and hone it down to a specific behavior in a specific stetting.

It is useful to write down goals in behavioral terms. Many coaches call this a development plan. This plan formalizes the desired change, giving the client an opportunity to envision

Managing People	Positive Responses (%)			
	25	50	75	100
12. Gives clear direction	+ + + + + + + + + + +			
13. Empowers others to make decisions	+ + + + + + +			
14. Delegates appropriately to others	+ + + + + + +			
15. Gives specific and accurate feedback	+ + + + + + + + + + +			
16. Gives feedback in a way that makes improvement possible	+ + + + + + + + + +			
17. Gives praise that increases awareness of strengths	+ + + + + + + + +			
18. Rewards and recognizes people for good performance	+ + + + + + + + + + + + + +			
19. Encourages and supports staff in developing their skills	+ + + + + + + + + + + +			
20. Motivates others to do their best	+ + + + + + + + + + + +			

Source: Discovery Consulting/Partners in Human Resources International.

themselves actually putting the behavior into practice. The goal statement also creates a common language for the new behavior that the coach can ask about and refer to in future conversations. The words in the development plan also serve to remind the client to think about and try out the new behavior. The goal statement should be specific enough to be shared with the client's manager and stakeholders, initially as a verbal contract and later as a reference point for ongoing feedback and reinforcement.

When the client has specified their goal statement, the coach can ask them to commit to it—commit to themselves, to the coach, to their manager, and to selected stakeholders.

Committing usually signifies the transition from contemplation to preparation. The commitment signifies that the client is ready to develop and practice the new behaviors.

Behavior change requires commitment, hyperconsciousness, practice, and risk taking. Because it takes so much energy, clients are likely to be most successful when they focus on one or two new behaviors, rather than five or six. Most experienced coaches recognize this and work with the client, early in the process, to select the one or two developmental goals that will have the greatest positive impact. This can be a hard decision because it may mean ignoring one seemingly compelling behavior pattern because it is not as powerful as another.

For example, Alice and I selected developing a more powerful presence and building organizational structure as her two goals. We decided not to address becoming more organized because its impact on the company and her career would not be as great as the others.

One goal, however, may involve several component behaviors. For example, Craig's efforts to become more influential included three different behavior sets: attending to others, involving them in the idea, and refraining from negative judgments. Becoming skillful at these three behaviors would be take considerable effort and take up our whole coaching program.

Step 5: Preparing for Change: Invention and Rehearsal (Month 2)

There are six tasks that will help the client prepare to put a new behavior into action:

Determining the setting in which the new behavior will be used

Formulating a new mental model to guide the behavior

Inventing a new behavior that fits the goal, the setting, and the client's personality

Identifying and overcoming barriers to using it

Practicing it in coaching to an adequate level of skill and comfort

Begin practicing it in the workplace

Determine the Setting

As described in Chapter Five, identifying the settings is helpful because the settings facilitate defining the specific behaviors. Bill identified two settings as triggers for his new empowerment behavior: when he delegated projects and decisions and when project managers asked him for advice or help.

Formulate a New Mental Model

To be effective and long lasting, the new behavior needs to be rooted in a new mental model. Bill's new model affirmed that the more he enabled the project managers to make their own decisions, the more ownership and initiative they would take and the more satisfied and effective they would be in their job. He would use this model to determine exactly what to say in the two trigger situations.

Invent a Specific New Behavior

Even though the client has defined the behavior in their development plan, they still need to pinpoint its specifics before putting it to use. It is sometimes helpful to ask, "Given what you now know, what would you like to do in this situation?" This gives the client an opportunity to draw on their new knowledge and invent their own behavior. If the client needs help, I may offer a suggestion or refine their proposal. Sometimes it might be useful to select a role model who is particularly skillful in these situations and ask the client to picture how the role model would act. It is important to remember that the client needs to believe in and feel comfortable with the new behavior; if it comes too much from the coach, the client may be less likely to use it. But since the coach does have a solid understanding of the situation at this point, they can view this as a collaboration in the invention of the new behavior.

Sometimes the client may not be able to invent the new behavior by themselves. The challenge might call for a series of new behaviors used together. In these cases, the client needs to add the coach's knowledge and skill to their own in order to invent a new pattern that will work.

Practice Case: Craig #3 New Influencing Behaviors

Craig's goal was to be more effective at influencing people. As we examined his current behaviors, we realized that it would take several new behaviors used together to achieve the effect he wanted. Like any teacher, I broke the lessons into small, digestible parts. First we focused on the nonverbal and emotional skills of making a connection with people. These included eye contact, body posture, and being genuinely interested in their experience. Next we focused on facilitation skills: asking questions, active listening, and reframing. Finally, we addressed adopting a nonjudgmental attitude toward his constituents, no matter what their ability. Over two months, Craig practiced each behavior and attitude, first one at a time and then in combination. He began to master each of the microskills, gradually becoming a skillful influencer.

Identify and Overcome Barriers

Sometimes practicing new behavior exposes a barrier. The barrier may be a personal one, as with Peter recognizing the unconscious strength of his anger response (see Chapter Fourteen). In other cases, it is organizational, as with Bill's recognition that his empowerment initiative would be countercultural and possibly frowned on by senior management. The emergence of the barrier to a desired change presents an excellent opportunity for the client to understand and address it. Because the barrier is appearing in the present, the coach and client can work in real time to trace it to its source. With a personal barrier, they can look for the antecedents that cause the feeling that leads to the behavior. They can memorize the flow of energy from the antecedent to the emotion and finally to the behavior and use this self-awareness to attempt to weaken the pattern at its roots and replace it with an alternative pattern. With an organizational barrier, they can plan ways of circumventing the barrier or camouflaging the new behavior to make it culturally acceptable. Even if their efforts don't fully eradicate the barrier, they build an awareness that enable the client to continue to progress.

Practice with the Coach

Here is where coaching justifies it name. Any new behavior improves with practice. Whether the new behavior is a tennis serve, a golf swing, or a way to lead a meeting, the client will perform better on the field if they practice off the field. I often introduce the practice by reminding the client that they will be more competent and more comfortable if they practice the behavior before using it. Because we have already identified a setting, we can role-play the behavior to give the client a chance to it try out in a simulated setting, to actually say the words and experiment with the content. After an initial role play, clients often want to try it several more times to refine their approach. When they look confident and feel comfortable, we will declare them ready, and plan their first trials of the new behavior in the real world.

Practice Case: Keith #7 Practice, Practice, Practice

Keith was ready to practice expressing his opinions in meetings and defending his team's work. I first asked him to describe a conversation in which he might weigh in. He scripted some words that would express his opinion without sounding redundant. Then I asked him to select a project that a client had rejected and to explain, in language that would appeal to them, why his team chose this creative approach. We added to that what he might say as a comeback in case the client didn't buy in to his first explanation. Keith felt that the practice session gave him a new set of behaviors that he could use in these meetings. He noted that it felt exhausting, just like a workout at the gym, but worthwhile.

Begin Practice in the Workplace

With the setting, the mental model, and the specific behavior in place, the client can now try out the new behavior on the job. It often takes many attempts and many missteps to learn a truly effective, skillful behavior. All the work at defining and practicing it with a coach speeds the process and reduces awkward and costly attempts in the workplace.

Change makes life more energized, more challenging, and more interesting. For some people, this feeling can be uncomfortably intense. Heightened self-consciousness is necessary, especially when clients are trying out new behaviors in the workplace. One client complained of feeling extremely self-conscious. She said she felt incompetent for the first time in her career. She hated the feeling and wanted it to stop. She wanted to know if her old behaviors were really "that bad" and if she could return to them to end her distress.

Step 6: Action and Maintenance (Months 3–6)

As clients begin to experiment with their new behavior in the world, they begin a new phase of their learning in which they are less reliant on the coach and more reliant on themselves and their relationships with their stakeholders. Writing down their learnings and observations can deepen and strengthen their learning. Many clients will keep a journal of their experiences, including a description of the setting, who was there, the nature of the topic, what they said and did, what they thought and felt, how people reacted, and what they might do differently next time. Journaling shortly after a behavioral trial intensifies the experience and burns its lessons more deeply in their memory.

Debriefing the client's experiences also adds to continued learning. At this stage, the coach and client are meeting less frequently, often every few weeks. Over these weeks, the client is trying out their new behavior multiple times. Each of these experiences can become fodder for learning. After preparing in the safe and possibly simplified environment of the coaching room, the client is now gaining experience in the real and imperfect world.

The coach can begin reinforcing the new behavior by honoring and examining the client's efforts. When the client describes using a new behavior, the coach and client have an opportunity to strengthen it by talking about and examining the incident. The coach can stimulate the client's analysis of their experimentation by asking questions similar to those in the journaling exercise:

"Where were you?"

"Who was there?"

"What did you do?"

"What reminded you to do it?"

"What did you think about before doing it? While you were doing it? After doing it?"

"How did you feel?"

"How did people respond?"

"Did things go as you hoped?" or "Did something unexpected happen?"

"What might you do differently next time?"

Answering these questions enables the client to relive the experience and strengthen their neural memory of it. Talking about the experience brings the behavior and its underlying mental models into consciousness and therefore makes it easier to repeat in the future. Both expected and unexpected outcomes provide opportunities for deepening the learning. When things go as hoped, the client can remember what they did, thought, and felt so that they can repeat it. When things don't work out, the client can alter their behavior and even possibly their underlying mental model to get a different outcome.

WHY SOCIAL LEARNING TAKES SO LONG: EXPLICIT AND IMPLICIT MEMORY

Why does it take months to learn a new social behavior so that it sticks when we can learn an equation or a poem in less than an hour? Neuroscientists would explain that the reason lies in the two different types of memory. We use explicit memory to record specific facts or events, like what we had for dinner last night or the name of the new British prime minister. With explicit memory, it usually takes no more than one trial for learning to take place.

We use implicit memory when we gain knowledge to learn a social behavior or a new way of relating to others. Binding a new social behavior in implicit memory takes practice over time. But once it is embedded in implicit memory, the behavior becomes automatic, relieving us of the need to consciously think through its steps before using it. This is because the mental models and neural pathways that support implicit memory change slowly over time in response to experience. Each trial changes the neural pathway a little bit in the direction of the new experience, rather than completely remodeling it in response to one new input. So it can take many trials, over many months, for the new behavior and its underlying cognitive and neural structures to become rewired.

Chapter 9

Coaching Skills and Techniques

In conversation, ask questions more often than you express opinions; when you speak offer data and information rather than beliefs and judgments.

—Will Durant

The Art of Questioning

Coaching enables clients to grow by facilitating changes in their thinking that lead to changes in behavior. If we view thinking as the way people talk to themselves about their interpretations of their world, then creating opportunities to talk to themselves differently becomes the engine for the change process. Of the two primary modes of conversation, statements and questions, questions are the coach's more useful tool. Questions are also more likely to promote learning because they acknowledge that we don't know something; they actively promote thinking by encouraging people to answer with a statement of their own.

Statements are static because they describe what we already know. Statements made by the coach express what the coach already knows and are less likely to inspire new thinking by the client. Statements also assert the power of the coach and are therefore less empowering for the client. Questions stimulate involvement because they ask the client to participate and contribute. Questions thus encourage involvement, learning, and new thinking.

Questions empower both the coach and client. Coaches get to leverage their expertise and intuition by asking questions that lead clients to an appropriate next step. The power of questions for coaches comes from the initiating focus of the questions. Clients get to use their knowledge and insight to formulate answers that move them in the direction of growth. The power of questions for clients comes from the information, emotion, and insight generated by their responses. Generally, both participants work hard and enjoy the give-and-take of the question-and-answer process. Questioning also draws on the strengths of both parties; using the coaches' ability to observe and sense what is important and the client's ability to make sense of their environment.

Questions can facilitate behavior change by leading the client to look at themselves and their environment differently. Questions can encourage fresher ways of looking at things or a more detailed perspective or provide opportunities to fit thoughts and feelings together in a different way. Probing into what is working well can cause the client to learn more about their strengths. Questions about what is troubling can enable them to deepen their understanding of opportunities for improvement. Questions about a particular behavior can lead to identifying its underlying motivations. And questions about its impact on others can crystallize a motivation to change. Fitting this information together in new ways elicits new thinking that leads to learning and change.

A Map to Guide Questioning

Coaches can determine what to ask by using the map of behavior change presented in Figure 9.1 to guide their choice of questions. As with any map, one begins by locating one's current position and then determines where to go next and formulates a question that will lead there. For example, the coach may think, "We have just described the critical behavior in some detail; now I think we are ready to explore her underlying thoughts and feelings."

Exhibit 9.1 presents an excerpt from a coaching dialogue that has been annotated to highlight the intent of the coach's questions. The sequence of questions has been modified to demonstrate how a coach might follow the pyramid in Figure 9.1 to formulate questions, moving from the client's current behavior to their underlying thoughts and feelings to alternative feelings, alternative thoughts, and finally alternative behavior.

Open and Closed Questions

One way to categorize questions is by the degree to which they delineate the response. Open questions give the client a lot of leeway in their response. For example, "What was the most important thing you did last this week?" Closed questions direct the client's attention to a topic selected by the coach. "Did she get upset when you said that?" Most skilled coaches and interviewers follow a line of questioning that begins with a broad,

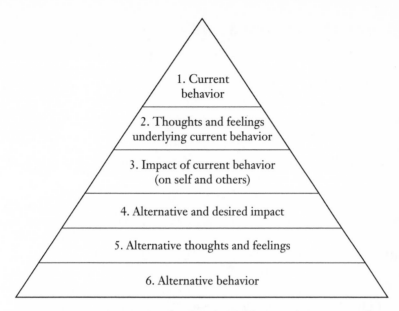

FIGURE 9.1 Map to Guide Coaches' Choice of Questions for Behavior Change

open question on a topic. With each client response, the coach asks more closed questions that delve more deeply into the topic until a valuable, new understanding is reached.

Presupposition Questions

One of the biggest barriers to change is clients' habituated relationship with their current behavior patterns. These patterns reflect the way they view the world, including their emotions and their optimism or pessimism about the likelihood of change. A coach can nudge the client's attitude toward change by asking questions that presuppose a desirable change. A question like "What would it look like if you gave a terrific presentation?" gives the client an opportunity to "experience" the

EXHIBIT 9.1 Annotated Coaching Dialogue

Coach's Questions and Client's Responses	Goal of Question: To Learn About . . .
COACH: So what happens in a meeting when someone says something you disagree with? CLIENT: I usually snap back at the person by saying something like, "How could you say that?" or "Didn't you read the research?"	Current behavior (see pyramid in Figure 9.1, level 1)
COACH: And what were you thinking when you said that? CLIENT: I was thinking that either the person was really stupid or hadn't done his homework.	Thoughts underlying current behavior (level 2)
COACH: How did you feel at that moment? CLIENT: I felt angry that I had to be working with someone like this and insulted that he hadn't read or understood my research report.	Feelings underlying current behavior (level 2)
COACH: And how do you think he felt about having you on his team? CLIENT: He was probably offended by me and wouldn't want to work with me very much.	Impact of current behavior (level 3)
COACH: How would you like your teammates to see you? CLIENT: Naturally, I'd like them to respect me, value my work, and actually use my work.	Alternative impact (level 4)

desired state before they actually attain it. Answering the question enables them to imagine a new reality, one that can compete with their old reality. Such presupposition questions are especially valuable for clients who are pessimistic or have trouble imagining change.

Coach's Questions and Client's Responses	Goal of Question: To Learn About . . .
COACH: Given that you can't control your teammates' actions but you could control your own reactions, no?	
CLIENT: Where are you going with this?	
COACH: I'm wondering if there is another way you could interpret his statement, not agreeing with it but being a bit more tolerant of him?	
CLIENT: But I still think his statement is ridiculous and antiquated.	
COACH: What kinds of experiences do you think he has had that led him to form these ideas?	
CLIENT: He does come from a different background than me. He spent twenty years in sales and distribution and probably had some very different experiences.	Alternative thoughts (level 5)
COACH: And do think those different experiences might have led him to form a different point of view from yours?	
CLIENT: Yes. He worked in the field all those years, counting delivery trucks and returns and things like that. He must have learned some lessons from that.	
COACH: So could you look at his experiences and ideas as just dissimilar, rather than stupid?	
CLIENT: When I look at it that way, he just becomes different. He doesn't feel as threatening or insulting.	

(continued)

EXHIBIT 9.1   *(continued)*

Coach's Questions and Client's Responses	Goal of Question: To Learn About . . .
COACH: If you held on to that view of him as different, what might you say to him next time? CLIENT: From that perspective, I might say, "Stuart, can you tell me how you came to that idea?"	Alternative behavior (level 6)
CLIENT: And how do you think he would respond to you when you treated him that way? COACH: He would probably find it more pleasant and even enjoyable, working with me.	Alternative impact (level 4)

Determining Which Question to Ask

The goal of good questions is to cause the client to look at topics in new ways. Useful questions ask the client to delve more deeply into fruitful topics. The best questions often follow the coach's hunches or hypotheses. They resemble the hypotheses of a research scientist in that the questioner forms a hypothesis and then asks questions to elicit answers that will either prove or disprove the hypothesis. This working hypothesis is an assumption about the nature of the dominant theme in the client's development.

To form a working hypothesis, the questioner uses logic and intuition to think about possible causes underlying the issue. Then they ask about that issue. For example, if the coach hypothesizes that open-minded listening is central to a client's development, they will ask questions about listening: When do you listen? What do you do when you listen? To whom do you listen and not listen? What do you do with what you have heard? What do you say after you have listened? What do you feel when you are listening? And so on.

For example, in a recent meeting, a potential client stated, "My colleague thinks I should work with an executive coach." I hypothesized to myself, "I think she is wondering if hiring a coach would be beneficial or a waste of time." I suspected that she had not thought much about what she would do with a coach. She had probably been viewing it as a yes-or-no decision. So I responded by asking, "What would you want to gain from a coaching relationship?" In answering my question, she began to give herself reasons to enter a coaching relationship. She started to give herself more information about a possible coaching process. She talked about some of the challenges she faced as the president of a newly acquired company and about her leadership style. These topics later became the themes of our coaching program.

The working hypothesis can come from the client as well as the coach. A simple question like "What do you think is important?" can provide the client and coach with a focus for their efforts.

Working hypotheses can be very valuable guides for the coaching dialogue. However, they carry the risk that the coach can leave the client behind. By asking the question from the coach's working hypothesis, the conversation may move in a direction that is not interesting or valuable to the client. The client could play along, attempting to please the coach, moving the conversation toward a solution that the client will ultimately resist because it came from the coach and not from inside themselves.

Because of this possibility, it is important to stay in sync with the client when asking a line of questions. To stay in sync, the coach can ask or assess whether the direction of the conversation seems meaningful to the client. If it is not, the coach can ask the client what direction would be more meaningful. The goal of staying in sync is to explore topics that seem valuable to both the client and the coach.

Powerful questions maintain an equilibrium between delving into the client's statements and pursuing the coach's working hypothesis. For example, my colleague Lilian Abrams was working with a first-level manager in an insurance company. She had come to understand that her client had a difficult relationship with his boss that would hurt him in the long run. But the client didn't consider this relationship important and wanted to focus on other issues.

At the beginning of one session, the client described a troublesome conversation with his boss. Lilian responded to this cue by asking about his feelings toward his boss. The client said that he didn't respect his boss and generally avoided her. Lilian followed by asking about the consequences of this attitude. This question led to a valuable conversation about his attitudes and behaviors in relation to his boss's needs and her power. As a result of answering these questions, the client came to recognize the importance of his relationship with his boss, and it has become a central focus of their coaching project.

EMPATHIC LISTENING

Empathy means feeling another person's feelings—or coming as close as you can to doing so. Empathic people make the other person's experience important and invest their energy in experiencing what the other might be experiencing. People who are empathically gifted unconsciously experience a version of the other person's feelings. Those who are empathically less gifted can develop this ability by consciously concentrating on the other person's words, body language, and condition and attempt to re-create, through the filter of their own emotions, what the person might be experiencing.

The coach can use empathy to help a client expand their self-awareness and eventually their ability to manage their actions. A coach can help clients understand their emotions and mental models more fully through empathic listening. Empathic listening entails paying sharp attention to each new client statement, listening for clues to the client's emotions and their mental models, and continually generating hypotheses about underlying meanings. The coach can then share these hypotheses with the client, often adding content to what was actually said. Through active, empathic listening, a coach can help the client increase their self-awareness, motivation, and consistency in thoughts, emotions, and actions.

Increasing awareness of their emotions and mental models helps clients in two ways. It enables them to act more confidently and influentially in expressing their ideas and goals. It also enables them to alter mental models in ways that make them more effective leaders.

Empathic Listening by the Coach Case: Greg #3
Resolving Conflicting Emotions

Empathic listening is especially helpful when a client has contradictory motivations. For example, in our initial coaching sessions, Greg expressed two contradictory motivations about his career ambitions. One part of him wanted to move into more senior, responsible, and influential roles in his organization. Another part of him felt comfortable in his current middle-management role and didn't need the additional risk or challenge that would accompany a promotion.

In our first few meetings he alternated between wanting more influence and power with senior management and wanting to stay where he was. Both paths had attractions and drawbacks. By listening empathically, I helped him clarify the attractions and drawbacks of the two directions and confirmed that he was conflicted. Exhibit 9.2 summarizes what I heard from Greg.

Even though Greg knew that only he could decide which path to take, he asked me for advice. I felt that any influence I exerted would dilute his motivation in the long run and possibly give him someone to rebel against. I resisted giving advice, restating that this decision would be entirely his. Instead, I proposed that I would act as his sounding board and partner.

We decided to progress, leaving the decision in abeyance and focusing on things he could do that would both increase his effectiveness in his current role and still position him for a larger role. Fortunately, there was a lot of overlap between these actions. Every third meeting or so, Greg would bring up his indecision. He would talk, and I would listen. He was having a debate with himself, and I was the moderator. In these debates, he was free to be as bold or as cautious as he felt. He was able to air both parts of himself. He was able to try on both roles in the light of day and decide which felt better.

After five months, he had made considerable progress in developing his new skills and expanding his relationships. He began the next meeting with a proclamation about his intention to seek more influence and a

EXHIBIT 9.2 Greg's Feelings About a
Possible Job Promotion

Path	Attractions	Drawbacks
Gaining influence	Growing as a leader	Feeling less competent as he tried to influence; possibly failing in his effort
	Using his expertise to shape technology decision making	Working less with technology and more with organizational decision making
	Getting promoted, earning more	Exposing himself to greater political risk
Staying put	Continuing to work in his comfort zone	Becoming stagnant and plateaued
	Staying close to the technology	Feeling left out of major decision making; watching as the organization might make poor technology decisions
	Remaining content with his income and organizational level	Always wondering how far he could have gone

more senior role in the organization. Then he went on to summarize his plan for achieving that. The plan included all of the skills and attitudes we had worked on and more. Somehow his indecision had disappeared. And he was fully committed to the advancement path, even though it would be difficult. He had made his decision.

Two nineteenth-century psychologists, William James and Carl Lange, described the two different ways that behavior and emotion interact. In the more common path, behavior follows emotion. People feel emotion first and then behave in a way that expresses that emotion. For example, if someone is nice to me, I will feel warmly toward them. Then I'll express that feeling by acting friendly toward the person. The second path works in reverse: emotions follow behavior. If I act in a friendly manner toward someone, I will begin to feel warmly toward them. The emotions-follow-behavior path can be especially useful for clients who are stuck between contradictory emotions.

In Greg's case, he was initially caught between the contradictory emotions of ambition and tranquility, effectively short-circuiting his ability to act on either. In our coaching work, he followed the path in which emotion follows behavior. He began acting as if he felt ambition. After a few weeks of trying out and refining some ambitious behaviors, the emotion took hold and he became truly committed to his ambition. When the emotion took hold, it was amazing to watch and listen to the strength of his commitment. He outperformed the textbooks.

REFRAMING

Leaders and coaches have much in common. Among other similarities, both manage meaning; that is, they seize an everyday event and interpret it in a new way, a way that reflects a new, more comprehensive view of the environment, a way that is likely to lead to positive, successful change. The act of reframing can create new meaning from a situation or help someone else create meaning.

In coaching, reframing can serve as a cornerstone of change because it changes mental models. The coach and client examine the client's behavior and environment with an eye toward improving the fit. When they find such an opportunity, they look at the behavior and its underlying mental models. Then they try to reframe the situation in a way that leads the client to change that mental model.

For example, Bob reframed his view that his colleagues were wrong and ignorant into a view that his colleagues merely had different experiences and beliefs than he did. This shift in his mental model enabled him to work more patiently and collaboratively with them.

Reframing is useful not only as a coaching skill but also as a leadership skill. One of the foundations of organizational success is that the whole organization acts in a concerted fashion. It is the leader's role to shape a shared set of mental models and shared sense of meaning that become the basis of these concerted efforts. The leader helps shape this shared meaning by reframing everyday events to facilitate the formation of shared mental models. For many leaders, learning to create meaning by reframing is part of their development. For individuals who are used to the less senior role of managing work and events, learning to reframe can be a skill that transforms them from manager to leader. Reframing is also important in the initiation of new business strategies. In these situations, the organization needs to shift its collective mental model from an old view of the world to a new one.

When leaders decide to help people make this shift, they first need to understand where the employees are today and plan how to help people reframe. They can begin by asking questions like these:

"What are the predominant models held by the organization's members?"

"What events and beliefs created these models?"

In planning to reframe, leaders can look into themselves and ask:

"What new events and data am I aware of that can shed a different light on the situation?"

"What language can I use to introduce the new view that can lead others to adopt a new mental model?"

"How will I recognize opportunities for reframing?"

Reframing by the Leader Case: Alice #2
Connecting with Others' Mental Models

Alice took the helm of Cybern following its acquisition by PharmaSci. The acquisition period had been tumultuous, rife with multiple offers and broken promises. Most of the staff were disgruntled because they had lost their opportunity to make money on their now worthless stock options and because they felt they would lose their autonomy under their new parent company. Alice saw the promise in the acquisition. She believed that the resources and expertise of PharmaSci, combined with the creativity of Cybern, could lead to the discovery of profitable new drugs. She knew that the whole Cybern staff would need to learn more about full-cycle drug discovery and take greater ownership of the key decisions on their projects. To do this, they would need to develop new mental models of their situation.

In our coaching process, we identified as her key mission to influence the predominant attitudes and views (mental models) of the organization's employees in a way that enabled them to successfully manage their drug discovery projects. She hoped she could help people shift from a passive attitude of expecting their bosses to make decisions for them to an active mind-set whereby they took ownership of their decisions and their projects. I use the word *hoped* because she had never done this before.

We began by examining her mental models about Cybern and their situation. We analyzed them in some detail to enable her to fully understand them, to connect her multiple beliefs into a coherent whole, and to put words to these beliefs. After articulating the significant components of her mental model, we looked for opportunities to communicate it. The opportunities fell into three categories: large meetings, small meetings, and one-on-one conversations. In the large meetings, her least favorite, she planned to describe her vision and strategy and support it with observations and examples that would be familiar to everyone. In this reframe, she would be calling up shared experiences and reinterpreting them through a different lens.

In smaller meetings, she would lay out her vision and strategy and then ask members for their reactions and for personal experiences that either supported it or refuted it. In listening to their beliefs and experiences, she would tactfully reframe them to reflect her own beliefs. She would seek both to understand the mental models of the members and to influence them by reinterpreting their experiences.

One-on-one conversations would be different because they occurred more spontaneously. She not only needed to plan for them by clarifying her beliefs and updating them with recent events but also needed to look for opportunities to reframe.

READING PERSONALITY:
RECOGNIZING PATTERNS AND TYPE

The client is the star of the coaching process. Their success is partly dependent on how well the coach understands them and how well they understand themselves. Both coach and client need to have a good understanding of the client's usual behavior patterns, needs, values, and reactions to stress. Talking about the client's career history and perceptions of their current situation can give the coach an initial understanding of the clients' personality traits and expand the client's view of themselves. Conducting 360° interviews provides another valuable perspective. Personality assessments are a third way to accelerate and deepen knowledge about the client. Together, these techniques form the basis for a useful understanding of the client.

Personality Assessments

Personality assessments provide a quick, albeit stereotyped, picture of the client. The tests are based on a set of personality characteristics, preselected by the instrument's authors. The tests generally ask the client a series of questions about their behavior, preferences, or beliefs. The tests are then scored to produce a personality profile providing a description of the client in terms of each of the selected characteristics. Some tests, like the Myers-Briggs Type Indicator, are based on eight characteristics, while others, like the Birkman, are built around more than twenty behavioral and psychological patterns. The questions are usually forced-choice and multiple-choice, which ask the test taker to choose among a few options, each representing one of the predetermined behavior patterns.

Because personality theory is not a hard science with a single, universally accepted model, different instruments measure different characteristics. Consequently, no one instrument provides a definitive assessment of anyone's personality. Some of the tests have been more rigorously validated statistically, and others are more theoretically appealing. Some are short, and some are longer. Coaches have their own personal favorites and use these with most of their clients. Coaches who are skilled with several instruments may select a particular instrument to work with a particular client.

There are more than twenty-five hundred personality assessment tests on the market today, representing a multibillion-dollar industry. Because assessment instruments are so efficient at revealing valuable information about people's behavior and motivational patterns, most coaches use at least one instrument with clients. Similarly, most clients like them because they find the results relatively accurate and appreciate the validated view of who they are. On the other hand, some clients don't like these instruments because they dislike being forced into the boxes of particular personality types or because they believe that their behavior is determined more by a particular situation than by their personality. But all in all, clients and coaches find them a good investment of a few dollars and a few hours of their time.

Most coaches administer assessment instruments early in the coaching process so they can use the information in expanding the client's self-knowledge and creating a relevant development plan. They usually spend one session interpreting the assessment feedback. Then it is often up to the coach to bring the assessment to life in the rest of the coaching process. The coach will look for opportunities to connect the personality feedback to the clients' descriptions of their behavior and their challenges during coaching sessions. Because the tests use memorable and validated personality labels, they can speed the clients' growth by enabling them to interpret ordinary events through the filter of the test. As a coach, I like to use personality assessments but stay on my guard never to become too dependent on them.

Reading Personality: Connecting Strengths and Weaknesses

Successful change requires that the client maintain a balance between comfort with themselves and the desire to change. If the client feels too self-satisfied, they will not be motivated to self-reflect or invest the energy in changing behavior. On the other hand, if they become too dissatisfied with themselves or focus too much on their need to improve, they lose confidence, energy, and courage. The balance is indeed delicate.

One of the most remarkable phenomena in coaching is the symbiotic relationship between strengths and weaknesses. Most people's weaknesses result from an overuse of their strengths. For example, Bob's analytical and conceptual intelligence enable him to sort through reams of data to identify new ways to market his company's products. His strength lay in his ability to grasp concepts and generate ideas. His talents in this arena earned him the praise and attention of senior management. On the downside, he had little patience for people who didn't grasp things as quickly as he did and was unable to consider ideas different from his own. This arrogance alienated people from him. His weakness was a direct outgrowth of his strength.

Bill demonstrates another example of the relationship between strength and weakness. As an experienced research executive, Bill had become proficient at making decisions about his business. His strength lay in designing studies that generated critical data and using those data to make decisions. His overuse of this strength led him to make too many decisions. His staff felt micromanaged because he made decisions for them and for their projects.

Perceiving Traits and Patterns

One of a coach's most important roles is to enable clients to expand their understanding of themselves. The coach attempts to fit together all their observations about their client in the same way that physicians piece together information about their patients. The coach looks for patterns that will help the client develop successfully. For example, Craig was working on influencing skills. After listening to several situations in which he tried to influence people, I recognized that Craig was least successful when he is the most excited about his idea. Craig understood this right away. We were able to use this understanding to speed up Craig's development into a skillful influencer.

Focusing on Behavior

Organizations invest in coaching to change the behavior of their leaders. Even though behavior change is the visible result of a successful coaching project, much of the time in coaching is spent laying the groundwork for behavior change, working on thinking patterns, perceptions, motivators, and other matters that are not actual behaviors. The coach must balance their focus on the client's thoughts and perceptions with a focus on behavior. They need to talk about these nonbehavioral components long enough to lay a proper foundation and then migrate the conversations into plans for behavior change. To accomplish this, they need to know what a behavior is and what it isn't and at the appropriate times move the process toward working on new behaviors. In the early stages of the coaching process, the coach and client work primarily on the context, attitudes, mental models, goals, and challenges related to the desired behavior change. At a certain point, they need to move from the conceptual to the concrete by homing in on a specific new behavior. The coach usually needs to lead this effort.

For example, in working with Bill on empowerment, Bill and the coach needed to progress from a conversation about the need for empowerment and its underlying attitudes to defining the specific things Bill would do and say to promote empowerment. These behaviors might include encouraging people to make decisions and supporting their decisions even when he might not agree with them. Once he had specified these behaviors, he could plan the actual words and actions that will lead to empowerment. He could then practice these behaviors and address barriers to their successful implementation.

IDENTIFYING ALTERNATIVES

Just as there are several ways to skin a cat, there can be a number of behaviors that will lead to a desired outcome. When identifying new behaviors, it is worthwhile to consider more than one alternative. Since they are new behaviors, neither the client nor the coach should have a vested interest in any one of them. Coming up with new behaviors involves creativity. Selecting the best alternative involves deciding on the one that both parties feel will work best in the environment and fit best with the client's style. Even if the coach is very experienced in this particular area, it is important for the client to generate some of the alternatives. It is human nature that if someone comes up with an idea, they will be more likely to remember it and try it out. If the alternative selected is not one suggested by the client, the coach will need to make sure that the client feels comfortable with it. The coach and client may want to consider the following criteria when choosing the best alternative:

How likely is it that the behavior will achieve the desired outcome?

How comfortable is the client with the behavior?

How well does the behavior fit the culture?

CLIENT-CENTERED TEACHING

Coaching is learning. Clients unlearn certain behaviors and learn new ones to replace them. Reshaping interpersonal behavior can be more difficult than learning a new software program or a business technique because it involves changing a comfortable pattern. Teaching involves asking people to expand or change their ways of looking at the world and doing things. People tend to resist this intrusion. A coach needs to respect this potential for resistance while still leading clients toward a new way.

Setting the Stage for Learning

Although coaches are not experts in every topic addressed in the coaching process, there are topics that they know a lot about. If clients need to know more about a topic in order to be successful, it becomes a teaching opportunity. One of the secrets to teaching adults, and children as well, is that they need to be interested and ready to learn. When a client hits one of these learning opportunities, the coach can do a couple of things before jumping into teaching. First, the coach can point it out as a learning opportunity and relate it to the behavior change goal. This should reinforce the client's motivation and readiness. Second, the coach can ask the client if they want to explore and learn about this topic now. By granting this permission, the client is taking ownership of the process and preparing themselves for the open-minded and vulnerable process of learning.

It is helpful if the coach recognizes that adults, unlike children, are used to feeling competent at things. Learning a new behavior throws them into a state of incompetence, and the resulting discomfort can interfere with the learning process. One technique for reducing the discomfort is to relate the new behavior to other areas where the client feels competent. For example, when Tom began grappling with the need to control his angry outbursts, he felt completely overwhelmed and discouraged by the size of the task and the self-discipline it would require. He had told me about his success at losing weight and keeping it off. So I drew a connection between his past success at weight loss and his current challenge with controlling his anger. Not only did he see the parallel, but he also gained confidence and planned to borrow some self-management skills from his weight loss and use them to manage his anger.

Client-Centered Teaching Case: Greg #4
Tapping into the Client's Learning Style

Greg and I experienced one such learning moment. For months, we had been talking about his need to speak more concisely and understandably. And for months, he had been making only slow progress at this. Then, at the beginning of a session, something fortuitous happened. In our introductory small talk about our families, he described a scenario involving his son moving in with him. As he described the situation and all of its possibilities, I became confused. Even using my best listening skills didn't help. Greg's explanation left me quite baffled. When I told him about my confusion, we recognized this as a learning opportunity. I asked him if we could use this as a coachable moment.

I knew that Greg was a visual thinker, so I decided to use visuals to help him learn to speak more lucidly. I asked him to reconstruct his son's move back with Greg. As he spoke, I wrote down the elements of his story, with each element displayed in an oval. When we looked at the ten ovals displayed on the page, it was clear that his original sequence was meandering. So Greg began to resequence the elements in a more understandable way. For ten minutes, he shifted around the ten ovals containing elements of his story until he found a sequence that made the story logical and easy to follow. I then asked him to retell it using the new sequence. It worked. The new story was crystal clear.

Greg learned some important lessons from this episode. He learned that his natural explaining style was circuitous and leapt around too much for other people to follow. He learned that he could prepare a story in advance to make it extremely understandable. And he learned a technique for outlining a story before he told it. As a technology executive who needs to explain complex information to nontechnical people, this skill has become especially valuable to Greg's future success. In the following weeks, he used this technique several times to explain potentially complicated ideas in comprehensible ways.

Using Labels in Teaching

Initially, learning is a conscious activity. The more conscious clients are of the change, the more likely they are to make that change successfully. Because language is the medium whereby people store and access most information, skilled coaches will help clients learn by verbally labeling their relevant behaviors and attitudes. Labels make it easier for clients to change their behavior because the labels remind the clients to think and behave in the new way. The labels serve as reminders. The advertising industry uses this phenomenon when it inundates us with repetitive verbal messages or sound bites that enter our memory and guide our purchasing behavior. Clients can use similar verbal reminders to guide their leadership behavior.

Labels are powerful because they represent a lot of important and meaningful information, particularly future wishes, past experiences, and situational cues. For Bill, the "empowerment" label reminded him of hours of thoughts and feelings about the benefits of empowerment, the consequences of disempowerment, and the situations where he would be tempted to make decisions for his staff. On his second behavior change goal, he used the label "context" to remind him to tell people about his reasons for asking them a particular question. By giving them a meaningful "context," he would counteract their perception that he was secretive and untrustworthy. Because it was important to him and his business to increase autonomy and trust, he kept the "empowerment" and "context" labels in his active memory during his workday. These labels reminded him to think and act differently in key situations.

Practicing New Behaviors

Once the coach and client have invented new, more constructive behaviors, it is time to prepare for applying them in the workplace. Practice enables the client to become skillful and comfortable with the new behavior and to use the behavior repeatedly over time. For behavior change to last, the client needs to gradually erase old memories and the associated neural pathways and to form new memories and pathways. Behavioral psychologists, neuroscientists, and athletic coaches have taught us that this takes repetition and practice. Coaches can create opportunities for clients to rehearse their new behaviors. The practice may be as basic as asking the client, "What would you say if one of your staff asked you to make a decision for them?" Or it may involve a lengthier practice of responding empathically to a staff member. It may also take the form of a role-play in which the coach plays a significant other. What is important is that the client actually try out the new behavior by saying the new words, thinking the new thoughts, and experiencing the new sensations. This is the kind of practice that builds new neural pathways.

Role-playing is an excellent form of practice, especially for interpersonal behaviors. Usually the coach plays the stakeholder and the client plays himself or herself. The client invents a realistic scenario. Depending on the difficulty of the situation and client's skill level, the coach may want to give the client a few minutes to prepare. Then both players play their parts. The coach becomes an actor, trying to portray the constituent as accurately as possible. When they have finished, they debrief the exercise, asking questions like "What worked well?" "What were you thinking or feeling?" and "What would you do differently next time?" If the client doesn't yet have the skill or confidence for role-playing, the coach can introduce reverse role-playing, in which the coach plays the client and the client plays the stakeholder. This way the coach models the new behavior and the client gets to empathize with the stakeholder. They can then work up to a full role-play.

Clients differ in their need and appetite for behavioral practice. Some clients quickly understand the new behavior and are able to readily translate it into words and actions. It is important for the coach to recognize the client's abilities and suggest just enough, but no more, practice than they need. Some clients may actually need to practice the new behaviors but find this type of practice simplistic or rinky-dink. In these situations, a good coach will hang tough and persuade the client to practice. This resistance to practice can come from a fear of failure or of feeling incompetent at the new skill. The coach can respond to this by acknowledging the client's discomfort and describing advantages of making mistakes with the coach over making them in the workplace.

Chapter 10

Coaching Perspectives

The goal of coaching is behavior change. The social sciences provide us with many theories and much research on behavioral change. A quick survey of the field reveals several separate perspectives and approaches to human behavior. Each perspective is uniquely valuable in coaching because each describes different forces that contribute to a person's actions. A pragmatic coach will use several perspectives and approaches in helping a client develop into a more effective leader.

BEHAVIORAL PERSPECTIVE

This approach addresses only observable behavior and the ways in which reward and punishment shape certain behaviors. It is derived from the behaviorism of B. F. Skinner. Learning theory, an outgrowth of behaviorism, describes the process through which people acquire new or complex behaviors. We don't need to look far for evidence of the power of behavioral psychology in shaping our behavior. Our society uses financial reward or public recognition to encourage socially desirable behaviors and threat of punishment to discourage antisocial behaviors. A behavioral approach is particularly useful in coaching because the goal is always some form of observable behavior change.

Coaches working from a behavioral perspective will focus on specific behaviors to establish a client's patterns of action. What do they do and say? Under what conditions do they do and say these things? What are their favorite actions? What are their least favored actions? For example, if the client is working on listening the coach will attend to how the client listens, when they listen (for example, in one-on-one conversations), when they don't listen (in meetings), and what they do instead of listening. The coach will look at the other people who are the recipients of the listening behavior: peers, senior managers, direct reports, and clients. And they will also look for the positive or negative reinforcers of the behaviors—for example, how limited listening saves the client's time by keeping conversations short. All in all, the coach focuses on the tangible, observable aspects of the client's actions.

Cognitive Perspective

This approach focuses on the thought processes that drive behavior. It is derived from the work of Jean Piaget, Jerome Bruner, and others. Cognitive psychology is based on the premise that humans are inveterate thinkers. Some call us the "sense-making" animals. Because of this, thinking is a powerful shaper of behavior. People form thoughts and mental models that shape their behavior in nearly every aspect of their lives. They have thoughts about what kind of car to buy, the best ways to interact with their bosses, and whom to copy on an e-mail. Some thoughts lead to successful actions, while others lead to actions that fail.

There are three types of thinking that I find particularly valuable in coaching:

- *Mental models:* The thinking patterns and rationales that underlie the client's behavior; the motives and intentions that drive their behavior
- *Beliefs:* Attitudes about the way the world works and how the client relates to the world; the sense of why people act as they do; the sense of how their industry and discipline work and why things work the way they do
- *Self-concept:* How the client views themselves; how they believe others view them; how they would like to view themselves; the degree to which they respect and feel good about themselves; the degree to which they feel shame and inadequacy; their awareness of their own behaviors and the rationales for these behaviors

When taking a cognitive perspective, the coach and client examine the thinking patterns that underlie the client's significant behaviors. They determine which patterns lead to successful action and decide to hold on to this thinking. They can also look at the thinking that underlies problematic behavior and find one or more alternative ways of thinking about these situations. In many instances, the new thinking will lead to an array of new behaviors. Because one thinking pattern can shape several behaviors, a cognitive approach can be faster and more comprehensive than a purely behavioral approach in which each behavior is addressed separately.

Unlike behavior, thought is invisible. So cognitive structures may just be a useful metaphor for what goes on in someone's mind. For me, understanding a client's cognitive structure is so important that I will create a graphic picture of their cognitive structures and use this picture to guide our work. Because of my own background and personality style, I rely heavily on the cognitive approach.

Cognitive Approach Case: Mitch #1
A Thinking Man's Path to Change

Mitch is a senior editor for a national publication. His goal in coaching was to develop more social relationships at work and break his habit of isolating himself from his peers. For example, he planned to lunch and network with his colleagues rather than eating lunch alone while surfing the Internet.

In our third session, it became clear that Mitch had some strongly held beliefs that were keeping him from initiating lunches. The first was a dislike for ambiguous conversations that did not have a discrete business purpose, since they left him feeling insecure about what to say. The second was his notion that salespeople were slick con artists. The third was his belief that it was politically dangerous to join cliques, stemming from his memory at a previous job of an entire clique that was fired by a new management regime. The fourth was his belief, passed down from his mother, that small talk was a waste of precious time.

No wonder Mitch ate lunch alone. He had a solid, four-legged, cognitive foundation for avoiding informal work relationships. As much as I wished, these foundations weren't about to disappear. But I believed that Mitch could weaken them by talking about them. As he described each belief, he became more aware of its almost haphazard evolution and the current risk it created. Examining his four mental models weakened their unconscious power over him. The more he talked, the more he realized that they were old, personally held beliefs, even superstitions, rather than inviolable facts. Mitch was skillful at self-reflection and motivated to change his behavior, so this approach eventually gave him greater freedom of choice over his social behaviors. He soon began scheduling meetings with his peers and seniors, building important new relationships, and generating new ideas and building political support for some of his projects.

One tool that was particularly valuable in working with client's mental models is the "ladder of thinking" model (see Figure 10.1), which describes how people form their points of view. The ladder concept is based on the cognitive psychology of Jean Piaget and has been adapted to organizational psychology by Chris Argyris and Peter Senge. (Senge labels it the ladder of inference.)

The ladder describes how people form their points of view, or conclusions, by inferring meaning from their own experiences, assumptions, and beliefs. Moving up the ladder:

1. We make observations on the basis of our experiences.
2. We select relevant data from these observations.
3. We use these data to form assumptions and beliefs.
4. We combine our beliefs to form conclusions and points of view.

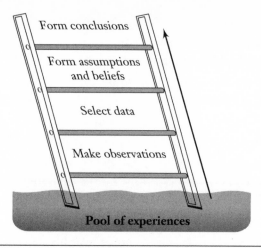

FIGURE 10.1 The Ladder of Thinking: How People Form Ideas

Throughout history, humans have been drawn to self-confident people as leaders. Although self-confidence does contribute to leadership, it's very easy for a naturally confident leader to step over the line into arrogance. These leaders overuse their self-confidence to the point of squelching the ideas and needs of others. Overconfident people are different in that they truly believe that they are right and that their point of view is the only reasonable one. Overconfident people regard their own ladder of thinking as the only way to look at a topic. They see their conclusion as the only possible truth. They are often unaware of the source of their conclusion and similarly unaware of the possibility that others could arrive at equally sound yet different conclusions.

Cognitive Approach Case: Mark #1
Confidence as a Road Block

Mark was one of these leaders. He was smart and assertive but overconfident. Other members of his organization were less confident and sometimes more thoughtful than he. His confidence was amplified by his extroverted personality. He had naturally high energy and liked to talk a lot and think out loud in a group. It was easy for him to dominate a room. More often than not, his ideas overshadowed the ideas of others. The ideas of others became lost or never even spoken. His colleagues grew to resent him for short-circuiting conversations with his confident pronouncements. Over time, they began to feel left out or undervalued. They learned to contribute less because their ideas didn't seem to matter. The group's innovation suffered because it had fewer ideas available.

This is how his constituents described Mark. "He says everything in such a confident manner. He always believes he is right. He is very opinionated. He is absolute, too absolute. He is not even interested in walking people through his thinking process."

Mark's colleagues saw him as a bully. Their resentment caused them to reduce their commitment and engagement in his project teams. Some left his group. Others simply stewed silently.

Mark's overconfidence reduced his credibility in another way. Since he was very enthusiastic and confident about all his opinions, his constituents couldn't differentiate between opinions and facts. Gradually, they came to doubt him, not knowing which ideas were true or which were simply Mark blowing smoke.

In coaching Mark, I employed several strategies, most of them cognitively based, to help him lose his overconfidence and reach a constructive equilibrium between confidence and curiosity. I chose to use the ladder of thinking in our coaching work because I believed it could give him some perspective on his own thinking.

I began drawing the model and explaining it to Mark as a way to increase his awareness of other people's ladders of thinking. This enabled him to develop a broader perspective on his conclusions. Through this awareness, he came to recognize that his ideas are simply his ideas, not necessarily "the truth." He also recognized that others could have different experiences, assumptions, and beliefs and therefore reach different conclusions.

Mark took his new understanding very seriously and used it to change the way he related. It enabled him to become curious and ask more questions about other people's points of view. His understanding of his own ladders of thinking enabled him to provide a more logical rationale for his ideas and to present them less stridently. He began to shift his behavior from arrogance to receptivity.

His colleagues responded quickly to this new stance. They felt freer to introduce their own ideas. They became more willing to collaborate because they felt more equal. The climate changed from resistance to exploration.

Cognitive Approach Case: Bob #2
Dialogue, Don't Dismiss

Bob is intelligent, well educated, and opinionated. As a marketing manager in the publishing industry, his knowledge of statistics and market research are important to the success of his company. Yet he had developed a reputation for being arrogant, harsh, and critical of others. When I met Bob, he countered these remarks by saying that his views were crucial to the future success of his company and that he "didn't suffer fools gladly." Even though peers and managers regularly criticized him, he was kind of proud of his reputation. This criticism actually strengthened his belief that he was right and that others were not smart enough or progressive enough to understand him.

Bob was not going to easily abandon his strongly held belief that "I'm right and they're ignorant." His motivation to work with me came from his desire to wield more influence and to advance his career. After the fourth session, we began exploring this core issue of his intellectual arrogance.

Bob prided himself on his analytical, intellectual style much more than on his ability to form relationships. So I began working with him on the cognitive foundations of his belief that he was right and others were wrong. Using the ladder of thinking model, we walked through the process by which people form opinions. I asked him to describe a business opinion so we could trace its origins. I asked him questions that encouraged him to describe its various sources. A light bulb seemed to go on as he came to recognize that even his opinions were founded on individual experiences and beliefs rather than absolute truths.

As a next step, I gave an example of one of my strongly held opinions and asked him to ask me questions that would reveal the source of my idea. In asking and listening, he coached me as he learned about how I came to hold my cherished opinion. Through this exercise, Bob developed two new strengths. First was his realization that ideas derive from an individual's experiences, assumptions, and beliefs and that different experiences can lead to different opinions. Second, he learned how to ask questions that encourage colleagues to reveal the sources of their ideas. This would enable him to establish dialogues with people with whom he disagreed, dialogues that could serve as a valuable substitute for dismissing them and their ideas. They would become the building block of a new way of relating.

VALUES PERSPECTIVE

A common definition of values is "things that are important to a person" or "things that they cherish and want in their lives." Values seem to combine thought and emotion, though I do not know of any research to support this theory. They are partly derived from the cognitive ladder of thinking and partly related to a person's emotional life because they define what the person cares deeply about.

The following are some commonly held work-related values:

High earning potential
Power and authority
Ability to work well
   under pressure
Independence
Fast pace
Creative expression
Recognition
Competence
Status, prestige
Efficiency

Influence with people
Security
Competition
Change and variety
Affiliation
Decision making
Advancement
Challenge
Risk taking
Working on the
   cutting edge

The Role of Values

Values play a major role in shaping people's behavior. People who value efficiency will invest a lot of energy in making their workplace efficient. People who value relationships will spend a lot of time cultivating and maintaining them. People who value creativity will regularly seek out opportunities to innovate. Like emotions, values shape behavior. Values, however, are enduring, whereas emotions are temporary.

Values Perspective Case: Tamara #1
Modifying Values to Achieve Success

Tamara is the manager of a corporate travel department. She places a lot of value on external rewards. This has been an important force in her career, motivating her to work hard in pursuit of promotions, raises, and formal recognition. Her next goal was to become a vice-president. As hard as she worked and as much as she accomplished, the promotion remained elusive. Her manager was the vice-president in the department and was not about to leave, retire, or get promoted.

As time went on, she worked harder and harder and accomplished more and more. She received kudos from senior management but no promotion. She became upset and depressed. She grew angry with her management and frustrated with herself. She wasn't sleeping well and was becoming distracted at work. To deal with the pressure mounting within her, she began interviewing outside the company.

In our coaching conversations, we explored the cause of her pain. It became clear how much she valued external rewards. She defined her life by physical evidence of the approval of others. When that was forthcoming, her system worked. She felt motivated, liked herself, and felt committed to her reward givers. When, through no fault of her own, the rewards slowed, she felt stymied, practically traumatized.

Tamara began to recognize the problems with being so externally focused. We pondered the possibility of providing herself with approval. She realized that although she got some satisfaction from doing a good job, developing useful new products, and managing people well, these couldn't compare to tangible rewards from others. She became more conscious of her own contribution to her dilemma. For the next few months, though she remained disappointed with her career progress, she experimented with a more internally focused reward system. Slowly, the new value began to take hold.

When I saw her two months later, she was a new person. She was in the same job, with the same manager, and still in the same position. But she was very happy. She was getting great enjoyment from developing products and from building relationships with some senior people. She had started a graduate program in marketing and was thrilled with it. She was getting so much satisfaction from her work and school that her need for external rewards had receded into the background. She had become a happy person and a more effective leader.

Beliefs and Values

Beliefs are the cognitive cousins of values. They include a mix of our values and the more cognitive conclusions we have drawn about life, work, people, and other things. They form the second-highest rung on the ladder of thinking and are often connected to our values. We form beliefs by drawing conclusions from a series of related experiences. For example, I believe that it is possible for people to change their behavior because I have witnessed such changes a number of times. Also, I grew up believing strongly in the improvability of people and societies. For most of us, our beliefs and values are congruent because our values bias the sample of experiential data we choose to perceive.

Combining Cognitive and Values Approaches Case: Tamara #2 Working with Beliefs

Tamara experienced another dilemma caused by her beliefs. Growing up, her father taught her that hard work would lead to success. She took this message seriously and worked hard at every job she held, earning respect and success throughout her career. She passionately believed that her company was, or should be, a pure meritocracy in which hard work, good judgment, and honesty would earn continued success. But at this point in her career, the formula didn't seem to be working. She was doing all the things that had worked for her in the past but was experiencing some negative results. Her boss was acting threatened by her productivity and trying to keep her down. A colleague felt oppressed by her high standards and was working to undermine her. And she was getting criticism from senior management for not getting along with others. Tamara reacted to this with disbelief and denial. Holding on to her belief in meritocracy, she simply worked harder and felt purer, which merely continued her political dilemma.

In our coaching, we examined her dogmatic belief in hard work and meritocracy. She walked down her ladder to trace the belief to her father and to the early part of her career. Then we compared this belief to her actual experiences as a middle manager in a large corporation. She recognized that some of her recent experiences didn't fit her beliefs. Pure hard work with little self-promotion and an expectation of ultimate fairness were actually hurting her career in some ways. She realized that others had different work habits and different beliefs about the formula for success. Over a period of weeks, she began to see her old beliefs as somewhat simplistic. She started to refine her formula for success to include adapting her behavior to the style of others, subtly promoting her accomplishments, and avoiding stepping on the toes of others. To both of us, this change felt like a loss of innocence but a gain of realism.

Emotional Perspective

Many psychologists address the emotions and emotional drives that shape a person's current behavior. This perspective began with Freud and has been furthered by Fritz Perls and others. Some examples of emotions at work can be seen when people seek approval, feel afraid, get angry, and protect themselves from embarrassment. These emotions and needs lead to certain behaviors, some with positive and others negative impacts. To truly change critical behaviors, clients need to identify the emotions and motivations that underlie those behaviors. Once identified, the clients can then recognize those emotions when they arise and use this awareness to act more thoughtfully and less impulsively in the situation. The awareness gives them greater choice and flexibility.

Why address emotions? Isn't it more efficient and more professional to focus primarily on behavior? Coaches who work with clients on emotions understand that emotions shape behavior. One reason for addressing emotions is that if they aren't recognized, they can creep up and unconsciously influence the clients' behavior in ways that are counter to their conscious goals.

Moreover, leading comes more easily when leaders know their feelings. Decisions and actions that feel right emotionally seem more comfortable and flow with less effort than those based solely on thought. Emotions also enable leaders to act authentically. Leaders who say or do things in a way that expresses feelings are more compelling than those who express themselves unemotionally. Such leaders feel more energized, and colleagues are more receptive to the things they say.

In working with emotion, I seek to understand what the client feels as they move through their work life. What is their awareness of the events that stimulate their feelings? What makes them happy, sad, scared, anxious, or angry? What motivates or energizes them? Similarly, what do they value? I will bring these data into the mix with the other information we learn about the client and use it all to expand the clients' self-knowledge and eventually their ability to master their behavior.

Anger

Anger is a particularly powerful emotion that crops up in organizational life. By nature, the boundaries between people's territories frequently overlap, and their interests may often conflict. Even in the best-managed organizations, people who are doing their jobs will step on the toes of others. Because they lead functions or departments, managers experience these overlaps more often than others with less responsibility.

The most effective response to these incursions is to assert one's boundaries and tell the other person to back off. But some people cannot do this. They cannot protect themselves from these infringements. They are usually aware that others are making them look bad or encroaching on their sphere of influence, but they can't respond with an appropriate, self-protective response. The result is that others then continue to sully their reputation and whittle away at their power because they haven't been told to stop.

Why do people allow this encroachment? The cause is often an inability to express anger or disapproval toward others. I have worked with several people with this pattern. In every case, the pattern reduces their effectiveness and damages their career.

Emotional Perspective Case: Jim #1 Helpless Anger

Jim is an upbeat, cheerful guy with a generally positive outlook on life. He is smart, friendly, and service-oriented. He had been successful as a manager of installation and repair in the software industry. In his last few jobs, he had started strong, developing a reputation as a skilled manager of technology and client relationships. In each situation, however, his reputation plummeted as others, especially salespeople, shifted blame to him for poorly conceived contracts. Clients blamed him when they didn't fulfill their role in a project. He was very successful when he had senior managers who would stand up for him. But without this protection, others continued to take advantage of his inability to protect himself.

Jim saw himself as a nice guy who enjoyed working hard, solving problems, and helping others. He relied on being friendly and accommodating. And most people appreciated him, except those who found it convenient to scapegoat him. Once they learned that Jim actually permitted this scapegoating, they employed it whenever it served their interests.

Jim knew what was going on, but without a behavior to counteract it, he was helpless in the face of these attacks. Instead he became silently resentful of his trespassers and the managers who wouldn't protect him. He developed long-standing grudges toward those who hurt him. He ceased contact with them, which naturally further hurt him politically. In addition, he began to lose confidence in himself and to become anxious about his career.

Jim's first learning step was to recognize this pattern, how people encroached on him and how he responded or didn't respond. We also explored the damage that he suffered from this pattern. My initial goal as his coach was to strengthen his motivation to address this issue. I believed his avoidance of anger was probably long-standing and deep-seated. It would take considerable diligence to overcome this strong psychological habit.

My strategy was to help Jim recognize exploitive situations, connect with his anger, and learn some behaviors that would send a "don't tread on me" message. I suspected he would need to abandon his unilateral nice-guy image and develop a more flexible set of behaviors, including expressing anger. I encouraged Jim to feel righteous anger against individuals who trespassed on him. It took several conversations for Jim to evolve from a passive, past-tense resentment to a more active, present-tense anger.

We both knew that raw expressions of anger would be inappropriate in his work environment. But feeling his anger would be an important signal to do something or to protect himself. We first invented and then practiced politically acceptable ways to express anger. Jim learned to channel his anger at work. His reputation had become so weak that he needed to leave his company, but he learned his new behaviors well and used them successfully in his next job.

Neuroscientific Perspective

For simplicity's sake, I will combine behavioral, cognitive, emotional, and psychodynamic psychologies with the latest findings in neuroscience. In doing this, I assume that behaviors, thoughts, mental models, feelings, and unconscious drives all have neural foundations. As a client learns new things about themselves, thinks new thoughts, and feels new emotions, these are all accompanied by the creation of new neural pathways. By working in all these perspectives over the course of a coaching process, the client grows new pathways. Because they are working on several levels, the new pathways and new behaviors will be interlinked and therefore firmly embedded in the client's mind.

The neuroscientific perspective guides my coaching in each of the phases. In moving from precontemplation to contemplation, I look to create opportunities for clients to repeat their new belief in the possibility and desirability of change, hoping that repetition will deepen their new neural pathways. Similarly, in the preparation phase, I will intentionally use labels that enable the client to quickly locate new thoughts, behaviors, and settings in the geography of their brain. Most important, I will ensure that the client has practiced enough for the new behaviors to form new neural pathways deep enough to use under the pressure of a work situation.

Developmental Perspective

Several psychologists have focused on the developmental stages that people go through over their lives. These "age and stage theories" state that people's needs and purpose changes over their life span. The goals and interests of a forty-five-year-old are usually different from those of a thirty-year-old. The theories were originated by Erik Erikson and Carl Jung, then expanded on by George Valliant and Daniel Levinson and differentiated for women by Nancy Schlossberg. Their theories are supported by cases that describe the typical life and career goals of people at various stages of life. These age and stage theories provide another lens through which a coach can interpret clients.

Developmental Perspective Case: Valerie #1
Moving into a New Life Stage

Valerie was a forty-year-old pharmaceutical scientist. She had built a successful career on scientific competence and a strong work ethic. Through high school, college, graduate school, postdoctoral work, and ten years of corporate life, her achievement came from her knowledge of science, her dedication to research, and her pleasant demeanor.

When I started working with her, she had become dissatisfied with her job. Though she still liked science, it didn't motivate her as it once had. She wanted to do something different, but she wasn't sure what. I gave her some career assessments to complete. As we reviewed these assessments, it became clear that she wanted to do work that was more engaged with people. She wanted to help and teach people. She wanted to use the knowledge she had gained to guide and mentor younger people. Supervising her one lab associate was satisfying but not enough. She wanted leading and teaching to be a major part of her job, not just a sidelight.

We thought about her seeking to become a manager in her company, but she was not on the "management track" and determined that it would take too many years to position herself for a management role there. She looked to academia and found a position managing a research lab that employed ten people and teaching a graduate course in her discipline. It had everything she wanted—teaching, mentoring, and science—at nearly the same salary as her corporate job.

"Doing science" was satisfying for her at thirty but not at forty. Valerie had moved into a new life stage, one that emphasized giving back more than producing. As she became more aware of her new goals, she knew she needed to change her job in order to fulfill them.

INTEGRATING THE PERSPECTIVES

Developing the whole person often involves working from most or all of these perspectives. It involves working with the various dimensions of the person. When integrating, a coach might ask and answer questions such as these:

"How are the dimensions connected?"

"Where and how do the dimensions support or reinforce each other?"

"Where do they interfere with each other or pull the person in opposite directions?"

Chapter 11

Forces That Interfere with Growth

We do not "kick out of the house" any subself or part of the personality but rather understand and integrate its energy and its functions back into the self organization. . . . There are no outcasts and no prisons to lock up the deviants.

—STEWART SHAPIRO, *The Selves Inside You*

There are many reasons why people don't change. Outwardly, many people resist change with tough demonstrations of disinterest or annoyance. However, underlying these hard emotions are often more vulnerable ones.

Anxiety is one of these emotions. People's existing mental models and behavior patterns are familiar and comforting to them. The models are supported by neural pathways that have become ingrained, even addictive. People know intuitively that giving these up will involve discomfort, even distress. They also recognize that in forging new patterns, they may feel strange or out of control. The anxiety they feel about giving up the old and embarking on the new is enough to make them want to avoid the whole endeavor.

Fear is the cousin of anxiety. Contemplating change can stimulate fear of failure, fear of embarrassment, fear of looking bad. As adults, we are used to feeling competent. When we attempt a new behavior or a new pattern of thinking, we feel awkward, even clumsy. In order to save face, we may avoid the new pattern and stick with the familiar, the tried and true.

People often avoid the discomfort of anxiety and fear by defending themselves and their traditional ways. They do this because the self is being challenged to become restructured. The best way to overcome it is to understand the nature of self-defense and work with resistant thoughts, feelings, and behaviors. In this chapter, we will define some common expressions of resistance and explore some ways of dealing with them.

Resistance

Almost all clients resist the coach or the coaching at some point. People vary in the ways they resist. Some will deny the existence of a need or minimize its importance. Others will ignore issues by discrediting the feedback from others. Others will agree to the need but then not act. Others will argue with the coach. And others will sit quietly, keeping their resistance to themselves. However people express it (see Exhibit 11.1), resistance is a real and natural reaction to the challenge of change. Unless it is addressed and weakened, it will undermine or even doom the coaching process.

EXHIBIT 11.1 The Many Faces of Resistance

Type of Resistance	Sample Comment	Analysis
Denial of impact—refusing to acknowledge the need, problem, or potential benefits of an alternative; insisting that things are fine the way they are	"I've been doing it that way my whole career and it has worked fine."	Individuals strongly identify with their current behavior pattern. They believe there is no obvious problem. Recognizing the undesirable effects of their behavior and contemplating change involve feeling bad and engaging in hard work. It is easier to believe that things are fine and that there is no need to change.
Restating the old mental model	"The firm is not well managed. It wasn't straight with me, so I don't have to do anything differently."	Individuals avoid considering alternative perspectives by repeating their current perspective, sometimes in a chantlike manner. This repetition reinforces their old perspective and attempts to ward off other ways of looking at the situation.
Arguing or anger—insisting that someone else's idea or perception is wrong and that one's own way is the only correct one; attacking the other person's credibility	"Your approach is wrong. It is too soft and won't work with my people. They need to be told what to do."	Individuals refuse to consider a new perspective by convincing themselves that it is wrong and that their perspective is the only correct one.

(continued)

EXHIBIT 11.1

(continued)

Type of Resistance	Sample Comment	Analysis
Self-deprecation, defeatism	"I'm just not a good manager. I let people push me around. I just keep screwing up."	This kind of defeatism gives people an excuse to avoid stretching themselves and developing a new behavior or thinking pattern.
Blaming others	"Management put me in an impossible situation with unrealistic deadlines and incompetent staff. I had to bully everyone to get the work out."	By completely externalizing the cause of their behavior, people absolve themselves of all responsibility and limit the opportunity to look at their own motives and attitudes.
Making weak attempts at change	"I tried what you said, but it didn't work."	By making half-hearted attempts at change, people feel they have done something, but they are avoiding the real work of changing their behavior and underlying attitudes.
Agreement without follow-through	"I'll try to do it."	Individuals agree with the coach to take the pressure off in the coaching session but do not change their thinking or make any serious attempts to change their behavior.
Forgetting—committing, then not remembering to follow through	"Oh, I had a very busy week and didn't get to it."	People are not sufficiently motivated to remember their commitments in between coaching sessions.

Why Do People Resist?

Resistance is a way for the self to protect itself from change. Clients recognize that the coach, the organization, and even parts of themselves want them to change. But even clients who want to change can feel that outsiders' attempts to change them are assaults on the self, on their existing way of perceiving, thinking, feeling, and behaving. The existing self resists being restructured, sometimes mightily.

Resistance to change is similar to the ways that all living things protect themselves from physical threats. Clients view their current behavior patterns as living organisms that are being threatened by the prospect of change. Living things respond to such threats by protecting themselves, either by attacking like a bear or hiding like a turtle or refusing to move like a mule.

Sources of Resistance

Resistance to change can have many sources:

- Defense of a familiar and comfortable self-concept and behavior patterns
- The anxiety that accompanies letting go of the old, learning and integrating the new, or facing something that appears to be beyond one's control or about which the outcome is uncertain
- Fear of failure, of embarrassment, of looking bad, awkward, or clumsy
- Pessimism about the ability to change
- Not truly understanding what needs to change or feeling

overwhelmed by overestimating the extent of the needed change

- Not having people in their corner to listen and provide support and encouragement
- Ambivalence about the goal
- Fear of unleashing personal "demons"

Dealing with Resistance

The coach's role in overcoming resistance is to listen, support, and collaborate—not to try to talk the client out of their resistance. The coach can present a different perspective on reality, one that is less self-protective but still optimistic. They can introduce perspectives and options not previously available to the client.

The best way to overcome resistance is to understand its nature and to work with resistant thoughts, feelings, and behaviors. Resistance is usually energized, which means that is an expression of something important to the person. Even though resistance can feel like an attack or a disappointment to the coach, it can actually express useful information and represent a necessary step in the change process. By resisting, the client reveals information about themselves, particularly about the values and beliefs that feel challenged by the change. The skillful coach will address resistance with respect and curiosity.

Labeling the resistance is another way to use it in the growth process. Other professionals use labeling to move through resistance. Conflict mediators label areas of agreement, disagreement, and shared desires as a way to focus on what the parties have in common. Psychotherapists work with clients to define and label problematic parts of themselves, such as the angry part or the jealous part. Even salespeople use labeling when they ask their customers to talk about what they are looking for and what they like and don't like about a particular product. Labeling enables both parties to isolate particular parts of the self. Labeling the resistant part enables clients to broaden their perspective by examining the resistance with a degree of distance, thus giving them the power to lessen its influence if they wish.

Resistance can also be seen as one side of an inner debate the client is having with themselves, sort of their pros and cons regarding the change. By giving the con side a voice, they can address it and through this conversation between these two parts of themselves discover a new stance that incorporates both parts.

Resistance Case: Ethan #1
Everything's Black and White When You're Angry

Ethan is a project manager in a mid-sized architectural firm. He has a reputation at the firm as heroically rescuing difficult projects by hard work and disciplined architecture. Last year, the firm took on a difficult project for a demanding client with a nearly impossible deadline. When the project ran into trouble, Ethan was assigned to manage it. He approached it with his usual diligence, high standards, and attention to detail. When a deadline loomed, he insisted that the junior architects stay late to finish and admonished anyone who balked. When a junior architect handed him mediocre work, he critiqued it and handed it back. If his architects continued to make errors, he verbally criticized them, sometimes loudly.

Ethan's team did complete the project successfully, but at great cost. The junior architects felt demeaned and abused by Ethan; two of them eventually left the firm. Some complained to management about the way Ethan treated them on the project. Management, who took pride in the firm's respectful, humane culture, came down hard on Ethan, threatening to withhold his annual bonus and insisting that he work with a coach to change his leadership style.

This is where Ethan and I began. He felt very angry and hurt—angry that the firm had given him the nearly impossible project and then castigated him for rescuing it the only way he could, and hurt for giving the firm fifteen loyal, hardworking years, only to be punished for trying to do the right thing. He felt rejected and wondered if this firm was the right place for him.

His anger and hurt affected his mood. When we would discuss his situation or his leadership style, his response was first anger and then hurt. When we tried to examine others' reactions to his behavior, he would agree with their accounts and then shift to blaming it on the impossible situation. He portrayed himself as the force of good, trying to produce high-quality work against all odds. And he characterized the firm as basically a force of evil, tolerating mediocrity and espousing civility while making Herculean demands on him and not providing him with the people resources to get the work done. Within his tight system of villain and persecuted hero, there was no room to even consider change.

Ethan saw no motivation to change because he ascribed all of his difficulties to the firm. He would not, or could not, examine his own contribution to his situation. His anger and righteous hurt protected him from the greater pain of looking at himself.

I tried to get us unstuck by offering to end our coaching project. But he decided to continue, I believe to save face. Then one day, as we were discussing his relationship with a difficult client, he mentioned his struggle with self-esteem. When we explored it further, he described his self-esteem as being particularly low now but being shaky for most of his life. We spent the rest of the session acknowledging his problems with esteem and beginning to label it as a condition. This conversation seemed like the first real opening in our two-month relationship. Ethan was open, nondefensive, and apparently asking for help.

I hoped that our focus on his self-esteem would become the pathway to a valuable experience for Ethan. When I discussed this with a clinically trained colleague, he suggested that Ethan's shaky self-esteem could be the cause of his desire for perfection and his intolerance of anyone who didn't meet his standards. I hoped that if Ethan saw his perfectionism as his way of manufacturing self-esteem, he could become more adaptable to imperfect situations. I hoped that he could stop seeing himself as the martyr of quality and adopt a more pragmatic approach to his work. I imagined that he might see how his desire for perfection damages his work relationships and his career. I approached our next session with a new, hopeful hypothesis.

But alas, it went nowhere. Ethan's interest in his self-esteem lasted about two minutes before he returned to his anger and resentment. I went back to the drawing board searching for another way to reach Ethan and wondering if I should resign from the project. Ethan had decided to stay at the firm until he could start his own architectural practice. Part of me believed that leaving the firm and venturing out on his own was the best path for him. But another part of me felt deeply disappointed that he did not overcome his resistance to coaching and to change. Ethan's resistance was too powerful to penetrate. I consider the project a failure.

THEORY OF PARTS OF THE SELF

As Virginia Satir (1978, p. 63) has observed, "You probably have many parts that you have not yet discovered. All these parts, whether you have owned them or not, are present in you. Becoming aware of them enables you to take charge of them rather than be enslaved by them. Each of your parts is a vital source of energy. Each has many uses and can harmonize with many other parts in ways to add even more energy."

Many schools of psychology recognize that people call on different parts of themselves to deal with different situations. These different parts of the self refer to the various aspects of a person that express themselves through the different aspects of their personality: patterns of thought, feeling, and behavior. (Parts of the self should not be confused with multiple personality disorder, a mental illness in which a person is completely and unconsciously possessed by entirely different personalities.)

The parts of the self can be seen as subpersonalities. A person can possess different subpersonalities that come out in different situations or in response to different moods. One subpersonality might be hardworking and responsible, while another is fun loving and mischievous. One might be gentle, while another is aggressive. One might be curious and open-minded, while another is inflexible and closed-minded. One might be very ethical, while the other is self-serving. All people have different parts of themselves that come out in different situations, sometimes stimulating the emergence of a useful subpersonality and at other times a dysfunctional subpersonality.

A knowledge of subpersonalities helps in understanding the full range of people's actions and in helping them bring out useful but previously dormant parts of themselves.

Subpersonalities are created by some combination of our genetic psychological predispositions and our responses to different experiences. These forces of nature and nurture also determine which subpersonalities become more dominant. As we mature, we develop an awareness of our patterns of behavior, thoughts, and feelings. This self-awareness becomes our "identity," or who we think we are. Because most of us have a desire to feel consistent, we generally exaggerate our dominant and more conscious subselves and underexpress our less dominant, less conscious ones.

This phenomenon of over- and underexpression holds potential for coaching. The underexpressed subpersonalities have the potential to become relief pitchers, entering the game when their special talents are needed. Similarly, the overexpressed parts can be seen as members of a somewhat tired starting lineup who need to be relieved in order to win the game.

Physiologically, multiple selves probably exist as neural connections within the brain. Neuroscientific studies of the brain support this theory. Michael Gazzaniga (1986, p. 195) describes the brain as having "a modular-type organization. . . . The brain is organized into relatively independent functioning units that work in parallel. The mind is not an indivisible whole operating in a single way to solve all problems. Rather, there are many specific, and identifiably different units of the mind."

Working with subpersonalities can be a fast path to growth because these parts of the self can become the foundation for new behavior. The coach can help the client develop these new attitudes and behaviors by tapping into one of their previously dormant subpersonalities. By locating and expanding their awareness of one of these minority personalities, the client can get to know this part of themselves and prepare to use it in selected situations.

In most behavior change situations, the client is seeking to replace an overused, problem-causing part of themselves with a less-used, more fitting part. Increasing awareness of both of these subpersonalities makes it easier to let go of the old and bring in the new. To increase awareness, it can be useful to access the parts of the self through multiple senses—visual, verbal, and body-kinesthetic. For example, to become aware of an overused subpersonality, a coach might ask a client to imagine the problem situation by describing, verbally, what it looks like visually and what it feels like physically. Next, the coach would ask the client to describe a "better" scenario in which the client acts in a more desired manner. The client pictures and describes the characteristics of that state visually, verbally, and kinesthetically. The coach might ask for more detail about the client's actions, thoughts, emotions, and sensations in order to help the client flesh out this emergent subpersonality. The coach can then ask the client to hold this image, this subpersonality, in mind as a desired goal and to store it for future and continued use.

Recognizing that people both seek and resist change, the coach can then explore the sources of resistance. The coach can ask the client to place the desired behavioral goal in a high location in their mind's eye and begin a journey to reach this desired place. As they travel to the goal, the coach asks the client to notice and label the impediments. After the client has reached the goal, the coach debriefs with them, asking about each of the impediments. Some impediments may be easily overcome as soon as some attention is paid them. Others might be more formidable, existing as attitudes or beliefs that disagree with an aspect of the desired behavior. In this case, coach and client would address each one as a subpersonality, ask it what it wants, and negotiate with it to find a way of addressing its needs while still achieving the goal. This journey gives the client a concrete experience with both trying out the new behavior and letting go of the old.

After becoming acquainted with the new subpersonality and negotiating with the resistance, the client can now prepare for trying out the new behavior in the world. The new behaviors will come more easily because they express the essence and needs of the emergent subpersonality. As the client starts to express it, they will likely keep using it because they are satisfying this part of themselves. The new behavior will probably be further reinforced, over time, as the individual recognizes and receives the rewards of its constructive fit with the environment.

Parts of the Self Case: Craig #4
The Other Side of the Coin

Craig, the research manager, was working at becoming more influential in his company. Besides paying attention to his audience, his ability to influence was also being hindered by his tendency to judge people who didn't agree with him as uninformed or unintelligent. Regardless of whom he judged this way, he would then treat them with a type of disdain that naturally interfered with his ability to influence them.

We began working on this trait by identifying it as a part of him. We labeled it his judging self. As soon as we did this, Craig breathed a sigh of relief because we were acknowledging a real yet unattractive pattern that had been with him most of his life, and by calling it a *part* of him, we were saying that he was more than this pattern.

Next we started looking for another part of him that could serve as an alternative to the judging self. Considering that he was a neuroscientist with a deep curiosity about the causes of human behavior, it didn't take us long to identify the part of himself that was curious about why people acted as they did. He labeled this part his curious self and began to describe how he would think and act when his curious self was guiding him. He would think, "I wonder what is making this person think like that. What filters is this person using to arrive at that point of view?" He recognized that thinking these curious thoughts would lead him to ask interested questions and listen attentively to the answers. His curious self would serve as a constructive alternative to judging and dismissing. Craig learned to bring out another part of himself in order to achieve his influencing goals.

Coaches can follow several steps in helping the client become more conscious of their subselves and use them more intentionally.

1. The first step is locating a relevant subself that will help the client successfully adapt to their new situation. Sometimes the client may give clues about its existence. At other times, the coach may need to ask questions that seek it out.

2. The next step is getting to know the subself. By asking the client to describe the undiscovered subself, they become more familiar with this aspect of themselves. By asking them to experiment with expressing the subself, they give it a voice and allow it to become stronger and more familiar. In getting to know the new subself, the client grows to appreciate it and experience it as an authentic part of their whole.

3. A newly emerging subself may come into conflict with the more dominant parts of the self. The coach can ask the client to observe the conflict between parts so as to understand how they had kept one hidden and one expressed.

4. Once the background is understood, the client can negotiate a new arrangement between the parts that enables them to be a better leader as well as more integrated as an individual.

5. Now the client can practice, first in the coaching session and then on the job, acting from their new subself. For example, Alice rehearsed presenting the company's mission and strategy and intervening in political disagreements.

The coach can also use the concept of multiple selves to work with a client's resistance. Some clients begin coaching ready and eager to change, some start out completely unwilling, but most clients fall somewhere between these two extremes. They are both interested in and resistant to changing a behavior. It is with this large group of clients that the concept of many subpersonalities becomes useful.

A coach might address resistance by naming and describing it. This labeling enables a client to begin to see the resistance as one aspect of themselves, rather than their whole being. The coach and client can then talk about the resistance as a separate part of the self. They can learn more about it, notice how it is expressed and when it is expressed, and trace its evolution throughout the client's career. In answering these questions, the client gains a greater understanding of the resistant part of themselves and therefore gain the ability to alter the intensity and duration of their resistance.

Sometimes getting past the resistance might take more effort. The resistance might be the result of different subpersonalities that are in conflict. This conflict can be invisible to people because they are not fully conscious of their opposing subpersonalities. A coach can help a client resolve this by asking them to give a voice to different, often minority parts of themselves—for example, asking them to speak from the part of themselves that wants efficiency or feels angry. The coach can then ask the client to speak from the part that cannot tolerate the expression of this other self. They can ask it what it needs and negotiate with it to keep it from interfering. By playing out this internal dialogue, the client can make progress toward overcoming their resistance and accepting and even embracing change.

Chapter 12

The Timing of
Learning and Change

Over the past fifty years, educators and psychologists have come to recognize the importance of readiness in the processes of learning and behavior change. Children learn to read when they are ready. People stop smoking when they are ready. And leaders learn new skills when they are ready. Readiness is often motivated by changes in the person's environment, such as a new position for a leader, peer pressure for a young reader, or a doctor's stern warning for a smoker. Readiness can be accelerated through coaching conversations. But largely, it is up to conscious and unconscious forces within the individual to determine when they fully engage in the process of learning and change.

Learning and change are usually slow. People have views of themselves and the world that were formed over time. The first indications that one of their strategies for dealing with the world might be ineffective usually go unnoticed. If they do notice them, they often write them off as anomalies or blame them on someone else. Or they might recognize a pattern that is ineffective and decide that it is too hard to change and not worth the effort.

Then something happens that makes people ready to learn and change. The stimulus could be becoming fed up with the repeated disappointing effects of a behavior. Or it could be a more immediate pain of a difficult situation or an awareness of a contradiction between behavior and values. Whatever the catalyst, the person becomes ready to examine and alter one of their behavior patterns. The coach can help them to transform this wish into long-lasting learning.

In their coaching sessions, clients prepare for change by developing awareness and deciding to behave differently. Insight is an apt label for these realizations because of the sudden and often stunning flash of truth. An insight can reveal a completely new perspective about oneself, others, or both. And insights can occur quickly.

As quick as insights can be, the resultant behavioral changes are usually slower. Even though the new behaviors represent a clear outgrowth of a brilliant insight, they often take a while to realize. When classical trigger events occur, people usually respond with old and familiar behaviors. It can take time for the new behavior to become strongly connected to the trigger.

Similarly, the new behaviors are weak. People are not used to them. They are not familiar with the words, thoughts, feelings, and actions that accompany them. Even though the person believes in the new behaviors and intends to use them, they are often pulled back toward the familiar.

Successful development results from persistence, trial and error, and diligent awareness. People will successfully use the new behaviors some of the time. At other times, the old behavior slips out. Sometimes the event happens so fast that they don't even have a chance to exert their newfound will.

This is the point when observation, self-awareness, and debriefing play a valuable role. Each situation becomes a potential learning event. Using the new behavior successfully, the person can celebrate and become conscious of the thoughts, feelings, and conditions that surrounded their success. In instances when they have reverted to the old behavior, they can examine the factors surrounding the missed opportunity. We can all learn by examining each situation.

Gradual Change Case: Alice #3
Integrating New Behaviors

In January, Alice and I decided that becoming a stronger leader would be her major development goal. Her reticence to assert authority and her tentativeness and silence in meetings were hindering her ability to lead the organization through a crucial period. Over several meetings, we first examined her current behaviors and their impact. Then we worked on more powerful alternatives, including her choice of words, the tone and pitch of her voice, hand and body movements, and the timing of her statements.

As we modeled and practiced the power behaviors, she experienced a normal awkwardness. She was motivated to make these changes. But when she tried them out, she said they felt showy, strange, and not like her. As we worked on integrating the new behaviors as new parts of herself, she became more comfortable with the concept but still self-conscious about the behaviors. As the weeks went on, she slowly put them to use in meetings and gradually became more comfortable exerting a more commanding presence. In September, she faced a high-stakes meeting in which she would make a case for taking over two key product areas. She spoke authoritatively and convincingly to persuade senior management and her peers at the parent company to move these product areas over to her division. She succeeded. She seized another opportunity in November when she told her direct reports about a controversial decision she had made regarding the company bonus plan. She appeared as strong and convincing as any leader I have seen. When I commented on her successful use of the new behaviors, she explained that it had taken this long for them to sink in. She gradually progressed from intention to awkward initial attempts to sporadic practice to more confident use. After eleven months, she had become able to consciously and comfortably use the new behaviors when she saw fit. It took nearly a year for her implicit memory to gradually, one step at a time, build these new neural pathways.

Gradual Change Case: Bob #3
Taking Responsibility for Change

Once he decided to address his intolerance and anger, Bob became an eager client. He liked the cognitive-behavioral approach because it appealed to his analytical, intellectual style. With my help, he traced the origins of his intolerance toward others' ideas and recognized how it quickly morphed into anger. We outlined the steps he could take to stay aware of his emotions and use this awareness to behave differently. He took notes on the steps for cognitive and emotional awareness in order to remember and practice them. He worked hard at the tasks of contemplation and preparation. He was on a roll.

After taking August off for vacation, I expected that he would pick up in September at a similarly fast pace. But Bob surprised me by suggesting that we slow down. He said we had gotten ahead of ourselves. He had done a tremendous amount of preparation but had had little chance to practice. He had great plans rolling around in his head but no opportunity to put them to use. Besides the usual summer slowdown, his company experienced a public relations crisis that put his major projects on hold. He wanted to forge ahead but was missing opportunities to apply his learning.

Bob had taken responsibility for his own change. With himself in charge, he had determined to slow the pace of our work to match the opportunities in his environment. I had a mixed reaction to his proposal. My trusting, client-centered side believed that it made perfect sense, and I was pleased he was being so astute about his change process. My skeptical side wondered if this was a clever form of resistance, designed to help him avoid changing. My trusting side won out, in part because it seemed more reasonable and in part because it was outnumbered. By November, he had returned to his plan and had made such visible changes that his colleagues were commenting on it.

Delayed Learning Case: Carl #2
A Long Learning Curve

Carl asked to work with a coach to assist him in his transition from scientist to manager. As he entered his second year as a manager, along with other goals, he wanted to feel and act more confidently in his new role.

This concept of feeling and acting managerial became one of the themes in our coaching process. We addressed his feelings of self-confidence, and he practiced ways of acting managerial in conversations and meetings. After several months, we both believed that he had made some minor progress in this area.

When I saw Carl in a meeting nearly a year after we had completed our coaching, he described a surprising experience. He explained that he was just beginning to feel like a manager. He was now aware of his important role as a link between line scientists and senior management. He was beginning to take seriously his position as a representative of the corporation to his staff and a translator of the staff's perspective to his management. He seemed different, a bit more sure of himself, and subtly taking an informal leadership role in the group. He told me that only recently had he had this revelation about what it meant to act like and feel like the leader of a group. Once he identified the feeling, all our learning came back to him and became easy to fit into his actions. It was a case of delayed learning that kicked in when he was truly ready.

He confessed that a year earlier, he had claimed that he understood his role and even practiced some behaviors, but he didn't really get it until now. His learning on this topic had been delayed. Perhaps he hadn't been ready to learn this lesson the year before. Apparently our conversations and behavioral rehearsals had sat in his subconscious waiting for the right moment. Now they were coming out. He was now feeling and acting in new ways.

Part Three

Coaching Applications and Marketing

Chapter 13

Distinctive Approaches to Coaching

The classic model of coaching, and hence most organizational consulting, has been deficit-based. It follows the medical model based on the concept that something is wrong and needs to be fixed. In the deficit approach, the coach and client diagnose a problem in the client's behavior patterns and then seek to repair the problem through behavior change. This fits with the Western civilization view that humans are flawed and need to be healed. It is familiar but a bit depressing and old-fashioned.

Appreciative Coaching: Playing from Strength

New research has challenged the medical model. Some organizational psychologists, led by David Cooperrider at Case Western University, have found that no matter how well intended, a problem focus discourages people and saps their energy away from positive change. The Appreciative Inquiry model encourages people to focus on their strengths, high points, and wishes. Then it challenges them to extrapolate from them to build a better future. This differs from the deficit model, which focuses primarily on solving problems or improving on weaknesses. While both approaches appeal to the desire for something better, the appreciative approach concentrates on moving toward the desired, while the deficit approach focuses on moving away from the undesired.

The Appreciative Inquiry approach was created to guide organizational change. The research demonstrates considerable success with this approach at an organizational level. It is tempting to apply the appreciative approach, lock, stock, and barrel, to individual coaching. But traditional coaching has been so problem-focused, so tied to constructive feedback and a remedial development plan, that it is not obvious how an appreciative approach would yield the same results.

When I took the Appreciative Inquiry training several years ago, I was deeply affected by the positive philosophy that it embodied. It fit with the constructive, supportive, optimistic underpinnings of my own values and many of the values of organizational psychology. Since then, I have been attempting to apply the appreciative approach with my clients.

An obvious first impact has been an increase in my positive regard. Although this concept, popularized by Carl Rogers, has formed the foundation of coaching and counseling for decades, coaches can sometimes give it a backseat in their attempts to help their clients improve. Viewing my clients as sound and legitimate leaders rather than flawed ones has both improved my relationships with them and facilitated their progress. Holding unilateral positive regard still leaves plenty of room for learning and development. It just keeps the conversations more supportive and, well, appreciative.

Another way to apply Appreciative Inquiry is to keep the conversations focused on the dream, the desired future. The coach can facilitate these conversations by asking questions about the details of the clients' desired state, questions like "What would your ideal team look like?" "What could you do to create that kind of team?" or "How could you gain support for this effort?" In answering these questions, the clients will be building a clear road map to their goal. They will also be thinking thoughts and saying words that are forming the neural connections necessary for behavior change.

The other insight from my experiments with Appreciative Inquiry has been a recognition that people's strengths are closely and inexorably tied to their weaknesses. When Bill overused his decision-making ability, his staff felt powerless. When Mark overused his action and results orientation, he was seen as a bully. When clients can appreciate their strong suit and understand it well enough to avoid overusing it, they bring more energy and self-confidence to their change process.

Appreciative Case: Bruce #1
When Enthusiasm Scares People

Bruce's enthusiasm was one of his greatest assets. When you first meet him, he greets you with an excited smile and a big, welcoming hello. He brings this same extroverted passion to his work, caring deeply about doing smart research and becoming excited about positive results and new ideas. The flipside of this enthusiasm is his ability to intimidate people. When Bruce hears an idea that he thinks will move the project forward, he energetically supports it, sometimes at the expense of its doubters. Similarly, if someone wants to follow a slower, more cautious path, he becomes impatient and critical.

In coaching Bruce, I first focused on appreciating his strength, recognizing it as a source of energy for himself and for his team. He enthusiastically liked people, enjoyed action, and deeply wanted success for his project. The flipside of his strength was his impatience, which could quickly change into intimidation. He would put his enthusiasm to succeed above rapport and harmony with his team members.

We explored Bruce's enthusiasm in a spirit of appreciation. Recognizing that rapport with his team members was important, we looked for ways that he could focus his enthusiastic energy on staying in rapport with each member. He liked this idea because it was energetic and because it would lead him to the larger goal. He practiced active listening, keeping eye contact, and pacing. Over the months, he became more successful at staying congruent with his team members and leading the team toward greater commitment to a shared strategy.

Appreciative Case: Frank #1
Separating the Messages

Frank's ability to empathize made him an astute manager who could interpret the needs of all of his constituents, including staff, peers, and senior management. He could quickly sense what was important to them and what was needed to make them happy. Most people liked working with Frank because he understood and connected with them.

Then Frank's department entered a period of rapid organizational change. It was scheduled for a radical reorganization, and people would be moved to new departments not of their own choosing. Some would be working with new clients and new managers. Part of Frank's job was to deliver these messages of change to employees and to work with each department to plan new goals and strategies. During this period, Frank saw his reputation decline. People began perceiving him as weak and were feeling confused by his messages.

In a moment of intuition, I realized that Frank was indeed mixing his messages. On the one hand, he was laying out the new structure and challenging people with new goals. Yet on the other hand, sometimes in the very next sentence, he was empathizing with them and the difficulties he knew they would face. Taken together, the two messages were canceling each other out. The empathy was detracting from the challenge, and the challenge was detracting from the empathy. Both were well intended, but neither was getting through.

Frank recognized this and worked at separating the two messages. He decided to have two different conversations, one about the challenges and the other, at a later time, expressing empathy. The new strategy worked. Within months, Frank had rebuilt the respect of his people and his reputation. His department soon became one of the top performers in the division. Recently, Frank was promoted to lead a large division of his company.

THE COACH'S USE OF SELF

So far in this book, I have portrayed the coach as a neutral observer and an objective thought partner. Such objectivity is impossible. Individuals see things through their own eyes and experience things through their own mental models. Coaches are people with their own sets of opinions, feelings, and values that influence how they operate. A coach may identify strongly with a particular client and therefore overlook certain behaviors that are important to the client's development. Or the coach may negatively judge a client who holds very different values and fail to notice some of their strengths.

Self-Awareness

How can a human coach be competent in light of these built-in biases and distractions? As with clients, the key is self-awareness. By becoming aware of their own feelings, values, and biases, coaches can be alert to situations that provoke them. They can use this awareness to make more conscious choices about what they perceive and how they act. For example, a new client who is angry and aggressive might scare me at some level. If I were not aware of my fear, I might simply become defensive and allow the fear to detract from my coaching work. If I can feel my fear and become conscious of it, then I can choose how I want to act in light of my fear. I could choose to let the client know that his or her behavior is intimidating me and explore how it might intimidate others. Alternatively, I could decide that this disclosure would not be ineffective at this point and instead try to listen carefully for the client's needs. If I were not fully aware of my fear, it would probably distract me from listening. This awareness both gives me choices and removes the limiting effects of unconscious emotion.

Reflective Practice

Coaches, like leaders, exert a lot of power through their influence on their clients. And coaches, like leaders, benefit from reflection and learning from their experiences. This reflection on their practice often makes the difference between a coach who is rigid and doctrinaire and one who is flexible and effective in a multitude of situations.

Like all people, coaches build mental models and act from these models. Reflective coaches become aware of their mental models, act on them, and reflect on their actions. They examine both the visible results of their actions and the relationships to their own guiding principles. They seek to adapt both their models and their actions to this examined reality. This interplay of action and reflection enables coaches to consciously evolve their skills.

Reflection Case: Peter #2 When the Coach's Mental Model Differs from the Client's

My work with Peter provides an example of reflection in action. Remember, I had originally assumed that the way for Peter to control his anger would come through expanding his awareness of his feelings. This was my mental model early in the engagement. I knew that this model was rooted in my own psychotherapy and in my belief in Daniel Goleman's (1995) model of emotional intelligence. Even though I was philosophically committed to this model, I began to see that my strategy of behavioral control through emotional awareness might

not work with Peter. When Peter revealed the importance of his idealism, I observed another characteristic
of Peter's and used it to create a new strategy. Peter
seemed more comfortable examining his thoughts than
exploring his feelings. He might become more engaged
in delving into his idealistic thinking than into something more emotional. When I introduced the idea, he
responded with enthusiasm, and I used this observation
to move further down this path. It turned out to be a
successful path for Peter. Through this experience, I
recognized the value of letting go of some of my closely
held models when they don't seem to be working.

To summarize, reflective coaches

- Become aware of their own mental models, assumptions,
  and perceptual filters for ascribing meaning to coaching
  interactions
- Become aware of their own methods and techniques
- Commit to examining their actions, both effective and
  ineffective
- Regard each client as a new challenge to their models and
  continuously evolve these models

The Coach's Subpersonalities

Coaches, like clients, benefit from being able to integrate the
different parts of themselves and to flow smoothly between
them. Three of the frequently used subpersonalities are sensitivity, intensity, and playfulness. Coaches do need to be gentle
sometimes. We often share information that can be difficult for
a client to swallow. By empathizing with the client's experience,

we can help the client feel OK in the face of some critical feedback. Our gentleness can create a zone of safety that enables clients to feel confident enough to consider changing one of their customary behavior patterns.

Unadulterated sensitivity can make the client feel so safe that they have no impetus to change. There are times when the coach needs to be intense or tough. There are two aspects of the coaching process when the coach's intensity is particularly important. When interpreting 360° feedback and using it to identify behavior change goals, the coach needs to accurately represent reality to the client by directing their attention to difficult information. They need to remind the client that these perceptions are valid and important, worth attending to.

Similarly, in the later stages of the coaching process, when the client is practicing their behavior change in the real world, distractions can arise that draw the clients' attention away from their behavioral goals. This is a time for the coach to be intense and keep the conversation focused on the desired change. For me, this intensity is powered by my knowledge that changing a behavior requires a sustained effort and focus over several months. Introducing a new goal or following an interesting tangent could distract the client's attention from the target behavior before it has become fully learned and habituated. When these distractions arise, I will usually direct the conversation back to the original goals and make sure the client has made solid progress before adding something new.

Humor can play an important role in coaching. At one level, it can keep rapport and connection between coach and client. Being playful can also add a new perspective to the client's undertaking, one that is lighthearted and not so deadly serious. It also introduces flexibility. Being playful about their process focuses attention on it while transforming it into a more familiar and even fun-to-talk-about theme.

When coaches can embrace these three sides of themselves, they have the breadth to connect with the client on multiple levels. When they feel that the client is grappling with something difficult, they can bring out their sensitive side. When they feel that the client is avoiding something important, they call on their intense side. And when they sense that the situation could use some lightening up, they bring out their playful side. As the coach becomes more comfortable with these parts of themselves, they can use them to make the coaching more effective.

Intuition

Dr. Benjamin Spock advised new parents to trust themselves by explaining that they knew more than they thought they did. Intuition can be another valuable source of information for the coach. Intuition can be seen as knowledge that comes from an unknown source inside of us. Jung describes intuition as a way of perceiving information beyond the five senses.

Although much has been written about the existence of intuition, little has been proved about the way it actually works because of its invisible, untraceable nature. Nancy Rosanoff, in *Intuition Workout* (1998), describes three primary ways that people receive intuitive messages: mentally through words, thoughts, images, and symbols; emotionally through feelings; and physically through bodily sensations.

Mental messages come in the form of thoughts, words, images, or symbols. The difference between intuitive messages and rational thinking is that the thoughts appear without reasoning. For example, I was about to order dinner in a restaurant when such a message came to me. It said, "Don't order the special vegetable casserole. Get two appetizers instead." I pondered that idea for a moment, but then asked myself, "Why should I follow that intuition? Specials are usually very tasty. And there is no logical reason why I shouldn't order it." So I went ahead and ordered it, still wondering what that intuitive thought was trying to tell me. I soon found out. Over the next half hour, the waiter proceeded to bring everyone else's dish except mine. As I waited almost an hour, hungry, jealous, and stuffing myself with bread, I realized that my intuition "knew" I would have been served the appetizers more promptly.

As another example, a client told me how she had come up with a logo for an entertainment company. While she was listening to some rock music, an image of bigness and heaviness appeared in her mind. She decided to go with this intuition and expressed it visually. It turned it into a now world-famous logo.

Emotional messages come in the form of feelings. People may feel scared about a situation even though it appears safe on the surface. Or they may find themselves feeling sad entering a room and later learn that the sadness is the feeling of someone else in the room who is in the midst of a personal tragedy.

Physical messages take the form of bodily sensations, like unease in the gut or tightness in the neck. They can indicate whether a situation or person will turn out well or not. In a job interview, tightness can indicate that the job or the culture might not be a good fit. Conversely, a feeling of physical well-being can mean that the situation would work out nicely.

Whatever form it takes, intuition provides real and useful information about the world. The better we are able to use it, the better decisions we are able to make.

There are two skills to using intuition. One is to learn how to access it. If we assume that all of us have intuition, then accessing intuition relies on giving the intuition a path to our consciousness. This means becoming relaxed while staying aware. Breathing deeply and relaxing the face, shoulders, and abdomen can clear the path for intuitive messages. Intuitive messages travel through our nervous system, so relaxation clears the pathways by removing the tension that blocks them. Allowing intuition to appear is more useful than trying to force it out.

The other skill is learning to trust intuition. It is important, however, to remember that intuition is nonrational and non-linear, that you cannot use logic to ascertain the accuracy of an intuitive message. The trust will come from experience rather than logic. Developing trust in intuition is similar to developing trust in a person. Begin by giving it a chance to perform. Then, if it proves useful, consciously give it more chances. Over time, you will become more trusting to use your intuition to make decisions.

Coach's Intuition Case: Diane #1
Using Intuition to Help the Client Face a Reality

I was working with Diane in a two-hour coaching engagement as part of her company's leadership development program. The feedback data from direct reports were so uniformly negative that they couldn't provide any clear clues about what she should work on. In the first part of our conversation, she told me about her optimism and her belief that she and the company could always find a way to make things work out and to make people happy. I registered to myself that this seemed a bit overly optimistic for a manager. She reinforced this view by describing her attempts to find a bigger job for an employee whose performance was only average.

Her 360° ratings were mostly low, but without a discernible pattern that would indicate where to focus. As I looked back at her data, I felt an intuitive wave of anger and frustration. When I looked at these low ratings, I felt what I believed to be the employees' frustration with her unending optimism. When I empathized with her staff, I believed they saw her as unrealistic and Pollyannaish and even dishonest in the way she ignored difficult realities. I imagined the other employees being disappointed and even angry with her for not dealing realistically with the average performer. When I described my hunch to Diane, she let out a sigh of relief. She relaxed and began to seriously consider changing because she finally knew what was wrong.

Self-Revelation

The coaching process should focus primarily on the client. Most of the time, it is inappropriate and distracting for coaches to talk about themselves. But occasionally, it can be valuable for coaches to reveal who they are and what they have experienced. It can be especially useful when the coach has learned lessons or dealt with challenges that are similar to the clients'. When the coach tells the story of their journey through similar territory, the client can feel reassured that success is possible and that they are in the hands of an experienced professional. Clients have said that hearing about someone else who faced similar hurdles strengthens their confidence in dealing with it.

Self-revealing can also make the coach more human in the client's eyes. When the coach tells a relevant story about themselves, the client gains some glimpses of the coach's private life. It reveals the coach as an ordinary person with human flaws and the courage to face them. It can also strengthen the bond between coach and client by disclosing things that they have in common.

Self-Revealing Case: Jane #1
When the Coach Joins the Client

Jane sought coaching after being told by her senior managers that she was not meeting their expectations as a project manager. One of their criticisms was that she did not push her team members enough to do their work on time. Jane had wanted to stay on them but had been hanging back for fear offending them. Another criticism was that she had been neglecting to follow up on certain tasks. She did not have a system for writing down these tasks and recording who was responsible for what and by when. Third, her management criticized her for speaking in a meandering, roundabout manner. When she thought about developing these new behaviors, she felt overwhelmed. She had never been in a situation like this and simply didn't believe that she could change that much.

Though she did face a considerable challenge, I was more optimistic. I felt optimistic not only because I had successfully worked with other clients on these issues but also because I had faced and overcome a similar challenge early in my career. I decided to tell her my story. I described how I learned to be an assertive, detail-oriented project manager while still maintaining a pleasant demeanor. I also explained how I learned to communicate more succinctly. Finally, I followed with an example of coaching a client to speak in a more linear, logical manner.

As a coach, it felt awkward to talk about myself rather than the client. But it also seemed useful. When I finished my story, Jane broke into her first smile of the day and said she felt heartened, knowing that it was possible for people to change these kinds of behaviors. She said that she was glad to be working with someone who had actually been through it himself. I felt satisfied at having opted to reveal myself and glad that it worked.

Chapter 14

Coaching Themes
Familiar and Unique

Even though every leader is different, some leaders share the same developmental themes. Although my sample of one hundred clients is small, examining their developmental themes can be enlightening. It can tell us something about the challenges many leaders face. And it can give coaches some insight into how to work with clients facing similar challenges.

This chapter describes some of these recurring themes and summarizes cases of leaders who successfully addressed them.

HAVING TO BE RIGHT

Being smart and having answers can propel people into positions of leadership. However, once someone is in a leadership position, always having the right answers becomes a liability. Such certainty can damage organizations in several different ways.

- People tend to avoid leaders who appear to have all the answers. They don't seek them out or engage them in work conversations because they don't want to hear another one-way, know-it-all response. The effects of a leader's always being right are listed below:

  - Decision-making can suffer because the leader's certainty limits conversation. Decisions don't get the benefit of a variety of ideas; instead, they get made with the limited input of the leader's perspective.

  - Employees do not develop under leaders who have all the answers. They tend to abdicate decision making and problem solving to the leader because the leader has monopolized that role. Some employees actually come to believe that the leader really does have the best answers and don't even try to come up with answers of their own. Others simply give up voicing an answer, knowing that the leader will overrule it.

Having to be Right Case: Louise #1
She Was Respected—and Resented

Louise is a parts manager for an airline. Her department makes sure that vendors supply the parts needed to keep the planes in good repair and safely in the air. She knows everything about her department, including the name and function of every part, as well as how long it should take to repair each one. She also has relationships with all the vendors. She is quick-thinking, results-oriented, and extroverted. Whenever a problem occurs, she is quick to formulate an answer and act on it.

Her 360° feedback report indicated that her staff respect her knowledge and defer to her but resent her for making all the decisions. They don't feel she respects their ideas and certainly don't feel empowered to make their own decisions. Louise was not completely surprised by this feedback, but she didn't know what to do about it.

Louise believed it was her job to have the answers. When I probed further into this attitude, she revealed some more personal reasons for her belief. First, she enjoyed having the answers and being in the middle of the action, even if it meant marginalizing her staff. Second, she didn't trust her staff to come up with ideas that were as good as hers. Her third reason was the most personal yet held the greatest potential for change. She believed that she would not be valuable if she didn't have all the answers. She needed the answers in order to feel secure and respect herself.

Once she revealed this, it became clear to her that she was monopolizing the answers for personal rather than business reasons. She realized that it would still be an effort to change her pattern, but the pattern was no longer justified by business necessity.

We proceeded from that point. My contract with her company was for only two sessions. So I cut to the chase and asked her bluntly, "When will you feel confident enough to let other people make decisions?" Her face changed, and she said that she really wanted to change this. I saw this as signal that she was seriously contemplating changing this behavior.

Listening Case: Mark #2
Not Just One Listening Pattern

Two years after our initial coaching work, Mark decided to move out of his scientific management role and into a project management role in the burgeoning new field of bioinformatics. In his new role, he needed to persuade hundreds of scientists and managers in his company to document their work in a different way. He used his new skills and attitudes to make some headway. But he and his department still faced significant resistance. Mark realized that he needed to change more of his behavior in order to influence his clients.

We decided to focus on listening because Mark had gotten feedback about being a poor listener. When we explored this, he described three different listening patterns in meetings. When he was very interested, he listened well. When he was completely disinterested, he thought about other things. And when he was marginally interested, he drifted in and out, waiting for the conversation to become relevant to him.

He asked for help in appearing more interested in the marginal situations. I didn't think that appearing interested was a worthwhile goal, since it was not authentic and avoided the real issue of his disinterest. I suggested that we explore ways he could actually become more interested in the conversation. He agreed, so we continued on that path.

We recognized that it was not uncommon for people to be disinterested in certain topics. But in Mark's case, his moments of disinterest were damaging his credibility and his ability to achieve his larger goal of creating a successful bioinformatics system. That goal involved building trusting, collaborative relationships with his clients. Once he made this connection, he moved into the contemplation phase, deciding to try to feel genuine interest in his clients and their conversations.

The approach I took was essentially one of self-discipline through commitment to a larger goal. I suggested this approach because of a personal experience I had had the previous week. While my wife and I were on vacation driving through the Rocky Mountains, she mentioned that the mountains reminded her of a painful weekend she had spent in Vermont thirty years earlier. I was about to say, "Oh," and change the subject when I remembered that I had been wanting to feel closer to her for weeks. We hadn't spent much time together because she had been working long hours at her new job. I recognized that this was an opportunity to learn more about her life and reconnect with her. I began listening with interest and found myself empathizing with her experience, asking follow-up questions, and getting involved in her story. My desire for a closer connection motivated me to listen deeply and initiate an intimate conversation. My larger goal had turned me into an interested listener. Couldn't Mark do the same?

Mark used this new commitment to build very successful relationships with his customers. His desire to succeed led him to change both the behavior and the emotion of interested listening.

WORKING WITH EMOTIONS: EMPATHY

Emotional intelligence has received a lot of attention in the leadership literature in part because it has been shown to be critical to effective leadership. Empathy is the cornerstone of emotional intelligence. Daniel Goleman (1995) defines four components of emotional intelligence:

- *Self-awareness*—knowing your own emotions and their corresponding strengths and limitations
- *Social awareness*—empathy; sensing other people's emotions, understanding their perspective, taking an active interest in their concerns; recognizing your impact on others

- *Self-regulation*—keeping disruptive emotions and impulses under control; using self-awareness to adapt to changing situations and managing your motivation
- *Managing relationships*—using empathy and self-management to skillfully relate to others; adapting your approach and style to work well with others

Emotional intelligence is built on empathy. People who feel empathy understand other people's experiences. They often sense it in their body, feeling the same excitement, fear, or frustration the other person feels. When we empathize, we can connect with others, we understand and respect their experience, and they appreciate this understanding. This can form the foundation for trust, mutual influence, and open communication.

As with any other human trait, people vary in their ability to empathize. Some can tune in to others' experiences with such accuracy that they are more aware of their colleagues' emotions than the colleagues themselves. Others are so focused on facts and logic that they are practically oblivious to people's feelings.

Empathy is, in a sense, a judgment about another person's feelings. When we empathize, we make a hypothetical decision about what the other is probably experiencing. Myers-Briggs type theory identifies two different sources of judgment: thinking, an approach based on logic, and feeling, an approach based on empathy and values. Each can be a way for a client to understand another's feelings.

Clients who favor feelings are able to experience another person's emotions directly through their own emotions. By observing and focusing their attention on the other person, they experience actual feelings that are similar to the other person's. They are often very accurate in their readings of other people.

Clients who favor thinking may need to take a more logical road to empathy. I have personally found that empathy is a learnable skill. By breaking empathy down into its component skills and by practicing these skills, people can strengthen their ability to experience and respond to others' feelings. This empathy training can be extremely valuable because empathy, and the human connection it creates, is an essential aspect of leadership.

In empathy training, we engage in a process of developing the client's empathy muscles, not unlike training in an athletic skill. We begin the training by acknowledging that we can never really feel another person's feelings. Starting in the cognitive realm, we view empathy as making an educated guess about what the other person is experiencing. To make a good guess, clients need to be able to recognize and feel their own emotions. We often spend time on recognizing their own feelings. (This is not a snap for everyone; people who have considerable difficulty recognizing and feeling their emotions may need additional work with their coach or with a psychotherapist.) Once the clients have developed this fluency with their own emotions, they can project themselves into the other person's situation and ask, "How would I feel in this situation or if I were in this person's shoes?" Their own emotions can serve as clues.

Sometimes one question is not enough to understand the other person's state. In this case, we can slow down the empathy lesson by pondering a series of questions that will lead to an estimation of the other person's emotions—for example:

"What situation is this person in?"

"How would I feel if I were in that situation?"

"How have I reacted when I faced similar situations?"

"What is this person probably feeling?"

With thinking-oriented people, such a series of logical questions and answers can be the easiest and most direct path to empathy.

The second source of empathy is "reading" the other person. Nonverbal factors such as facial expressions, moistness of the eyes, tone of voice, breathing pace, skin tone, and body posture all provide clues to people's emotional state. Naturally, their words also furnish valuable information.

Learning Empathy Case: Stan #2
Recognizing the Importance of Feelings

Stan is a pharmaceutical research manager who was losing the trust of his department because of his insensitive behavior. He asked me to help him rebuild that trust. After interpreting his assessment and feedback, we determined that Stan was not very empathic and would benefit from learning this skill. Stan agreed that he wanted to strengthen his empathy.

In our first "lesson," we reviewed the role that feelings play in organizational life. We examined how people make decisions and form opinions through a combination of logic and emotion. Since this can come as surprise to some ultralogical people, I asked Stan to recount some of his work decisions, looking for their emotional component. I also shared the research on the centrality of emotions in decision making. We then examined the negative effects of being mistrusted by colleagues and considered possible causes. The goal of this exercise was to enhance Stan's recognition of the importance of feelings.

The goal of the next step was to strengthen Stan's ability to feel and understand his own emotions. We named some common emotions, such as joy, pride, hurt, and anger. I asked him to recall moments he had experienced these feelings and to describe the sensations. We also named each feeling in order to establish a language of emotion.

Once we had reinforced Stan's ability to identify his own feelings, we moved on to the big step of recognizing the feelings of others. I asked him to think of situations in which others probably had emotional reactions, including situations like getting promoted, being criticized, being listened to, and being ignored. (In a more elaborate empathy training program, the coach might show videos and ask the client to identify the emotions of the actors.) As Stan described each situation, I asked him to hypothesize what the person might be feeling. I also asked him to act out how they might express that feeling. After five or six scenarios, Stan was feeling pretty confident in his ability to make educated guesses about people's feelings.

As an assignment, Stan practiced empathy by guessing how people might be feeling in actual situations. He observed people in meetings, in one-on-one conversations, on the telephone, and responding to his e-mails. When possible, he would make an empathic remark to demonstrate his understanding and check his hypothesis. Statements like "That must make you worried" or "You seem enthusiastic" made people more comfortable with him. I asked Stan to practice this new skill as often as he could over the next months. Reading and understanding people's feelings became his new project, one that he could work on every day. As he practiced it, a whole new world of feelings and empathic responses opened up to him.

The final step in Stan's training was to learn to use his empathy to modify his own actions. Before saying something, he would ask himself, "If I say this, how might this person feel?" If he were comfortable with their likely response, he would say it. If he didn't want to evoke that feeling, he would change his words to something that would evoke a more desirable response. After practicing this skill in our coaching sessions, Stan started using it in his work life.

Can a person have too much empathy? Yes. Empathy, if overused, can interfere with a leader's need to give constructive feedback or to communicate other types of difficult messages.

Too Much Empathy Case: Ross #1
You Still Need to Have Those Difficult Conversations

Ross is an experienced public relations executive. He manages the press department for an entertainment company, providing press coverage for its shows and events. One of the keys to his success is his skill at meeting the needs of media people. He reads people, empathizes with them, and adapts his behavior to them. He is a master at keeping people happy.

His challenge came when he learned that his department's performance was at best mediocre. His staff of press professionals was producing incomplete or off-the-mark work and was not following up frequently with the press people. Improving the performance of his staff became our coaching goal.

When we talked about what he was doing to turn the situation around, Ross told me about a recent staff meeting where he laid out his expectations for department. His staff appeared to agree. But in the following weeks, Ross saw little improvement. I asked if he had spoken with each person to explain his expectations and where that person was missing the mark. He surprised me when he said that he had not given this difficult feedback because it would probably upset his people and might cause their performance to deteriorate even further. We had uncovered Ross's weakness. He empathized and sought to please so much that he dared not initiate difficult conversations.

My goal would be to help Ross conduct these difficult conversations. Ross wanted to succeed and agreed that this was an important goal but recognized that it would be a complete departure from his normal interpersonal style.

THE ANGRY LEADER

Many people feel anger at work. Both the workplace and the marketplace foster competition and bring out people's aggression. In their desire to succeed, people bump into one another and create situations in which some people are bound to be disappointed, dismissed, ignored or overruled. People become frustrated or angry in these situations. While their anger may be understandable, if it is expressed aggressively, it can damage work relationships and undermine a leader's effectiveness.

Anger, especially vicious anger, drives people away. It builds barriers between angry leaders and others. People avoid angry leaders and become very cautious about what they say to them. This leads to angry leaders becoming isolated from their staff, limiting their ability to influence as well as their access to information.

A pattern of anger also reduces a leader's credibility with senior management. Senior-level managers come to see angry leaders as lacking in people skills or, even worse, out of control. They might seek to reduce the angry leaders' responsibilities and keep them away from important and sensitive assignments.

Recently, I have been coaching two different angry leaders. Both are aware of how their anger is negatively affecting their careers. Both have tried to curtail their workplace anger on their own, with little success. Why is their anger so difficult to control? What can they do to channel their energy more constructively?

Anger Case: Tom #1 What Triggered His Outbursts?

Tom is a telecommunications manager with a securities trading firm. He is seen as very effective at managing large projects and completing them profitably and on time. But his career has plateaued because of his pattern of anger.

I was contracted to work with Tom for a ninety-minute coaching session as part of the company's leadership development program. As we went through his 360° feedback, Tom started elaborating on one of the written-in comments about his anger. It was clear that he wanted to work on this.

I followed by asking Tom to describe some of the situations in which he got angry. He described one in which an employee did not complete a task that had been assigned to him. He described another when a senior manager asked him to perform a task that Tom believed was useless. A third situation occurred when a peer did not complete his part of a critical project. In each situation, Tom expressed his anger by becoming judgmental and sarcastic and openly criticizing the person by saying something like "How could you be so stupid?" or "That's a terrible idea."

I asked about what he experienced when he got angry. Tom described his incensed reaction as being so sudden and so intense that it was impossible to control. When I commented on the speed of his reaction, Tom agreed that it happened too quickly to even be aware that it was coming on, not to mention consciously slowing it down.

I have come to believe that anger, for many people, is a form of protection against a more threatening feeling. Men especially become angry as a way of warding off the vulnerable feelings of fear, anxiety, or hurt. Since my coaching time with Tom was short, I explored with him the possibility that there might be an emotion lying behind his anger. I asked if there was anything that the anger-inducing situations had in common. He replied that each held the possibility of his failure. When I asked about his emotions that accompanied the possibility of failure, he explained, with some prompting, that they made him anxious. (It is interesting that Tom and others find it very hard to feel and identify vulnerable emotions such as fear or anxiety but have a much easier time feeling and expressing aggressive emotions like anger.)

Tom seemed both relieved and shaken by recognizing his anxiety: relieved at finding a way out of the grip of his hair-trigger anger and shaken by the vulnerability of feeling anxiety. I decided to focus on this anxious part of Tom to draw some of his energy and attention away from the accompanying anger. He talked about how, in each situation, the other person's actions would cause him to worry about failing on a project. He accepted and understood his anxiety in these situations. I encouraged him to use his awareness of his anxiety as stepping-stone in learning how to control his anger.

I believed that Tom would need to slow down his anger response in order to rein it in. Tom seemed to be a physical guy, so I chose to refer him to his body as a fast path to becoming aware of feelings. To heighten his awareness, I asked him where in his body he felt the anxiety. Tom indicated he felt it in his chest. We talked about staying aware of the sensations in his chest and his underlying anxiety as a way to slow down and moderate his anger response.

As we put these pieces together, Tom began to feel that he could actually conquer his anger pattern and advance in his career. He seemed hopeful for the first time. Then the resistance appeared. As soon as he recognized that he was truly capable of this change, he made a remark about retiring. At the peak of his optimism about conquering this pattern, which had plagued him throughout his entire career, he pulled back. It seemed that the part of him that didn't want to change was rebelling by speaking out. When I commented on his remark, Tom agreed that there was a part of him that did not want to put in the effort.

Seeing this rebellion as a motivational issue, I addressed it from two fronts: past successes and potential rewards. I asked him if he had made any other significant behavioral changes in his life. He told me about losing eighty-five pounds and keeping it off. That would serve as his model for this change. When I asked him what had motivated him to lose the weight, he said that he was afraid of dying young. Avoidance of a negative outcome had motivated him in the past. So I tried to use it again by asking how he would feel if he stayed at his current level for the rest of his career. He made a face and admitted that would be horrible, almost as bad as dying young from obesity. By focusing on his fear of the unwanted outcome, he became remotivated to continue working on his anger.

I wanted to give him more tools to succeed in his anger management effort, so I asked him how he had succeeded in losing the weight. He credited two actions he took. First, he developed and used a plan. Second, he made the process comfortable by setting a series of goals that were easy to achieve. We set about trying to replicate this approach to his anger management. We outlined a plan based on (1) awareness of the feeling the anxiety in his chest and then (2) waiting and (3) deflecting the anger by using the waiting time to plan a diplomatic and dignified response. Tom gave each step a label that he could easily remember and then went through each step to assure himself that he could practice it under fire. Everything checked out.

Since I was not contracted to meet with him again, we explored his sharing his plan with his manager and some selected peers. He liked the idea of meeting with them monthly to ask for feedback about their view of his progress on managing his anger. Involving them would serve two purposes. It would provide Tom with needed feedback and reinforcement. And it would speed up their perception of his change. Tom made a commitment to both himself and to me to work at controlling his anger. We both left feeling optimistic about his chances.

Anger Case: Peter #3
Preventing Hair-Trigger Reactions

Peter is a research executive at a biotech company. He is a youthful yet skilled manager with an energetic, engaging style. He came to the company expecting to shore up the chemistry department, as well as to help develop the company culture and integrate it with its parent. At the suggestion of his manager, Peter sought coaching because he was damaging work relationships with angry outbursts. His anger was causing people to fear and avoid him, diminishing his ability to lead. He had been aware of this pattern for several years but on his own had not made much progress in controlling it. His goal in coaching was to gain control of his anger.

In our initial meetings, Peter described some situations in which he lashed out at someone. In each situation, he would get angry in response to someone's doing something that disappointed or offended him. What first struck me was the speed of his angry reactions. The event would occur, and within seconds, he would lash out. When we explored this sequence further, it became clear that he was only vaguely aware of his emotions. All he knew was that he got angry. When I asked him to describe his feelings just prior to the outburst, he could only describe them as "upset." This seemed significant because, like Tom, identifying his emotions could become helpful in gaining greater control of them. As homework, I asked Peter to track the situations in which he was tempted to lose control, to describe the events, to name his emotions, and to suppress his reaction.

Peter liked the idea of controlling his reactions but balked at identifying his emotions. Even after several requests, he resisted this part of the assignment. His reluctance seemed important, however. I thought of the emotional intelligence model in which people begin with emotional awareness and then move to social awareness, self-regulation, and finally relationship management. I started believing that Peter's lack of awareness of his emotions might be related to his inability to control them. My initial strategy was to assist Peter in becoming more aware of his emotions so he could regulate them.

He seemed motivated to change his anger pattern, yet he had a strong aversion to examining his feelings. Because of this, I wondered if my initial strategy of helping him become more aware of his precipitating emotions might fail.

In our next meeting, another possibility emerged. Peter spoke frequently of wanting to build a great culture, wanting his managers to excel, and wanting to be an excellent leader. I wondered if there was a connection between his idealism and his anger. Did his high expectations for others mean that he could easily become disappointed whenever they did not live up to his ideals? Could his anger come from these deep and frequent disappointments? When I asked about his high ideals, he explained how important they were to him and how frustrated he became when people disappointed him.

In that session, we looked at Peter's idealism as an important part of himself while also looking for a more realistic part. We talked about his expectations for people, what was realistic and what was unrealistic. For example, he wanted a team member to become more detail-oriented and better at managing his time—rapidly. Upon examination, however, it seemed more realistic to believe that this change would take at least a year, if he achieved it at all. Peter came to see that by tempering his idealism with realistic expectations, he would be less prone to disappointment and therefore to anger. This approach did help Peter control his outbursts for a while.

Several weeks later, he had another embarrassing outburst. At a management meeting, Peter got angry with a colleague who had been lecturing the group in a condescending way. I was at the meeting and observed the tantrum at first hand. It wasn't pretty. Clearly, the idealism cure hadn't worked. Peter and I met again to address what had happened.

My only plans for this meeting were to try to understand what had happened and to look for another clue to prevention. Then Peter described how he acted in meetings at the parent company. He explained that he edited himself all the time in these politically sensitive meetings. He followed this by asking me if a radical change might work better than an incremental change. He referred to his experience as a trumpet player. When players needed to make a significant improvement in playing, the teacher would make them abandon their current style of breathing and fingering and adopt a completely new approach. Playing would initially feel quite awkward but would result in significant improvement after a while. He wondered if the same type of sweeping change might help him control his anger. Would staying aware of his thoughts and feelings and editing his behavior do the trick?

Initially, I had mixed feelings about his idea, thinking it seemed a bit radical. I was glad that he had taken charge and come up with a workable idea. He was proposing to act more like a seasoned executive and less like an impulsive young man. I was concerned, however, about his giving up his spontaneity and wondered what he might lose in the process. But the more we talked about it, the more sense it made. I supported Peter in trying out his "editing himself all the time" approach.

APPLYING USE OF SELF

Following my session with Peter, I reflected on my own actions. I asked myself why I had not completely supported his idea when most executives I knew regularly edited themselves. I realized that even though I deeply wanted him to gain control of his emotions, I was also attracted by his quick, energized, emotional spontaneity. I had lost my own spontaneity early in my life and may have wanted him to preserve his boyishness as a way of preserving my own. Whatever my reasons, I had almost gotten in the way of my client's progress. My little talk with myself enabled me to get out of the way and help Peter progress.

MOTIVATION AND LEADERSHIP

Most leaders wish for a motivated staff. I have worked with several clients on creating an environment that is maximally motivating to their staff. The first operating principle is that one size doesn't fit all, that no one motivator is likely to appeal to every member. Our first task is to identify the key motivators for each staff member. With a little questioning, clients can usually identify these motivators, but many have not used this knowledge so pragmatically before. Next we talk about the kind of highly motivated, "stretch" effort they would like to see from each person and identify a specific motivator that could propel that person to the next level of performance.

Motivation Case: Bill #6
Choosing a Motivator That Fits the Person

In a motivational analysis session, Bill identified the motivators for his three key project managers. Since manager A would clearly be motivated by a promotion, Bill planned a conversation with him describing the new behavior he was hoping for and tying it to a promotion to director. Manager B wanted to stay on the cutting edge of her field and share her expertise with other people. So Bill set out a development plan for her that included a senior technical role. Manager C wanted more visibility. So Bill's plan for him included more presentations at meetings with senior management. Six months later, Bill's department had become one of the top performers in the division. Morale was high, and turnover had slowed to a trickle.

GAINING AND USING POWER

Organizations need their leaders to guide members' actions toward common goals. Leaders need to exercise power in order to influence their actions. When leaders don't exert this influence, employees begin moving in their own sometimes disparate directions. This causes the organization to flounder. For this reason, the skillful and judicious use of power is one of the important lessons of leadership.

Some people are naturally drawn to acquiring and exercising power. Others hold back from obtaining or using it. Both types of people can learn about power. The power-oriented people can learn to temper their appetite and to share power with others. The power-reticent people can learn the value of using power wisely and become skillful at knowing how and when to exercise it.

Organizational psychologists define five sources of power:

- *Position*—role in the organizational structure
- *Control of resources*—ability to use and distribute money, equipment, data, or people
- *Expertise*—superior relevant knowledge

- *Personal behavior*—actions that inspire confidence and attract followers
- *Relationships*—communication and trust with significant people

Personal behavior and relationships are the sources of power that are most malleable and therefore the ones most likely to be addressed in coaching. People can project, or not project, power through their personal behavior. How they speak, ask questions, project their voice, and hold their body all contribute to their interpersonal power. A loud voice is more powerful than a squeaky voice. An upright posture is more compelling than one that is hunched over. Large, expressive arm movements appear more powerful than twiddling fingers. Direct eye contact is more commanding than darting eyes, and so on. Leaders who want to appear more powerful can learn these personal behaviors and put them into practice.

But these physical behaviors are not enough. If they are merely tacked on to a person's personality, they may gain temporary attention but can also seem hollow. Authentic power comes from within. Truly powerful people use their behavior to express something personally and organizationally important. Clients who are seeking to develop a more powerful presence learn to connect their behaviors to an idea that is internally meaningful. When they combine the power behaviors with a meaningful message, they become authentically powerful leaders.

Persistence and consistency are additional aspects of power. A persistent leader will stay with an idea, regularly raising it in order to gain support. If leaders abandon ideas in the face of resistance or back off to avoid disagreement, their ideas will fall by the wayside, and their perceived power will diminish. A powerful leader recognizes when to persist and when to negotiate. For some, that means being more persistent, more often.

Power Case: Alice #4
Refitting Her Presentation Style as a Manager

Alice needed to lead Cybern through a significant transition from being a biotech firm designing promising technologies to a pharmaceutical company that develops marketable drugs. To succeed, managers would need to manage differently, scientists would need to learn new skills, and the whole company would need to adopt new practices. To lead this behavioral and attitudinal change, Alice would need to be a more powerful voice at Cybern.

The first challenge she faced was influencing her staff to support the new strategy. Transitioning to a drug discovery company meant that most people would need to leave their comfort zones and learn new skills. When she initially communicated the new strategy, she communicated it only once and a bit tentatively.

The first skill on our agenda was persistence and repetition. As a creative scientist, Alice wasn't fond of repetition. She liked to solve a problem and move on. In our coaching, she recognized that her staff would need to hear the new strategy several times in several different formats before they abandon their old mindsets and habits to embrace it.

Our second project was her personal behavior in groups. Five foot one, with a soft, high pitched voice, Alice was hardly a commanding presence. On top of that, her conceptual intelligence and broad knowledge caused her to question everything and look at topics relativistically. This meant that she that she treated many ideas with a measure of doubt. When she expressed an idea, it would be tentative, always leaving open the possibility that it might be wrong.

We began working on developing a more definitive and commanding presence. The first target was her voice. When she expressed an idea, she would often raise her voice at the end of the sentence. This "uptalk" in effect turns every statement into a question. After pointing this out, she practiced lowering her voice at the end of her sentences. It is a simple technique with concrete results. Instantly, she sounded more authoritative.

Next we worked on her body movements. We realized that the gesture of moving her hands downward at the end of a statement made it more definitive. So she began to weave that into her style.

In meetings, her tendency was to speak only when she had something unique to add. As a team member, this is a fine strategy. But as the leader, her silence made her seem passive and left her constituents wondering where she stood on the issues under discussion. Acknowledging this, she began to weigh in on each topic in meetings. This wasn't particularly hard, since she did have opinions. But it did take some practice to make it into a new habit.

Power Case: Marianne #1
A Creative Learns to Use Her Power

Marianne is a design director at a publishing company. A year earlier, her company had launched a new magazine. Now she was charged with managing its redesign to attract a broader readership. The job was not easy, since it involved a makeover into a new type of magazine, and there were no models to follow or even adapt.

Besides the design and branding challenge, Marianne and her team also faced a tight deadline because the company had promised its advertisers a new look in the next four months.

Marianne and the magazine's editor-in-chief contracted with a design studio to do the redesign. The studio created a wonderful logo that all the publishing executives loved. But when it came to designing the magazine's interior, the studio kept missing the mark. After a third failed presentation, Marianne had a feeling in her gut that the studio just wouldn't be able to do the job. She mentioned this concern to the editor, who agreed. But instead of acting on her feeling, Marianne kept plugging along, giving the studio her feedback and asking them to try again.

Three precious weeks went by, and the studio submitted three more off-target designs. Finally, the editor called Marianne into his office and told her he wanted to fire the design studio and hire another one. He also decided to take over the role of managing the studio. Marianne gulped and agreed. She knew that firing the studio was the right thing to do and wished she had been more forceful about it three weeks earlier. As a result of her not exercising her power, the magazine had lost three weeks and several thousand dollars. Furthermore, she had lost some power as the leader of the design function. Her manager was disappointed that she had not been swifter and more decisive in exercising her power.

As we reviewed the episode, Marianne learned an important lesson from this experience. She had the right idea but diluted its impact by neglecting to act on it. She retraced her thoughts and actions to identify what she could have done differently. She realized that she had been too patient, too nice to the studio, and not aggressive enough in using her power to pursue the path that was right for the magazine. She had been reluctant to use her natural power.

A Caveat on Management Power

Leadership is demanding work. Even when they empower others, leaders assume responsibility for the whole undertaking. They plan, review, and coordinate the work of their staff and take responsibility for the overall result. It is a big responsibility, often accompanied by a lot of pressure. One of their rewards for this investment is increased influence over the direction of the enterprise. If a person values leading, influencing, responsibility, and decision making, leadership can be a satisfying job. People who enjoy power can learn to exercise it well and get pleasure from exercising it. But for people who do not value power, management can be a punishing job with little reward other than the salary.

Power Case: Brian #1 Not a Happy Manager

Brian was a team leader in a pharmaceutical R&D organization. He managed a team of eight senior and fifteen junior scientists seeking to come up with an obesity drug. He had developed a reputation as being brash and overbearing. He entered the coaching process to become more skillful and comfortable in leading his team.

In our initial conversation, he expressed some frustration with his management role. He explained that he wasn't very comfortable managing his team and managing his superiors. He wondered if it was the right role for him. We agreed to keep this question on the table and address it through our coaching work.

In the first phase of our work, we examined the assessments he had undertaken in a recent leadership training program. The FIRO-B is an assessment instrument that looks at three aspects of a person's needs: affiliation, the need to belong; control, the need for influence, responsibility, and power; and affection, the need for openness and trust. Brian's control orientation was the lowest score in his profile.

There were now two signals regarding Brian's interest in leadership: his expressed doubts about being a manager and his low control score. As we talked about Brian's relationship with power, he realized that he was not particularly interested in directing the efforts of others. He realized that some of the tension he felt in managing resulted from his dislike for influencing the behavior of others and of the pressure exerted on him by his management. These aspects of his job were simply not satisfying for him. He was much more interested in his own scientific creativity and achievement. About half an hour into the conversation, he said, "I don't want to be a manager anymore." I felt that his decision was sudden and possibly impulsive, so I asked him to postpone making any big decisions until he was truly sure. We continued to explore it over the next month. Over that time, he became more certain of his decision. Four weeks later, he announced it to his manager and returned to being a research scientist.

Competition and Conflict Case: Valerie #2
Dealing with Challenge

Valerie, the scientist who took a research and teaching job on a college campus, eventually left academia and transitioned into a management position at a biotechnology company. There she excelled at hiring and developing junior people as she built a department and taught the staff the needed skills. But her new role brought a new array of challenges, particularly in the political arena.

Her first challenge came from Len, a peer who was to provide the raw material (synthesized proteins) needed by Valerie's department. Len was not delivering all the proteins needed, and those that he did provide were often six months late. Their director had left the company, so Valerie was essentially on her own in her efforts to secure the proteins. Len had adopted a stance of agreeing to her requests and then ignoring them. When she reminded him, he grew angry with her "meddling" and even made some comments about wanting Valerie to fail so that he could take over her department.

When we began our coaching, Valerie had tried a number of strategies to get the proteins from Len's lab, but none was working. When she tried regularly reminding Len of his commitment, he saw her as a nag and complained of her interfering with his autonomy. When she made a comment in a meeting about the situation, she was dismissed as "not a team player." The absence of an immediate supervisor made her job even more difficult. Yet her department desperately needed these proteins to do its work.

We decided on a two-pronged strategy. One involved talking with the president about her challenge. The second involved rebuilding some kind of alliance with Len and his staff. In going to the president, she was careful to present the situation as a difference in priorities rather than a condemnation of Len. This alerted the president to the risks and rewards and induced him to talk with Len about the importance of his protein synthesis.

Rebuilding the collaboration with Len was more difficult because he and Valerie had become adversaries. Valerie needed to let go of her anger and spend time with Len, listening to his concerns and talking about protein synthesis. In our coaching sessions, she explored new mind-sets for relating to Len and then put them into practice in conversations with him. She found it useful to picture herself as a mature, patient leader who had the power to get what she needed. This differed from her previous perception of herself as a victim who expected to be disappointed.

The new approach started to work. Len delivered the next batch of proteins on time. Valerie made point of continuing her regular conversations with Len and lauding him and his lab at the next management meeting.

During the same month, Valerie faced another challenge from George, one of her direct reports. She had hired George for his talent and ambition, and he was performing well, both in the lab and in the interpersonal arena. After a year, he was chomping at the bit, wanting more visibility and power.

George had begun to go around Valerie to deal directly with the president, to challenge her in meetings, and to work on his own priorities rather than hers. She knew that she needed to do something to stop his challenges, but she didn't know what. She considered confronting him about his recent behavior but held back because that seemed inelegant and possibly even desperate.

We began by examining the situation, the players, and Valerie's attitudes and actions. She recognized that she often felt powerless in relation to others and that they sensed this inner weakness. We identified that her self-esteem and her ability to confidently express her needs lay at the core of this problem. I suggested that working on her self-esteem would be best addressed in psychotherapy, but we could work on attitudes and behaviors that would communicate her needs and be likely to influence others.

She commented that her self-esteem issues had plagued her for most of her life and that this would be a good time to address them with a psychotherapist. In the meantime, we began working on her feelings of power and confidence. She came to acknowledge the physical differences between her powerless posture of stooped shoulders, sunken chest, and shallow breathing and the powerful stance of a full chest and head held high. As she practiced communicating the attitude that "my wishes are important," she accompanied it with the improved physical postures.

With the powerful attitude as her base, we planned things she could say to George that would bring him back into allegiance with her. We considered the age-old combination of the carrot and the stick, using her control of rewards as a source of power. She would look for opportunities to give George recognition and exposure. Conversely, she would calmly take charge of meetings when he would attempt to hijack them from her agenda. These new behaviors felt within her repertoire, both bold enough to expand her power and subtle enough for her to feel and seem calm and confident.

Coaching in the Political Arena Case: Greg #5
Learning to Play the Game—and Get What You Want

Several months after Greg made his personal commitment to develop himself, his manager, Mitchell, left the company. Greg and most of his peers believed that

Mitchell would not be replaced, with some of his direct reports reporting directly to Beverly, Mitchell's manager, and some not. This presented Greg with an immediate challenge: to ensure that he became one of Beverly's new direct reports.

This was a real opportunity for Greg. He had been making progress on his skills in communicating succinctly and developing senior relationships, but it was probably too soon for them to be fully recognized and acknowledged by others. He believed that Beverly would be making her decision in the next two months. He saw two choices of action: do something to make a play for the position, or wait and hope that Beverly and the senior team would recognize his progress.

He chose to make a play. Greg had never done anything like this before. I had limited experience, both in my own corporate career and observing executives position themselves and lobby for a desired position. Together we planned his strategy.

We agreed that the most important action would be to talk with Beverly about his wish to report to her. But to frame it as his wish seemed too self-serving and not very appealing. He decided to focus on his belief that he could do a lot to help Beverly and the business succeed.

We also recognized that decisions like this are made more by group consensus than by a solitary person. Talking with Beverly's current direct reports about his goals and plans could move the consensus in his direction. But some of this group had self-interests in keeping the number of direct reports small. Talking with these people about his goals could cause them to lobby against him. As we went through the list of Beverly's reports, we identified two people he could approach to gain their support. For the rest of the session, we planned what he would say to each person.

COACHING AS AN ORGANIZATIONAL INTERVENTION

No person is an island, especially a leader in a modern organization. Leaders are important members of a social system that depends on shared goals and beliefs to coordinate the actions of its members. In such an organization, the actions of each member both affect and are affected by the actions of others. Because people look to their leaders for direction and as role models, they have a particularly strong effect on the actions of people around them. Similarly, the leader's senior management has a particularly strong effect on the leader's actions. Therefore, it is worth regarding a coaching program as an intervention with the whole system, since a change in the leader's behavior will both affect and be affected by the behavior of many others.

Systems Thinking Case: Bill #7
The Perp Is Part of the Culture

Bill was asked to engage in a coaching program because of unusually high turnover in his department. In interviews with his staff, I learned that the primary cause of the staff turnover was a deep dissatisfaction resulting from a lack of empowerment. The highly educated staff felt they were not allowed to make decisions about their projects. Although Bill was a perpetrator of the disempowerment, the staff indicated that it went far beyond him. It was characteristic of the whole division and of the whole company. In this company, it was the norm for senior managers to make the decisions and for project managers to implement them. It was also common for senior managers to reverse the decisions of project managers. What was originally presented as Bill's troublesome habit turned out to be powerful characteristic of the organizational culture. In working with Bill on empowerment, we needed to keep in mind the actions and beliefs of his senior management as well as his direct reports.

Involving Stakeholders: Who Is the Client?

Most leadership coaching is sponsored and funded by the organization. The organization generally views coaching as a way to develop its leaders, much like training or executive education programs. Organizations invest in it because they believe that it will result in more effective leaders. They have an interest in the coaching, and their sponsorship makes them important stakeholders in the coaching process. As sponsors and clients, they want information about the progress of the coaching assignment.

From the coach's perspective, every coaching engagement has at least two clients, the individual leader and the organization. Balancing the needs of both clients can be a source of concern, even conflict, for some coaches. The most apparent concern is the potential disparity between keeping certain information confidential and the need to keep the organization informed about the coaching process. Some coaches, especially less experienced ones, struggle with the decision about what information to share and what to keep confidential.

Underlying this struggle is an uncertainty about where one's loyalties lie. Some beginning coaches can feel more loyalty to their individual clients than to their organizational clients. This imbalance may stem from the values instilled in training counselors, the need for client-coach trust, and the amount of time the client and coach spend together. The imbalance, however, can lead to undercommunicating with the organizational client.

Undercommunicating with the organization can be risky, first, because the organization is the clients' environment, to which they must adapt in order to succeed, and second, because the clients' managers may see behaviors and situations that coaches and clients may not see. Third, as the sponsor and funder of the coaching project, the organization has a valid interest in knowing, within reason, what is going on.

One goal of the coach is to keep the organization informed while protecting the interests and trust of the individual client. One way to do this is for the coach to review with the client what the coach will say to the manager or HR manager. This accomplishes several goals. It preserves the trust and ensures that the leader will not be surprised or harmed by anything the coach says. It reinforces the connection between the coaching pair and the rest of the organization. And it makes coaching and personal development more acceptable by shedding some light on the process.

The noted coach Marshall Goldsmith (personal communication) has developed an approach to communication and evaluation that both increases the probability of behavior change and hastens the perception of this change by the stakeholders. In this model, the client assumes two roles, that of the behavior changer and that of a facilitator involving others in their behavior change. Early in the process, the client shares their development plan with selected stakeholders and contracts to talk monthly about their progress toward their goal. Then, each month, they go back to each stakeholder, asking for feedback on their behavior change and suggestions about the future. This approach ensures that the client maintains an accurate reading of how others see their actions. It also keeps the stakeholders observant about the key behaviors. And it strengthens the relationship between the client and each stakeholder. Stakeholders, leader, and coach become a team all working toward the leader's increased effectiveness.

Refocusing Using Stakeholder Feedback Case: Greg #6 Learning to Cut to the Chase

Greg's primary development goal was to communicate more succinctly with senior managers. His constituents clearly and frequently expressed this need though the 360° interviews. In our coaching sessions, I too noted the circuitousness of his explanations. We embarked on a rigorous behavioral learning process to help Greg tell a succinct, sequential story and get to the bottom line quickly. Greg worked hard at this, practicing it both in the coaching session and on the job.

As the coaching drew to a close, I called his manager, Beverly—yes, he succeeded in becoming her direct report—to ask for her impression of his progress. Beverly surprised me by saying that although he had been communicating more clearly on some topics, there was one topic on which he was still imprecise and circuitous. Whenever they talked about contracting with offshore programmers, he seemed vague, closed-minded, and eager to find reasons to avoid aggressively pursuing this path. Greg and I had been working on one behavior, clarity, but missing a related one, reading peoples' unspoken agendas. Had I not spoken with her, we would have concluded our coaching, declaring success prematurely. I wished I had spoken with her months earlier so that we could have begun working on this issue sooner.

The Client-Manager Relationship

Work relationships are central to getting things done. Each relationship is a partnership in which the partners collaborate. A client's relationship with his or her manager is one of the most important. Good boss relationships often accompany success. And bad boss relationships often lead to failure.

As with marriages, all client-manager relationships are different, coming in all shapes and sizes. This means that there is no simple formula for creating an excellent boss relationship. Like any relationship, learning and adapting to the other's style is a good place to start. Skillful subordinates learn about their manager's style, values, priorities, preferences, and blind spots. They then use that knowledge to guide the interaction. They find out how the boss likes to be communicated with. They allow themselves to be influenced and learn how the boss can be influenced. Sometimes a great boss relationship is easy. Sometimes it is hard. That is when it becomes a coaching theme.

Understanding and Adapting to the Manager Case: Greg #7 Who Makes the First Move?

When Beverly told me about Greg's lack of follow-through on outsourcing, I wondered if Greg was experiencing a values conflict between loyalty to his employees and his role as an executive in his corporation. But as I listened to her, I wondered if Beverly wasn't experiencing a similar conflict. I hypothesized that some of their relationship difficulties were being caused by something they had in common but neither could admit.

Both Greg and Beverly had become successful, in part, by building loyal, talented staffs. They valued their people and kept them appropriately challenged and rewarded. Now the corporation was asking them to determine the feasibility of eliminating some technology jobs by moving them to other countries. Greg was ready to do the analysis and make a recommendation, but did not want to take the initiative to actually begin the outsourcing process. He was waiting for Beverly to make this commitment. I believed that Beverly shared Greg's disinclination to take the initiative on the outsourcing effort but was not fully aware of this. She was waiting for Greg to make the commitment. So the project floundered, Beverly grew impatient with Greg's beating around the bush, and Greg grew increasingly confused by Beverly's mixed messages.

In a coaching session, Greg and I examined the possible causes of this problem. Only then did he realize that he and Beverly were both hesitant about the project—and that he needed to provide the initiative to get it going. Once he realized this, his job became clearer and easier. Within a month, he completed his analysis, presented his plan to Beverly, and took charge of moving some consulting positions to India. His relationship with Beverly improved rapidly. She began valuing him as a key member of her team—just because he was able to understand a tricky part of their relationship and act on it without even having to speak about it.

Because of the difference in their styles, Greg still needed to adapt to Beverly's pace and bluntness, but this was relatively easy compared to the challenge he had just surmounted.

Misreading the Signals Case: Michael #2
Just Report the Good Stuff—NOT!

After three months, Michael, the marketing director, had begun working on managing his staff more actively and being more organized in dealing with the consulting staff. He was focusing on communicating with his staff and empowering them to interact with certain customers on their own. He also talked about his efforts at giving consultants more lead time to prepare for client presentations. Each time we met, he described his progress in these areas. I believed that he was making good progress until I received a phone call from his HR manager.

She told me about a near revolt among the consulting staff resulting from Michael having given them last-minute assignments on two important projects and from the disrespect with which he treated them. She also said that Michael had neglected to manage a direct report, resulting in her working for months on the wrong aspects of a project. I was surprised because these stories contradicted Michael's descriptions of his progress in working with the consultants and managing his staff.

In my next meeting with Michael, I relayed the HR manager's account and asked him what was up. From his perspective, these incidents were minor slip-ups in a sea of real progress. I realized that he was a poster child for learned optimism. He focused his attention on his three successes and minimized his two failures. He had selected the events that made him feel and look good and had avoided or rationalized his setbacks. He avoided them so much that he neglected to mention them to me, and, probably successfully, moved them to the far corners of his memory.

Michael is a salesperson. In *Learned Optimism*, Martin Seligman describes how optimists distort reality to maintain a positive view of the world. They selectively filter out negative experiences in order to maintain their belief in the goodness of themselves and the world. In some jobs like sales, this optimism is a critical success factor; that is, optimists perform significantly better than pessimists. (In other fields, like law or finance, the "what could go wrong here?" perspective of pessimists is valuable.)

The phenomenon of optimism poses a challenge for coaches. We want to and need to believe in and trust our clients. Yet many have positively skewed perspectives that cause them to overlook their lapses. One way to correct for this is to get regular, ongoing feedback from the clients' constituents. Either the coach or preferably the clients themselves can ask the constituents to describe the clients' progress on their development plans. This practice has two benefits. It provides feedback on the clients' progress, and it also reinforces the clients' commitment to positive change and keeps the constituents as allies.

DOING NO HARM

There are some situations where sharing information could harm a client—for example, when the client expresses an intention of leaving the organization. If the coach were to share this information with the client's higher-ups, they could remove responsibilities in anticipation of the client's departure or worse, could terminate the client so they can start recruiting a replacement. In such cases, it is important for the coach to keep the client's secret, no matter how difficult.

SEXUALITY AT WORK

Now that the workforce has nearly equal numbers of men and women, there is more than ever the possibility of attraction and flirtation at work. Sometimes these attractions stay innocent; at other times they escalate into affairs and even marriages. I once knew a manager who boasted, "I like XYZ Corporation. I met all three of my wives there."

Flirtatious work relationships become troublesome when the sexual attention is unwanted, in which case it becomes sexual harassment. Trouble can also arise when there are differences in power and seniority between the two participants and when one or both is married. Allison's case plays this out.

Sexuality Case: Allison #1 Cooling Unfair Gossip

Allison has been a private coaching client for over a year. Over that time, we had worked on her decision to return to a career in politics, securing her position as advance manager in the mayor's office, and developing a leadership style that was direct, diplomatic, and influential. She called me one day in a panic.

She was upset because the members of the mayor's inner circle believed that she had been flirting with the mayor and were actively working to isolate her from him. Although she did not talk with the mayor very much, when they did talk, they had excellent rapport and enjoyed each other. They were both good at repartee; the mayor would say something clever or humorous, and she would respond by laughing and coming back with a clever remark of her own. Whenever the mayor's handlers or his wife observed these interactions, they became nervous and shooed Allison away. Even though she was the most senior member of the advance team, the inner circle had already barred her from out-of-town trips with the mayor.

It is important to note that Allison is an attractive, single woman with a warm and friendly style that can seem flirtatious. She is the kind of woman many men find attractive. The mayor, who had a reputation for flirtatiousness, did not seem to be hiding his attraction. Allison asked me what she should do. She felt that she was being unfairly labeled and wanted to do something to recoup her good reputation. As we explored her options, it became clear that the responsibility for repairing it lay completely with her. She was tempted to talk with someone higher up to explain her side of the story and rectify the situation. But as we considered this, it seemed like it would only lead to more trouble, because she would be spreading the word that she was a temptress.

Even though her intentions were innocent and the way she was being treated was unfair, no one other than Allison could put an end to people's speculation. We decided that she should stop the interpersonal sparks from flying by keeping her conversations with the mayor strictly professional. This would include not responding to his gestures, not laughing at his clever remarks, and limiting smiles and eye contact.

Allison thought about how she could act more coolly toward the mayor. She felt confident that she could do it. She also recognized the wisdom of telling no one about her concern, for fear of reinforcing her unwanted reputation. We estimated that it would take at least six months, probably closer to a year, for the inner circle to perceive her differently. But this was her only option. As she contemplated her new persona, she breathed a sigh of relief.

Chapter 15

The Business of Coaching

Coaching has existed as long as there have been leaders. Kings, tsars, and pharaohs had advisers to offer suggestions on the best ways to rule. Moses had Aaron, and Nixon had Kissinger. They gave both tactical counsel on economic and military matters and behavioral advice on political and interpersonal issues, instructing the ruler to communicate a message in a particular way or improve a relationship with particular person.

These advisers of yesteryear had a lot in common with modern coaches. They met regularly with the rulers. They addressed some of the stickiest aspects in the leaders' domains. They kept their conversations confidential. And they were paid for their services.

In the last twenty years, the leadership coaching industry has grown considerably. In its early days, coaching was provided primarily to only the most senior executives, often in a very secretive manner so that no one would know that their heroic leaders were getting help. As word spread about its effectiveness, coaching began to be offered to mid-level managers, both to those with increased responsibilities, as well as to those who were struggling with challenging situations or who had difficult management styles. In many organizations, coaching became so open that having a coach became perceived as an executive perk or even a status symbol, contributing to its rapid growth. In the 1970s, I encountered two different types of coaching. One took the form of a mentor or adviser providing interpersonal and political guidance to key executives. The coach was often a psychologist or former executive giving a very personal service to the client. The second type emerged from the world of training and development, through a desire to help leaders develop individualized approaches to the standardized content of the leadership training program. Both types appeared to be very effective at enabling behavioral change. And that made them even more popular.

The mentor or adviser form of coaching has evolved into the type of multimonth coaching engagement described throughout much of this book. These engagements are usually defined, contractually, as three-, six-, nine-, or twelve-month programs. The coach and client meet regularly, often weekly or biweekly, and progress through the behavior change process as described in Chapter Eight. Early meetings focus on building rapport, gathering assessment information, and setting goals. Midphase meetings usually deal with understanding the dynamics of the specific behavioral change and learning and practicing the new behaviors. Final stages usually address fine-tuning and reinforcing the behavior change and adapting it to fit a variety of situations. The coach and client generally meet more frequently in the beginning of the process and less often toward the end. This is the structure of most classic executive coaching.

In the training-based model, popularized by the Center for Creative Leadership, learners participate in an experience that blends training with coaching. This short-term model comprises a group workshop usually led by a trainer and individual work with a coach. Beforehand the company distributes 360° assessment instruments to a number of each participant's colleagues. In the workshop, participants learn and practice leadership skills. They also receive their individual feedback reports and work with a coach for one to two hours to interpret the feedback. With their coach they then select one or two skills that they feel are most crucial to their future success and work with the coach to develop these skills. Participants model or even practice these behaviors. The coach may ask the client to commit to the plan and may ask the client to write it down to share with the client's manager and possibly others. At the close the participant should feel ready to implement the new behaviors back at work. The coach may also follow up with a phone call or an e-mail to help the client stay focused on the plan. This type of short-term coaching combined with training can be very powerful, especially for clients who are in the contemplation phase, ready for change, and seeking help in understanding which behaviors to change and how to actually change them. A colleague, Judy Rosemarin, refers to this as "laser coaching" because of the speed and precision required to compress into one session what usually takes ten to twenty sessions.

"Laser Coaching" Case: Diane #2
A Fast-Track Success

Diane is the location manager at a regional airport for a rapidly growing airline. She manages ticketing, baggage handling, and ground operations in an eighteen-hour-a-day operation at this airport. She manages four supervisors with a total staff of more than thirty people. Her feedback showed very high scores from her manager and peers and very low scores, across the board, from her direct reports. As usual, I began by exploring her strengths and then sought to understand her development needs in relation to these strengths. Her strengths are her strong customer orientation; her upbeat, people-pleasing personality; and her optimistic management style in which she always looks for possibilities. She believes in and lives the company culture, which prides itself on its flexibility and the ability to think creatively to make the right things happen. The downside of her style is that she tends to avoid difficult conversations when she can't make the right things happen or might have to disappoint someone.

Our initial challenge was to identify a single area for development. This was not obvious; because the survey data from the direct reports provided little in specifics other than overall dissatisfaction, I knew I needed to read between the lines. I used two sources of information to form an initial hypothesis. The first was her own description of her very positive, optimistic style and her question about how she could use this style to deal with a negative situation. The second source was the unanimously low ratings from her direct reports. Remember, my intuition told me that these undifferentiated low ratings were expressions of anger and frustration. I voiced my hunch that she might have lost the trust of her people because of her avoidance of negative messages. She agreed strongly and became even more engaged in our process.

In talking about her need to deal with the negative aspects of work, she understood it immediately but recognized that it would be a considerable change in the way she looked at life. Addressing it would mean a shift from cheerleader to realist. Because of the size of this shift—and her body language, which signaled approach avoidance—I wondered whether she had the motivation to earnestly pursue this change on her own. When I asked whether she felt she had the motivation to sustain this change, she wavered. So we explored some possible motivators and found two, one internal and one external. If she learned to confront limitations by having the difficult conversations, she would feel better about herself. The gnawing feeling that people didn't fully trust her would go away and be replaced by everyone's knowing that she was doing the right thing. For employees to feel better over the long term, she would need to make some of them feel worse in the short term. The second motivator was external. The annual employee satisfaction survey was coming up, and she expected that the scores would be low, similar to her 360° feedback scores. She indicated that this would hurt her reputation as a manager and possibly even her job security. Because this was a one-session coaching relationship, I felt Diane would need strong reasons to progress on her own from contemplation to planning to action. She now had two real reasons to change.

The combination of training and coaching works because training and coaching address different needs. Through training, people gain the rationale, knowledge, and a summary of the key steps in the new skill. Through coaching, they integrate the skills into their personality, select the settings in which they will use the skill, practice it, and address their resistance to the change. Together, they cover most of the bases in the game of change. A study conducted by Xerox Corporation showed that training followed by coaching resulted in more than 85 percent greater behavior change than training alone.

The training-coaching model does not work so well with certain clients. Because it is a onetime meeting, it is less helpful for clients who are resistant to change and do not have enough time to fully explore and overcome their resistance. Laser coaching also comes up short when the new skill is so difficult that the client will need more than an hour or two to learn and integrate it.

Coaching has been successful because it does two things very well. It identifies the one or two specific areas for growth that are most critical to the client. And it provides practice and support over a long enough time frame so that lasting behavior change can take place. Because of this repeated effectiveness at producing visible results, coaching is used more and more as the methodology of choice to facilitate specific behavioral learning by leaders. However, coaching is not and should not replace leadership training or executive education in building the fundamental skills and knowledge of leaders. These are important and addressed well by those modalities. Coaching has, in a sense, created a new market for itself: behavior change in specific, usually interpersonal, arenas.

CURRENT TRENDS

As coaching has become more widespread, it has also been maturing and changing. As organizations used coaching more, they saw their expenditures on coaching grow considerably.

Let's do the math. A large organization that invests in one hundred coaching engagements at $10,000 to $15,000 each spends over $1 million a year on coaching. Organizations recognized that they were spending large sums of money on dozens of coaches without properly evaluating the results. Although there was a lot of positive, word-of-mouth press for coaching, there was no actual measure of behavior change or impact on the business. The organizations wanted a better understanding of the return they were getting on their coaching investment. They also wanted more openness about what their leaders were doing in the coaching process. They wanted to ensure that coaching assignments ended and didn't continue indefinitely.

Recently, organizations and coaches have initiated several new practices that bring greater accountability and cost effectiveness to the business of coaching. One change seeks to measure the behavior change with follow-up surveys or evaluations. Some coaching firms use minisurveys at the beginning and end of the coaching process to measure the degree of behavior change perceived by the clients' constituents.

Another innovation has been to offer flexible, shorter coaching services to fit different developmental needs and to provide coaching to more of the organization's leaders. With this flexible service, a leader might be offered six to ten hours of coaching to address a specific skill need.

Organizations that use many coaches have begun seeking some degree of consistency among coaching assignments. They have also begun looking for ways to retain the benefits of coaching while paying less or at least a better understanding of the return on their investment. Some organizations are bringing some of their coaching in-house by training internal human resource and management professionals to provide coaching to their leaders.

As the demand for coaching has grown, so has the supply of coaches. This increase in the number of coaches has resulted in an increased competitiveness in the coaching industry. It is now the norm for client organizations to interview several coaches and receive proposals from each before selecting one for a particular assignment. Some organizations have contracted with coaching firms that can provide them with certified coaches in several locations.

The increased competitiveness is causing coaches to become better marketers of their services. As with other professional services, organizations expect coaches to differentiate themselves by describing their strongest skills, their coaching style, and the types of people with whom they work best. Some coaches have begun to carve out specialty niches in particular market segments; for example, some coaches claim specialties in working with CEOs, technology executives, financial people, or creatives. As coaching grows, we should continue to see even more sophisticated marketing by coaches.

Like other industries, coaching has spawned a number of satellite industries that are growing along with it. One is the leadership assessment industry. There are now dozens, if not hundreds, of 360° assessment instruments on the market. Some are research-based, and some are not. Some can be customized to the culture and key success factors of a particular organization. Most produce attractive graphs that display the clients' results. Most are available with online administration. The variety of available instruments gives both coaches and organizations greater choice in selecting one that fits their needs and culture.

The coach training industry is another satellite industry that is growing like Topsy. In 2003, there were more than sixty private organizations offering training and certification for coaches. Many universities also offer courses and certification programs for coaches. Shortly there will be master's degree programs as well.

Research on coaching is another new and growing field. At this time, little research has been conducted on such topics as coaching outcomes, coaching approaches, or critical success factors. As coaching grows, more institutions will conduct research that generates more objective knowledge about the profession and its practice. This knowledge should enable coaches to become more effective.

The Future

Coaching is continuing to grow both in use and in sophistication. More articles and books will be written to spread knowledge of the field. More training programs will refine their curricula and train more and better coaches. More talented people will join the profession and add to it. Some coaches will invent new techniques and spread them to others. More leaders will become comfortable with the coaching process and ask for it at appropriate points in their careers. All in all, the field should continue to grow, both in quantity and quality.

Coaching will continue to contribute to the quality of leaders. These leaders will build organizations that are successful. They will also create work environments that are good places to work. They will develop employees who are competent and confident. All in all, coaches and their clients will create better workplaces and a better world.

Bibliography

Anthony, William P. *Managing Your Boss.* New York: AMACOM, 1983.

Arbinger Institute. *Leadership and Self-Deception.* San Francisco: Berrett-Koehler, 2000.

Argyris, Chris. *Knowledge for Action: Guide to Overcoming Barriers to Organizational Change.* San Francisco: Jossey-Bass.

Austin, George A., Bruner, Jerome S., and Goodnow, Jacqueline J. *A Study of Thinking.* Hoboken, N.J.: Wiley, 1956.

Bandler, Richard, and Grinder, John. *The Structure of Magic.* Palo Alto, Calif.: Science and Behavior Books, 1975.

Bass, B. *Leadership and Performance Beyond Expectations.* New York: Free Press, 1985.

Bateman, Thomas, and Organ, Dennis W. *Organizational Behavior: An Applied Psychological Approach,* 3rd ed. Burr Ridge, Ill.: Irwin, 1986.

Beck, Judith. *Cognitive Therapy: Basics and Beyond.* New York: Guilford Press, 1995.

Beer, Michael, and others. *Managing Human Assets: The Groundbreaking Harvard Business School Program.* New York: Free Press, 1984.

Bellman, Geoffrey. *Getting Things Done When You Are Not in Charge.* San Francisco: Berrett-Koehler, 1992.

Bennis, Warren, and Nanus, Bertram. *Leaders.* New York: Harper-Collins, 1985.

Benton, D. A. *Secrets of a CEO Coach.* New York: McGraw-Hill, 1999.

Blake, Robert, and Mouton, Jane. *Consultation.* Reading, Mass.: Addison-Wesley, 1976.

Blanchard, Kenneth, and Johnson, Spencer. *The One Minute Manager: The Quickest Way to Increase Your Own Prosperity.* New York: Berkley, 1981.

Block, Peter. *Flawless Consulting: A Guide to Getting Your Expertise Used.* Austin, Tex.: Learning Concepts, 1981.

Block, Peter. *The Empowered Manager: Positive Political Skills at Work.* San Francisco: Jossey-Bass, 1987.

Block, Peter. *The Answer to How Is Yes.* San Francisco: Berrett-Koehler, 2002.

Boden, Margaret A. *The Creative Mind: Myths and Mechanisms.* New York: Basic Books, 1990.

Bohm, David. *On Dialogue.* New York: Routledge, 1996.

Bolman, Lee, and Deal, Terrence. *Reframing Organizations: Artistry, Choice, and Leadership,* 2nd ed. San Francisco: Jossey-Bass, 1997.

Bolton, Robert. *People Skills: How to Assert Yourself, Listen to Others, and Resolve Conflicts.* New York: Simon & Schuster, 1979.

Bradford, David L., and Cohen, Allan R. *Influence Without Authority: The New Way to Get Things Done at Work.* Hoboken, N.J.: Wiley, 1990.

Brewi, Janice, and Brennan, Anne. *Mid-Life Psychological Perspectives.* Berwick, Me.: Nicholas-Hayes.

Burke, Warner W. *Organization Development: Principles and Practices.* Glenview, Ill.: Scott, Foresman, 1982.

Burley-Allen, Madeline. *Listening, the Forgotten Skill: A Self-Teaching Guide.* Hoboken, N.J.: Wiley, 1995.

Burns, James MacGregor. *Leadership.* New York: HarperCollins, 1978.

Buzan, Tony. *The Mind Map Book.* New York: Penguin, 1996.

Carter, Lewis, Giber, David, and Goldsmith, Marshall, eds. *Best Practices in Leadership Development Handbook: Case Studies, Instruments, Training.* San Francisco: Jossey-Bass/Pfeiffer, 2000.

Collins, Jim. *Good to Great: Why Some Companies Make the Leap . . . and Others Don't.* New York: HarperCollins, 2001.

Cooperrider, David. "Introduction to Appreciative Inquiry." In W. French and C. Bell (eds.), *Organization Development,* 5th ed. New York: Prentice Hall, 1995.

Covey, Stephen R. *7 Habits of Highly Effective People.* New York: Simon & Schuster, 1989.

Csikszentmihalyi, Mihaly. *The Evolving Self: A Psychology for the Third Millennium.* New York: HarperCollins, 1993.

Culbert, Samuel A. *Mind-Set Management: The Heart of Leadership.* New York: Oxford University Press, 1996.

Culbert, Samuel A., and Ullmen, John B. *Don't Kill the Boss: Escaping the Hierarchy Trap.* San Francisco: Berrett-Koehler, 2001.

Czarniawska, Barbara. *Narrating the Organization: Drama of Institutional Identity.* Chicago: University of Chicago Press, 1997.

De Bono, Edward. *Six Thinking Hats.* Boston: Little, Brown, 1985.

Denning, Stephen. *The Springboard: How Storytelling Ignites Action in Knowledge-Era Organizations.* Boston: Butterworth-Heinemann, 2001.

De Pree, Max. *Leadership Jazz.* New York: Dell, 1992.

Devanna, Mary Anne, and Tichy, Noel M. *The Transformational Leader.* Hoboken, N.J.: Wiley, 1986.

Dilts, Robert. *Modeling with NLP.* Capitola, Calif.: Meta, 1998.

Dixon, Nancy M. *The Organizational Learning Cycle: How We Can Learn Collectively,* 2nd ed. Brookfield, Vt.: Gower, 1999.

Donnelon, Anne. *Team Talk: The Power of Language in Team Dynamics.* Boston: Harvard Business School Press, 1996.

Drucker, Peter F. *Managing in Turbulent Times.* New York: Harper-Collins, 1980.

Erikson, Erik. *Childhood and Society.* New York: Norton, 1950.

Ertel, Danny, and Fisher, Roger. *Getting Ready to Negotiate: A Step-by-Step Guide to Preparing for Any Negotiation.* New York: Penguin, 1995.

Farrell, John D., and Weaver, Richard G. *Managers as Facilitators: A Practical Guide to Getting Work Done in a Changing Workplace.* San Francisco: Berrett-Koehler, 1997.

Farson, Richard. *Management of the Absurd.* New York: Simon & Schuster, 1996.

Finke, Robert A., Smith, Steven M., and Ward, Thomas B. *Creativity in Mind: Discovering the Genius Within.* New York: Plenum, 1995.

Fisher, Roger, and Ury, William. *Getting to Yes: Negotiating Agreement Without Giving In.* New York: Penguin, 1981.

Fitzgerald, Catherine, and Berger, Jennifer, eds. *Executive Coaching: Practices and Perspectives.* Palo Alto, Calif.: Davies-Black, 2002.

Flaherty, James. *Coaching: Evoking Excellence in Others.* Burlington, Mass.: Butterworth-Heinemann, 1999.

Fritz, Robert. *The Path of Least Resistance: Learning to Become the Creative Force in Your Own Life.* New York: Fawcett Columbine, 1984.

Fordyce, Jack K., and Weil, Raymond. *Managing with People: A Manager's Handbook of Organization Development Methods.* Boston: Addison-Wesley, 1979.

Foy, Nancy. *The Yin and Yang of Organizations.* New York: Morrow, 1980.

Friesen, G. Bruce, and Mills, D. Quinn. *Broken Promises: An Unconventional View of What Went Wrong at IBM.* Boston: Harvard Business School Press, 1996.

Gazzaniga, Michael. *The Social Brain.* New York: Basic Books, 1986.

Gentner, Dedre, and Stevens, Albert L., eds. *Mental Models.* Mahwah, N.J.: Erlbaum, 1983.

Gilligan, Carol. *In a Different Voice: Psychological Theory and Women's Development.* Cambridge, Mass.: Harvard University Press, 1982.

Goffee, Robert, and Jones, Gareth. "Why Should Anyone Be Led by You?" *Harvard Business Review*, September-October 2000, pp. 63–70.

Goldsmith, Marshall, Lyons, Laurence, Freas, Alyssa, and Witherspoon, Robert. *Coaching for Leadership: How the World's Best Coaches Help Leaders Learn.* San Francisco: Jossey-Bass, 2000.

Goleman, Daniel. *Emotional Intelligence: Why It Can Matter More Than IQ.* New York: Bantam Books, 1995.

Goss, Tracey. *The Last Word on Power: Executive Reinvention for Leader Who Must Make the Impossible Happen.* New York: Doubleday, 1996.

Hagberg, Janet O. *Real Power: Stages of Personal Power in Organizations.* Minneapolis, Minn.: Winston Press, 1984.

Hargrove, Robert. *Mastering the Art of Creative Collaboration.* New York: McGraw-Hill, 1998.

Heifetz, Ronald, and Linsky, Marty. *Leadership on the Line: Staying Alive Through the Dangers of Leading.* Watertown, Mass.: Harvard Business School Publishing, 2002.

Herman, Stanley M., and Korenich, Michael. *Authentic Management: A Gestalt Orientation to Organizations and Their Development.* Boston: Addison-Wesley, 1977.

Herzberg, Frederick. *Work and the Nature of Man.* Cleveland, Ohio: World, 1966.

Hillman, James. *Kinds of Power: A Guide to Intelligent Uses.* New York: Doubleday, 1995.

Hofstadter, Douglas. *Fluid Concepts and Creative Analogies: Computer Models of the Fundamental Mechanisms of Thought.* New York: Basic Books, 1995.

Holland, Bea Mah, Riley, Deanna, and Schiller, Marjorie, eds. *Appreciative Leaders: In the Eye of the Beholder.* Taos, N.Mex.: Taos Institute, 2001.

Hornstein, Harvey A. *Managerial Courage: Revitalizing Your Company Without Sacrificing Your Job.* Hoboken, N.J.: Wiley, 1986.

Hudson, Frederic. *The Handbook of Coaching: A Comprehensive Resource Guide for Managers, Executives, Consultants, and Human Resource Professionals.* San Francisco: Jossey-Bass, 1999.

Issacs, William. *Dialogue and the Art of Thinking Together: A Pioneering Approach to Communicating in Business and in Life.* New York: Doubleday, 1999.

James, William. *The Varieties of Religious Experience.* New York: Simon & Shuster, 1997.

Johnson-Laird, Philip N. *Mental Models.* Cambridge, Mass.: Harvard University Press, 1983.

Jung, Carl. *Collected Works. Volume 6: Psychological Types.* Princeton, N.J.: Princeton University Press, 1976.

Kahn, Robert L., and Katz, Daniel. *The Social Psychology of Organizations,* 2nd ed. Hoboken, N.J.: Wiley, 1978.

Katzenbach, Jon R., and Smith, Douglas K. *The Wisdom of Teams: Creating the High-Performance Organization* New York: HarperCollins, 1994.

Kelly, Joe. *How Managers Manage.* Upper Saddle River, N.J.: Prentice Hall, 1980.

Kennedy, Eugene. *On Becoming a Counselor: A Basic Guide for Nonprofessional Counselors.* New York: Continuum, 1988.

Kilhooly, K. J. *Thinking: Directed, Undirected, and Creative.* San Diego, Calif.: Academic Press, 1988.

Kinlaw, Dennis C. *Coaching for Commitment: Managerial Strategies for Obtaining Superior Performance.* San Francisco: Jossey-Bass/Pfeiffer, 1989.

Kirschenbaum, Howard, and Henderson, Valerie Land. *The Carl Rogers Reader.* Boston: Houghton Mifflin, 1989.

Kleiner, Art, and others. *The Fifth Discipline Fieldbook: Strategies and Tools for Building a Learning Organization.* New York: Doubleday, 1994.

Kohut, Heinz. *The Analysis of the Self.* New York: International Universities Press, 1971.

Kotter, John P. *The Leadership Factor.* New York: Free Press, 1988.

Kouzes, James M., and Posner, Barry Z. *Credibility: How Leaders Gain and Lose It, Why People Demand It.* San Francisco: Jossey-Bass, 1993.

Kouzes, James M., and Posner, Barry Z. *The Leadership Challenge: How to Keep Getting Extraordinary Things Done in Organizations.* San Francisco: Jossey-Bass, 1995.

Langer, Ellen J. *The Power of Mindful Learning.* Boston: Addison-Wesley, 1997.

Lawrence, Paul, and Nohria, Nitin. *Driven: How Human Nature Shapes Our Choices.* San Francisco: Jossey-Bass, 2002.

Le Doux, Joseph. *The Emotional Brain: The Mysterious Underpinnnings of Emotional Life.* New York: Touchstone Books, 1996.

Lepsinger, Richard, and Lucia, Antoinette D. *The Art and Science of 360° Feedback.* San Francisco: Jossey-Bass/Pfeiffer, 1997.

Levinson, Daniel J. *The Seasons of Man's Life.* New York: Ballantine Books, 1978.

Levinson, Harry. *CEO.* New York: Basic Books, 1984.

Lombardo, Michael M., and Eichinger, Robert W. *The Leadership Machine: Architecture to Develop Leaders for Any Future*. Minneapolis, Minn.: Lominger, 2000.

Lombardo, Michael M., and Eichinger, Robert W. *FYI for Your Improvement: A Development and Coaching Guide for Learners, Supervisors, Managers, Mentors, and Feedback Givers*, 4th ed. Minneapolis, Minn.: Lominger, 2004.

Lord, Robert G., Klimoski, Richard J., and Kanfer, Ruth, eds. *Emotions in the Workplace: Understanding the Structure and Role of Emotions in Organizational Behavior*. San Francisco: Jossey-Bass, 2002.

Mahesh, V. S. *Thresholds of Motivation: Nurturing Human Growth in the Organization*. New York: McGraw-Hill, 1994.

Maslow, Abraham. *Toward a Psychology of Being*. New York: Wiley, 1998.

McCall, Morgan W., Jr. *High Flyers: Developing the Next Generation of Leaders*. Boston: Harvard Business School Press, 1998.

McCall, Morgan W., Jr., Lombardo, Michael M., and Morrison, Ann M. *Lessons of Experience: How Successful Executives Develop on the Job*. San Francisco: New Lexington Press, 1988.

McGregor, Douglas. *The Human Side of Enterprise*. New York: McGraw-Hill, 1960.

Miller, James B. *The Corporate Coach: How to Build a Team of Loyal Customers and Happy Employees*. New York: St. Martin's Press, 1993.

Millman, Dan. *Way of the Peaceful Warrior: A Book That Changes Lives*. Tiburon, Calif.: Kramer, 1980.

Minsky, Marvin. *The Society of the Mind*. New York: Simon & Schuster, 1985.

Myers, Rochelle, and Ray, Michael. *Creativity in Business*. New York: Doubleday, 1989.

Neisser, Ulric. *Cognition and Reality: Principles and Implications of Cognitive Psychology*. New York: Freeman, 1976.

Nonaka, Ikujiro, and Takeuchi, Hirotaka. *The Knowledge-Creating Company: How Japanese Companies Create the Dynamics of Innovation*. New York: Oxford University Press, 1995.

O'Neill, Mary Beth. *Executive Coaching with Backbone and Heart: A Systems Approach to Engaging Leaders with Their Challenges*. San Francisco: Jossey-Bass, 2000.

Organ, Dennis W. *The Applied Psychology of Work Behavior: A Book of Readings*. Plano, Tex.: Business Publications, 1987.

Oshry, Barry. *Leading Systems: Lessons from the Power Lab*. San Francisco: Berrett-Koehler, 1999.

Osipow, Samuel H. *Theories of Career Development*, 3rd ed. Upper Saddle River, N.J.: Prentice Hall, 1983.

Pascale, Richard Tanner. *Managing on the Edge: How the Smartest Companies Use Conflict to Stay Ahead.* New York: Simon & Schuster, 1990.

Peltier, Bruce. *The Psychology of Executive Coaching: Theory and Application.* Philadelphia: Brunner-Routledge, 2001.

Perkins, David N. *The Best Mind's Work.* Cambridge, Mass.: Harvard University Press, 1981.

Perls, Fritz. *Gestalt Therapy Verbatim.* Moab, Utah: Real People Press, 1969.

Piaget, Jean. *Adaptation and Intelligence.* Chicago: University of Chicago Press, 1980.

Pinker, Steven. *How the Mind Works.* New York: Norton, 1997.

Prochaska, James O., Norcross, John C., and Di Clemente, Carlo C. *Changing for Good: The Revolutionary Program That Explains the Six Stages of Change and Teaches You How to Free Yourself from Bad Habits.* New York: Morrow, 1994.

Raelin, Joseph A. *The Clash of Cultures: Managers Managing Professionals.* Boston: Harvard Business School Press, 1985.

Robinson, Alan G., and Stern, Sam. *Corporate Creativity: How Innovation and Improvement Actually Happen.* San Francisco: Berrett-Koehler, 1997.

Rogers, Carl. *Client-Centered Therapy: Its Current Practice, Implications and Theory.* Boston: Houghton Mifflin, 1951.

Rosanoff, Nancy. *Intuition Workout: A Practical Guide to Discovering and Developing Your Inner Knowing.* Boulder Creek, Calif.: Aslan, 1998.

Rosen, Robert H. *Leading People: Transforming Business from the Inside Out.* New York: Viking, 1996.

Rosenberg, Marshall B. *Nonviolent Communication: A Language of Compassion.* Encinitas, Calif.: PuddleDancer Press, 1999.

Rowan, John. *Subpersonalities: The People Inside Us.* New York: Routledge, 1990.

Sadler, Philip. *Managing Talent: Making the Best of the Best.* London: Financial Times/Pitman, 1993.

Sapienza, Alice M. *Managing Scientists: Leadership Strategies in Research and Development.* New York: Wiley-Liss, 1995.

Satir, Virginia. *Your Many Faces.* Berkeley, Calif.: Celestial Arts, 1978.

Schank, Roger C. *Tell Me a Story: A New Look at Real and Artificial Memory.* New York: Scribner, 1990.

Schein, Edgar H. *Organizational Culture and Leadership*, 2nd ed. San Francisco: Jossey-Bass, 1992.

Schein, Edgar H. *Process Consultation Revisited.* Boston: Addison-Wesley, 1999.

Schlossberg, Nancy, and Entine, A. D. *Counseling Adults*. New York: Springer, 1995.

Schön, Donald. *The Reflective Practitioner: How Professionals Think in Action*. New York: Basic Books, 1983.

Seligman, Martin. *Learned Optimism: How to Change Your Mind and Your Life*. New York: Simon & Schuster, 1990.

Senge, Peter M. *The Fifth Discipline: The Art and Practice of the Learning Organization*. New York: Currency/Doubleday, 1990.

Shapiro, Stewart. *The Selves Inside You*. Berkeley, Calif.: Explorations Institute, 1976.

Shore, Bradd. *Culture in Mind: Cognition Culture and the Problem of Meaning*. New York: Oxford University Press, 1996.

Siegel, Allen. *Heinz Kohut and the Psychology of the Self*. New York: Routledge, 1996.

Siegel, Daniel J. *The Developing Mind: Toward a Neurobiology of Interpersonal Experience*. New York: Guilford Press, 1999.

Simon, Sidney B., Howe, Leland W., and Kirschenbaum, Howard. *Values Clarification: A Handbook of Practical Strategies for Teachers and Students*. New York: Hart, 1972.

Simonton, Dean Keith. *Genius, Creativity, and Leadership: Historiometric Inquiries*. Cambridge, Mass.: Harvard University Press, 1984.

Skinner, B. F. *Contingencies of Reinforcement: A Theoretical Analysis*. Englewood Cliffs, N.J.: Prentice Hall, 1969.

Spears, Larry C., ed. *Insights on Leadership: Service, Stewardship, Spirit, and Servant-Leadership*. Hoboken, N.J.: Wiley, 1998.

Sternberg, Robert J., ed. *The Nature of Creativity: Contemporary Psychological Perspectives*. New York: Cambridge University Press, 1988.

Sternberg, Robert J., and Wagner, Richard K. *Mind in Context: Interactionist Perspectives on Human Intelligence*. New York: Cambridge University Press, 1994.

Tannen, Deborah. *You Just Don't Understand: Women and Men in Conversation*. New York: Ballantine Books, 1990.

Vaill, Peter B. *Learning as a Way of Being: Strategies for Survival in a World of Permanent White Water*. San Francisco: Jossey-Bass, 1996.

Vaughan, Susan C. *The Talking Cure: Why Traditional Talking Therapy Offers a Better Chance for Long-Term Relief Than Any Drug*. New York: Henry Holt, 1997.

Vygotsky, Lev. *Thought and Language*. Cambridge, Mass.: MIT Press, 1962. (Rev. ed., 1986.)

Watkins, Jane M., and Mohr, Bernard. *Appreciative Inquiry*. San Francisco: Jossey-Bass/Pfeiffer, 2001.

Watzlawick, Paul. *The Language of Change: Elements of Therapeutic Communication.* New York: Norton, 1978.

Watzlawick, Paul, ed. *The Invented Reality: How Do We Know What We Believe We Know? (Contributions to Constructivism).* New York: Norton, 1984.

Watzlawick, Paul, Weakland, John H., and Fisch, Richard. *Change: Principles of Problem Formation and Problem Resolution.* New York: Norton, 1974.

Weisinger, Hendrie. *Anger at Work: Learning the Art of Anger Management on the Job.* New York: Morrow, 1995.

Wheatley, Margaret J. *Leadership and the New Science: Learning About Organization from an Orderly Universe.* San Francisco: Berrett-Koehler, 1992.

Whitworth, Laura, Kimsey-House, Henry, and Sandahl, Phil. *Co-Active Coaching: New Skills for Coaching People Toward Success in Work and Life.* Palo Alto, Calif.: Davies-Black, 1998.

Wycoff, Joyce. *Transformation Thinking: Tools and Techniques That Open the Door to Powerful New Thinking for Every Member of Your Organization.* New York: Berkley, 1995.

Zaleznik, Abraham. *The Managerial Mystique: Restoring Leadership in Business.* New York: HarperCollins, 1989.

Index of Cases

CHAPTER 2: WHAT IS LEADERSHIP?

Vision Case: Ralph #1 Finding a Vision to Guide and Energize the Work [pp. 20–21]

Managing Through Structures Case: Alice #1 Creating Structure [pp. 22–23]

Setting Expectations Case: Keith #1 Developing an Appropriate Writing Style [pp. 23–24]

Delegating Case: Bill #1 Empowerment Through Delegation [pp. 28–29]

Communicating Case: Richard #1 You Gotta Keep 'Em in the Loop [p. 30]

Influencing Case: Craig #1 Developing Influencing Skills [pp. 31–32]

Feedback Case: Martha #1 Confronting Conflict [pp. 34–35]

Rewarding and Recognizing Case: Dean #1 Using Positive Motivation [p. 38]

Team Work Case: Victor #1 Strategic Collaboration [p. 39]

Developing People Case: Paul #1 Concentrate on the People, Not the Task [pp. 40–42]

Building and Maintaining Relationship Case: Tom #1 Collaborating with Clients [pp. 42–43]

Recruiting Talent Case: Barry #1 Find and Hire the Right People [pp. 43–44]

Decision-Making Case: Peter #1 Thinking, Emotions, and Intuition— It Takes All Three [pp. 44–45]

Managerial Courage/Political Savvy Case: Bill #2 Risking Standing in the Culture [pp. 45–47]

Creating Meaning Case: Carolyn #1 Healing Discord/Renewing Commitment [pp. 48–49]

Navigating the Poles Case: Richard #2 Staying Connected [pp. 56–57]

CHAPTER 3: THE NATURE OF COACHING

Adaptation Case: Greg #1 Extending the Borders of His Tent
[pp. 66–67]

Talking Case: Keith #2 Uncovering Embedded Assumptions
[pp. 73–74]

CHAPTER 4: THE PROCESS OF BEHAVIORAL CHANGE

Mental Models Case: Bob #1 Understanding and Changing Mental
Models [pp. 79–82]

CHAPTER 5: THE PHASES OF CHANGE

Precontemplation Case: Bill #3 Getting Bad News [p. 89]

Precontemplation Case: Michael #1 Turning Up the Heat [pp. 89–90]

Contemplation Case: Keith #3 Looking Inside Himself [pp. 95–96]

Preparation Case: Bill #4 Making Progress [pp. 98–99]

Preparation Case: Keith #4 Explaining a Creative Approach [pp. 99–100]

Role Model Case: Keith #5 Selecting a Role Model [pp. 100–101]

Action Case: Keith #6 On a Roller Coaster [pp. 101–103]

Action Case: Martha #2 Back and Forth [pp. 103–104]

Maintenance Case: Martha #3 Success [pp. 105–106]

Maintenance Case: Greg #2 A New Motivation Leads to Self-
Maintenance [pp. 106–107]

CHAPTER 6: SELF-KNOWLEDGE

Self-Knowledge Case: Craig #2 Building New Influencing Skills
[pp. 110–111]

Self-Knowledge Case: David #1 Making New Inferences [pp. 118-121]

CHAPTER 7: MOTIVES FOR CHANGE

Motivation Case: Bill #5 Commitment to Change [pp. 128–129]

CHAPTER 8: STEPS IN THE COACHING PROCESS

Feedback Case: Stan #1 The Positive Use of Negative Feedback
[pp. 139–140]

Feedback Case: Carl #1 Using Feedback to Address Organizational
Issues [p. 141]

Practice Case: Craig #3 New Influencing Behaviors [pp. 148–149]

Practice Case: Keith #7 Practice, Practice, Practice [p. 150]

CHAPTER 9: COACHING SKILLS AND TECHNIQUES

Empathic Listening by the Coach Case: Greg #3 Resolving Conflicting Emotions [pp. 163–165]

Reframing by the Leader Case: Alice #2 Connecting with Others' Mental Models [pp. 168–169]

Client-Centered Teaching Case: Greg #4 Tapping into the Client's Learning Style [pp. 176–177]

CHAPTER 10: COACHING PERSPECTIVES

Cognitive Approach Case: Mitch #1 A Thinking Man's Path to Change [pp. 184–185]

Cognitive Approach Case: Mark #1 Confidence as a Road Block [pp. 186–188]

Cognitive Approach Case: Bob #2 Dialogue, Don't Dismiss [pp. 188–190]

Values Perspective Case: Tamara #1 Modifying Values to Achieve Success [pp. 191–192]

Combining Cognitive and Values Approaches Case: Tamara #2 Working with Beliefs [pp. 193–194]

Emotional Perspective Case: Jim #1 Helpless Anger [pp. 196–198]

Developmental Perspective Case: Valerie #1 Moving into a New Life Stage [pp. 199–200]

CHAPTER 11: FORCES THAT INTERFERE WITH GROWTH

Resistance Case: Ethan #1 Everything's Black and White When You're Angry [pp. 207–210]

Parts of the Self Case: Craig #4 The Other Side of the Coin [pp. 213–214]

CHAPTER 12: THE TIMING OF LEARNING AND CHANGE

Gradual Change Case: Alice #3 Integrating New Behaviors [pp. 219–220]

Gradual Change Case: Bob #3 Taking Responsibility for Change [pp. 220–221]

Delayed Learning Case: Carl #2 A Long Learning Curve [pp. 221–222]

CHAPTER 13: DISTINCTIVE APPROACHES TO COACHING

Appreciative Case: Bruce #1 When Enthusiasm Scares People [pp. 227–228]

Appreciative Case: Frank #1 Separating the Messages [pp. 228–229]

Reflection Case: Peter #2 When the Coach's Mental Model Differs from the Client's [pp. 231–232]

Coach's Intuition Case: Diane #1 Using Intuition to Help the Client Face a Reality [pp. 236–237]

Self-Revealing Case: Jane #1 When the Coach Joins the Client [pp. 238–239]

CHAPTER 14: COACHING THEMES FAMILIAR AND UNIQUE

Having to be Right Case: Louise #1 She Was Respected—and Resented [pp. 241–242]

Listening Case: Mark #2 Not Just One Listening Pattern [pp. 242–244]

Learning Empathy Case: Stan #2 Recognizing the Importance of Feelings [pp. 247–249]

Too Much Empathy Case: Ross #1 You Still Need to Have Those Difficult Conversations [pp. 249–250]

Anger Case: Tom #1 What Triggered His Outbursts? [pp. 251-254]

Anger Case: Peter #3 Preventing Hair-Trigger Reactions [pp. 254–257]

Motivation Case: Bill #6 Choosing a Motivator That Fits the Person [pp. 258–259]

Power Case: Alice #4 Refitting Her Presentation Style as a Manager [pp. 261–262]

Power Case: Marianne #1 A Creative Learns to Use Her Power [pp. 262–264]

Power Case: Brian #1 Not a Happy Manager [pp. 264–265]

Competition and Conflict Case: Valerie #2 Dealing with Challenge [pp. 265–268]

Coaching in the Political Arena Case: Greg #5 Learning to Play the Game—and Get What You Want [pp. 268–270]

Systems Thinking Case: Bill #7 The Perp Is Part of the Culture [pp. 270–271]

Refocusing Using Stakeholder Feedback Case: Greg #6 Learning to Cut to the Chase [pp. 273–274]

Understanding and Adapting to the Manager Case: Greg #7 Who Makes the First Move? [pp. 274–276]

Misreading the Signals Case: Michael #2 Just Report the Good Stuff—NOT! [pp. 276–277]

Sexuality Case: Allison #1 Cooling Unfair Gossip [pp. 278–280]

CHAPTER 15: THE BUSINESS OF COACHING

"Laser Coaching" Case: Diane #2 A Fast-Track Success [pp. 284–285]

Index

A

Aaron, 281

Abrams, L., 162

Acceptance, of need to change, 91–92. *See also* Precontemplation phase; Readiness to change

Acceptance drive, 54–57

Accountability demands, in coaching profession, 287

Acquisition drive, 12; leadership practices associated with, 15, 16, 17, 18

Action: change phase of, 85, 101–104; coaching step of, 151–153; self-consciousness in, 103–104, 151

Adaptation, coaching for, 4–5, 65–67

Age-and-stage theories, 199–200

Ambition *versus* vision, 54–57

Anger: healthy expression of, 195–198; idealism and, 256–257; intolerance and, 79, 220–221; in men, 252; nature of, 195–196; negative effects of, 250–251; resistance to changing, 207–210; self-editing approach to, 257–258; as sign of resistance, 203; underlying emotions of, 252–253; working with, 250–257

Anticipation, 101

Anxiety: anger and, 252–253; about change, 201–202, 205; about coaching, 132

Appreciative Inquiry approach, 225–229

Argyris, C., 185

Arrogance: in coaches, 8; about one's beliefs, 118–121, 185–190, 213–214; overcoming, 185–190. *See also* Egocentrism; Intolerance; Overconfidence

Assessment: in coaching process, 133–142, 265; personality, 169–173;

satellite industry for, 288. *See also* Feedback; 360-degree feedback

Assumptions: mental models and, 75–83, 182–190; semiconscious, 72–74; uncovering embedded, 73–74. *See also* Beliefs; Mental models

Attitude change, talking and, 68–69. *See also* Beliefs; Mental models; Thinking

Authenticity, 50–51, 195; power and, 260

Autocrats, 31

Awareness. *See* Emotional awareness; Self-awareness

B

Barriers, organizational *versus* personal, 149

Behavior change: coaching for self-knowledge and, 109–121; coaching steps for, 130–153; emotion and, 70–72, 115–116, 165–166, 194–198; focus on, *versus* conceptual change, 173–174; for gaining and using power, 260, 261–262; goal setting for, 143–146; map of, 156, 157; mental models and, 75–83, 182–190; multiple selves and, 210–216; neuroscience of, 70–72, 198; phases of, 84–108; process of, 75–83; questions and, 155–156; resistance to, 201–216; social science perspectives on, 181–200; talking and, 68, 70–72; thinking and, 75–83, 183–190; time frame for, 217–222. *See also* Change; Change phases

Behavioral psychology, 97, 181–182

Behaviors, new: acting with, 101–104,

151–153; defining, 143–146, 174–175; envisioning, 82; experimenting with, 83, 151–153; identifying and selecting alternative, 174–175; inventing, 98–100, 147–149; maintaining, 104–107, 151–153, 218–222; number of, 146; rehearsing and practicing, 83, 98–100, 149–150, 179–180, 219–222; role models for, 100–101

Behaviors, old: assessment of, 133–142; components of, 111–116

Beliefs: changing, 114, 184–190, 192–194, 213–214; as components of behavior, 113–114; holding *versus* letting go, 117–121; importance of, 183; ladders of thinking and, 185–190; overconfidence in, 79–82, 118–121, 185–190, 213–214, 220–221; reflecting on, 117–121; values and, 192–194

Bias: in coaches, 230; decision making and, 44–45

Birkman personality assessment, 170

Blake, R., 40

Blame and blaming, 90–91, 93, 196; as sign of resistance, 204

Body language, 62, 79; communicating power through, 260, 261–262

Body sensations, 235, 245, 253

Bonding drive, 12; leadership practices associated with, 15, 16, 17, 18

Boundary-setting, 195–198

Bruner, J., 182

C

Center for Creative Leadership, 283

Certification in coaching, 289

Change: of mental models, 77–82, 182–190; motives for, 122–129; organizational, 66–67, 167–169, 226, 270–271; process of, 75–83, 84–108; repetition and, 70–72, 153; resistance to, 201–216; talking and, 67–74, 68; transformational, 128–129; of values, 190–194. *See also* Behavior change

Change phases, 84–108; of action, 85, 101–104; coaching steps and, 130; of contemplation, 85, 86, 92–96; listed, 85–86; of maintenance and

termination, 85–86, 104–107; overview of, 84–87; of precontemplation, 85, 87–92; of preparation, 85, 86, 97–101; role of talking in, 69; self-development skills and, 5; skipping, 86–87, 108

Client-centered teaching, 175–178

Client-manager relationships, 274–277

Clients: of coaches, 271–274; of leaders, 42–43

Closed questions, 136, 156–157

Coaches: qualities of good, 8–10; roles and goals of, 64–67; self-revelation by, 237–239; subpersonalities of, 232–234; supply and demand for, 288; training and education for, 288–289; use of self by, 230–239, 257–258

Coaching: appreciative approach to, 225–229; approaches to, 225–239, 282–286; balancing individual and organizational client needs in, 271–274, 277–278; classic deficit, 225–227; classic executive, 281, 282; client-initiated *versus* imposed, 92–93; developmental themes in, 240–280; expenditures on, 286–287; goals of, 5, 63, 65–66; mentor-advisor approach to, 282–283; for motivation to change, 122–129; nature of, 61–74; as organizational intervention, 270–271; process of, 130–153; rationale for, 3–10; reflective practice in, 231–232; with resistance, 206–210; for self-knowledge, 109–121; short-term training-based, 282, 283–286; situations calling for, 4–5; skills and techniques of, 154–180; social science perspectives on, 181–200; talking and, 67–74; training combined with, 282, 283–286

Coaching profession: business and industry of, 281–289; competition in, 288; dangers of, 7–8; education and certification in, 288–289; evolution of, 281–282, 286–289; future of, 289; research on coaching and, 289; rewards of, 5–7; satellite industries to, 288–289; specialties in, 288; trends in, 286–289

Coaching steps, 130–153; of action and maintenance, 151–153; of assessment, 133–142; change process and, 130; of development planning, 131–133; of goal setting, 143–146; of initial meeting, 130–131; of preparing for change, 146–151; of rapport-building, 131–133

Cognitive-behavioral approach, 76–83, 220–221

Cognitive psychology, 76, 182–190, 192–194

Collaboration: in coaching, 62; team building and, 38–39

Commitment, 128–129, 145–146; resistance and, 204

Communication: avoiding difficult, 228–229, 249–250; balance in, 53; in client-manager relationship, 274–277; of coach with client organization, 271–274, 277–278; developing skills in, 30, 273–277; drives fulfilled by, 16; as leadership practice, 16, 29–30, 273–277

Competencies, leadership: leadership practices model of, 14–49; skill-based models of, 13–14

Competition, in coaching industry, 288

Confidentiality, 132, 271–274, 277–278

Conflict avoidance, 33, 34–36, 196–198, 284–285

Contemplation phase, 85, 86, 92–96; feedback and, 93–94, 95–96, 139

Contracting, 130–131

Cooperrider, D., 225–226

Core values. See Values

Cost effectiveness, 287

Creative guide role, 64

Creativity, in coaching profession, 6

Curiosity, as antidote to intolerance, 81–82, 187–188, 214

D

Darwin, C., 65

Decision making and problem solving: drives fulfilled by, 18; emotions and, 44–45, 247; intuition and, 44–45, 236; leaders' monopolization of, 241–242; as leadership practice, 18, 44–45; thinking and, 44–45

Defeatism, 204

Defending drive, 12; leadership practices associated with, 16

Defensiveness and defenses: to negative feedback, 138; in precontemplation phase, 88, 90–92; resistance and, 201–216

Delegating: developing skills in, 28–29; drives fulfilled by, 16; as leadership practice, 16, 25–29. See also Empowerment

Denial, 90, 203

Developing people: balancing task accomplishment with, 40–42; drives fulfilled by, 17; as leadership practice, 17, 39–42. See also Leadership development and training

Development plan, 131–133, 144–146, 171; sharing, with organization, 272

Developmental perspective, 199–200

Developmental themes, 240–280

Di Clemente, C. C., 84

Di Giorgio, R., 75

Discomfort: in action phase, 101, 102, 103–104; in change, 201–202; of changing mental models, 78–79; client-centered teaching and, 176; about coaching process, 132; in contemplation phase, 93; with feedback, 138; with giving feedback, 32–36; motivation and, 122–123; with practicing new behavior, 180; in precontemplation phase, 90–92; resistance and, 201–216; of self-awareness, 116–117

Discrepancy, feedback and, 89

Driven (Lawrence and Nohria), 12–13

Durant, W., 154

E

Egocentrism: decision making and, 44; humility and, 54; mistrust and, 27. See also Arrogance; Intolerance; Overconfidence

Einstein, A., 77

Embarrassment, fear of, 202

Emerson, R. W., 109

Emotion: awareness of, 115–116, 231–232, 244; behavior and, 165–166, 194–198; behavior change and, 70–72, 115–116, 165–166,

194–198; decision making and, 44–45, 247; empathic listening and, 163–166; expressing, 54, 195–198; feedback and, 138, 139; importance of, to leaders, 194–195; motivation and, 139; neuroscience of, 70–72, 198; resistance and, 201–202, 205; resolving conflicting, 163–166; in self-awareness, 116–117; talking and, 70; values and, 190, 191; working with, 244–258. See also Anger; Anxiety; Discomfort; Fear
Emotional awareness, building, 244–258
Emotional intelligence: components of, 244–245; emotional awareness and, 231, 255; empathy and, 244–247; feedback giving and, 36
Emotional messages, intuitive, 235
Empathy and empathic listening: balancing, with difficult communications, 228–229, 249–250; in coaching, 162–166, 232–233; developing skills in, 244–250; by feeling-oriented people, 245; sources of, 245–247; by thinking-oriented people, 245–249
Empowerment: delegating and, 25–29; developing skills in, 28–29, 45–47, 98–99; as leadership practice, 25–29; monopolization versus, 241–242; political savvy and, 45–47; systemic intervention for, 270–271. See also Delegating
Enterprise, in coaching profession, 6, 7
Enthusiasm, flipside of, 227–228
Envisioning, of new behavior, 82
Epictetus, 75
Erikson, E., 199
Expectations setting: developing realistic, 256–257; drives fulfilled by, 16; as leadership practice, 16, 23–25
Expenditures on coaching, 286–287
Experiences: debriefing, in maintenance phase, 105, 151–152, 219; examining beliefs and, 117–121, 192–194; integration of semiconscious, 72–74
Experimentation: with new behaviors and mental models, 83, 151–153; talking as first stage of, 73

Expertise power, 259
Explicit memory, 153
External rewards, as personal value, 191–192

F
Fairness, in reward systems, 36
Fear: awareness of, in coach, 230–231; of change, 202, 205, 206; in contemplation phase, 93–94; of failure, 180, 202, 252; in precontemplation phase, 87–88
Feedback: in assessment phase, 133–142; balance in, 53; conflict avoidance and, 33, 34–36, 284–285; constituent, 133–134; in contemplation phase, 93–94, 95–96, 139; to counteract learned optimism, 277; developing skills in giving, 34–35; drives fulfilled by, 17; gathering, 135–140; as leadership practice, 17, 32–36; for motivation to change, 88–90, 127, 128–129; obstacles to, 32–36; overly blunt, 35–36; for precontemplation phase, 88–90; purposes of, 133–134; vague, 33–34, 35. See also 360-degree feedback
Feeling approach to empathy, 245
Fifth Discipline, The (Senge), 76
Filtering, 53, 90, 276–277
FIRO-B, 265
Flexibility, 234
Flirtatious work relationships, 278–280
Focus versus open-mindedness, 53
Follow through, failure to, 204
Forgetting, 204
Four-drive theory, 12–14, 14–18, 126
Freud, S., 194

G
Gazzaniga, M., 211
Gentleness, 232–233
Goals, client: articulating, 124–125; commitment to, 145–146; determining, 143–146; initial talking about, 132–133; writing, in behavioral terms, 144–145
Goals and priorities setting: coaching step of, 143–146; drives fulfilled by, 16; as leadership practice, 16, 23–25
Golden mean, 52

Goldsmith, M., 272
Goleman, D., 244

H
Hair-trigger reactions, preventing, 254–257. *See also* Anger
Half-heartedness, 204
Hard work, belief in, 193–194
Harvard Business School, 12
Heifetz, R., 52
Herzberg, F., 37
Hiring. *See* Recruiting talent
Hope, in contemplation phase, 93–94
Humility: developing, 120; *versus* ego-centrism, 54
Humor, 233–234
Hygiene factor, 37

I
Idealism, 256–257
Idealistic thinking, 232
Identity, 211
Impatience, 86
Implicit memory, 153
Incompetence feelings, 78–79, 132, 151, 180; reducing, 176; resistance and, 202
Influencing: developing skills in, 31–32, 110–111; drives fulfilled by, 17; inventing new behaviors for, 148–149; as leadership practice, 17, 30–32; power and, 259–270; reframing and, 168–169; self-knowledge and, 110–111, 117–121; talking and, 68–69
Initial meeting, 130–131
Inner debate, 207
Insight, 218
Intensity, coach's, 232, 233
Interviews, 360-degree feedback, 135–136. *See also* 360-degree feedback
Intimidation, 228, 230
Intolerance, of others' ideas, 185–190, 213–214; curiosity as antidote to, 81–82, 187–188, 214; ladder-of-inference technique applied to, 118–121
Intuition: in coaching, 234–237; decision making and, 44–45, 236
Intuition Workout (Rosanoff), 234

J
James, W., 75, 165–166
Job promotion, conflicting emotions about, 163–165
Journaling, 103, 151
Judging self, 214
Judgment, empathic, 245–246
Jung, C., 199, 234

K
Kissinger, H., 281
Kohut, H., 54–55
Kouzes, J. M., 12

L
Labels and labeling: of behaviors and attitudes, 178; of emotions, 248; neural pathways and, 198; of parts of self, 214, 215–216; of resistance, 206–207, 215–216; using, in teaching, 178
Ladder of inference, 117–121, 185
Ladder of thinking, 184–185, 192
Lange, C., 165–166
Language, 62, 67
Laser coaching, 282, 283–286
Lawrence, P., 12–13
Leaderlike, acting more, 95–96, 99, 101–104
Leaders: benefits of coaching to, 4–5; demands on, 264; developmental themes of, 240–280; importance of emotions to, 194–195; importance of self-knowledge in, 109–111; organizational impacts of, 3–4
Leadership: arenas of, 49–50; checklist of practices for, 14, 15–19; definitions of, 12; dialectics of, 51–54; dimensions of, 14–58; management *versus*, 12; models of, 11–14, 49–50; motivation and, 12–14; organizational directions of, 49–50; personality styles and, 50–51; practices and skills of, 14–49, 53–54, 167; psychological polarities of, 54–57; situational applications of, 51–54
Leadership development and training: coaching combined with, 282, 283–286; competency models of, 13–14. *See also* Developing people

Leadership Development Survey, 144–145

Leadership on the Line (Heifetz and Linsky), 52

Leadership styles, 25–26

Learned optimism, 276–277

Learned Optimism (Seligman), 277

Learning: adaptation and, 65; client-centered teaching for, 175–178; of coaches, 6–7, 231–232; setting the stage for, 175–177; styles of, 176–177; time frame for, 217–222

Learning drive, 12; leadership practices associated with, 16, 17, 18

Learning theory, 181–182

Levinson, D. J., 199

Life stages, 199–200

Likert scale instruments, 142, 144–145

Linsky, M., 52

Listening: active, 99, 126; by coaches, 8–9, 62, 64, 162–166; developing skills in, 94–95, 139–140, 242–244; empathic, 162–166; using feedback to improve, 139–140

Logic, 69

Loss feelings, 78–79

Loyalties, in coaching, 271–272

M

Maintenance, 85–86, 104–107; self-, 106–107, 220–221; time frame for, 107, 218–219

Manager-client relationships, 274–277

Marketing, 288

McGregor, D., 25–26

Meaning: creating, as leadership practice, 18, 47–49; drives fulfilled by, 18

Memory: implicit and explicit, 153; semiconscious, 72–74

Mental messages, intuitive, 234–235

Mental models, 75–83; coaches' awareness of own, 230–232; cognitive psychology perspectives on, 182–190; empathic listening and, 163–166; formulating new, 147; influence of, 76–77; organizational change and, 167–169; reframing, 166–169; reinforcing new, 82–83; restating old, 203; steps in modifying, 82–83; understanding and changing, 77–82, 163–166; using feedback to revise, 138–139

Meritocracy, belief in, 193–194

Millman, D., 120

Mirror role, 64

Mixed messages, 228–229, 273–277

Moses, 281

Motivation: avoidance of negative outcome as, 253–254, 285; for change, 122–129; coaching goal and, 124–125; developing skills in, 38, 258–259; emotion and, 139; feedback for, 134; four-drive theory of, 12–14, 14–18, 126; goal setting and, 132–133; identifying, 125–128; internal and intrinsic, 36, 38, 106–107; as leadership practice, 14–18, 38, 258–259; leadership role and, 12–14; meaning and, 47–49; for power, 264–265; professional development as, 39; recognition and rewards and, 36–38; resolving conflicting, 163–165; self-psychology framework of, 54–57; for transformational change, 128–129; values and, 125–128

Mouton, J., 40

Multiple choice rating scales, 142, 144–145

Myers-Briggs Type Indicator, 170

Myers-Briggs type theory, 245

N

NASA, 32

Neural pathways, 70–72, 105, 153, 179, 198, 201

Neurolinguistic programming, 69

Neuroscience: behavior change and, 70–72, 198; multiple selves and, 211; social learning and, 153

Neutrality, 230

Nixon, R. M., 281

Nohria, N., 12–13

Norcross, J. C., 84

O

Objectivity, 230

Open-mindedness *versus* focus, 53

Open questions, 135–136, 156–157

Optimism, 103–104, 134, 136, 157, 236–237; learned, 276–277

Organizational change: adapting to, 66–67; Appreciative Inquiry approach and, 226; coaching for, 270–271; reframing technique for, 167–169

Organizational culture: empowerment and, 27–29, 270–271; high-trust *versus* low-trust, 27–29; political savvy and, 45–47

Organizational issues: systemic nature of, 141, 142, 270–271; 360-degree feedback used for, 141

Overconfidence, 79–82, 118–121, 185–190, 213–214; anger and, 220–221; as developmental theme, 240–244

P

Patience *versus* speed, 53

People orientation, in coaching profession, 5, 6

Perceptions, importance of, 140–141

Performance reviews, 32

Perls, F., 194

Persistence, as aspect of power, 260–261

Personality assessment instruments, 170–171

Personality patterns and types: assessment of, 169–173; integration of leadership practices with, 50–51; subpersonalities and, 210–216, 232–234

Pessimism, 103–104, 134, 157, 158, 205

Physical messages, intuitive sensing through, 235

Piaget, J., 182, 185

Playfulness, 232, 233–234

Political savvy: anger expression and, 197–198; coaching for, 10, 64; developing skills in, 45–47; drives fulfilled by, 18; flirtatious work relationships and, 278–280; as leadership practice, 18, 45–47; power and, 265–270

Position power, 259

Positive regard, 226–227

Positive view, 134, 277, 285. *See also* Optimism

Posner, B. Z., 12

Posture, 260, 268

Power: caveat on, 264–265; gaining and using, 259–270; indecision in exercising, 262–264; physical behaviors of, 260, 261–262, 268; political challenges and, 265–270; sources of, 259–260

Power behaviors, 219–220

Power-oriented people, 259

Power-reticent people, 259, 262–265

Practice, of new behavior, 83, 149–151, 153, 179–180, 198, 219–222. *See also* Action; Rehearsal

Practice partner role, 64

Precontemplation phase, 85, 87–92

Preparation: change phase of, 85, 86, 97–101; coaching tasks in, 146–151; determining the setting in, 97–98; inventing new behavior in, 98–100, 147–149; rehearsing in, 98–100, 149–150; role models in, 100–101; talking in, 69

Present, focus on, 65–66

Presupposition questions, 157–158

Problem solving. *See* Decision making and problem solving

Prochaska, J. O., 84, 86

Professional education in coaching, 288–289

Psychological perspectives in coaching, 9, 181–200

Psychological polarities, 54–57

Q

Questions and questioning: to analyze experimentation, 152–153; annotated example of, 156, 158–160; art of, 154–162; in coaching conversations, 9, 63; to integrate coaching perspectives, 200; map to guide, 156, 157; open and closed, 135–136, 156–157; power of, 154–156; presupposition, 157–158; selecting, 160–162; in sync with client, 162; in 360-degree feedback interviews, 135–136; working hypothesis and, 160–162

R

Rapport and rapport-building, 9–10, 62–63, 131–133

Readiness to change: determinants of, 127–128, 217–218; feedback and, 134; short-term training-based coaching and, 283, 286. *See also* Motivation; Precontemplation phase

Realism, 256–257, 285

Recognizing and rewarding: challenging for higher performance *versus*, 53; drives fulfilled by, 17; as leadership practice, 17, 36–38

Recruiting talent: development and, 39; drives fulfilled by, 18; as leadership practice, 18, 43–44

Reflective practice, 231–232

Reframing, 166–169

Rehearsal: with coach, 149–150; in preparation phase, 98–100, 149–151; in workplace, 150–151

Reinforcement: in maintenance-and-termination phase, 85–86, 104–107, 151–153; of new mental models, 82–83

Relapse, 104

Relationship, coaching, 9–10; nature of, 61–63

Relationship building and management: client-manager, 274–277; cognitive approach to improving, 184–185; developing skills in, 42–43; drives fulfilled by, 18; emotional intelligence and, 245; flirting and, 278–280; as leadership practice, 18, 42–43

Relationship power, 260

Relativist approach, 81, 261–262

Relaxation, 236

Reminders, 83

Repetition, 70–72, 153, 179, 198, 261

Reporting, on coaching progress, 271–274

Reputation, 140–141, 196, 278–280, 285

Research on coaching, 289

Resistance: to change, 201–216, 286; client-centered teaching and, 175; dealing with, 206–210; to emotional awareness, 253, 256; emotions of, 201–202; exploring multiple selves

and, 210–216; to practice, 180; short-term training-based coaching and, 286; sources of, 205–206; types and signs of, 202–204

Resource power, 259

Reward and punishment, 181–182

Reward practices. *See* Recognizing and rewarding

Right, needing to be, 240–244. *See also* Arrogance; Intolerance; Overconfidence

Risks, of managing with trust, 26, 27

Rogers, C., 226

Role models, 100–101

Role-playing, 179–180

Rosanoff, N., 234

Rosemarin, J., 283

S

Satellite industries, 288–289

Satir, V., 210

Scapegoating, 196–198

Schlossberg, N., 199

Self: coach's use of, 230–239, 257–258; polarities in, 54–57; subselves of, 210–216, 232–234

Self-awareness and self-knowledge: of beliefs, 117–121; in coaches, 230–232; coaching for, 109–121; of components of old behavior, 111–116; in contemplation phase, 92–95; difficulties of, 116–117; of emotions, 244, 248, 252–253, 255–256; empathic listening for, 163; importance of, to leaders, 109–111; influencing and, 110–111, 117–121; personality assessment for, 171, 173; in precontemplation phase, 87–92; self-psychology framework for, 54–57; of subpersonalities, 211–216, 232–234

Self-blame, 91

Self-concept, 183

Self-confidence, 186. *See also* Overconfidence

Self-consciousness, 103–104, 151, 219–220

Self-deprecation, 204

Self-development skills, 5

Self-editing approach, 257–258

Self-esteem: exercising of power and,

267–268; negative feedback and, 138; struggles with, 209
Self-promotion, 54
Self-protection skill, 195–198
Self-psychology, 54–57
Self-regulation, 245
Self-reliance, 151
Self-revelation, coach, 237–239
Self-talk, 95–96
Seligman, M., 134, 277
Selves Inside You, The (Shapiro), 201
Senge, P. M., 75, 76, 117, 185
Sensitivity, 232–233
Sensory exploration, 212
Session structure, 132
Settings: identifying, for behavior change, 97–98, 147; as triggers for old behavior, 112, 147
Sexual harassment, 278
Sexuality, in workplace, 278–280
Shame, 91
Shapiro, S., 201
Short-term training-based coaching, 282, 283–286
Siegel, A., 54
Skepticism, 93–94
Skinner, B. F., 181
Social awareness, 244. See also Empathy
Social learning, 153
Social sciences, 6–7; coaching perspectives from, 181–200
Speaking up: developing skill in, 99–100, 262; power and, 262
Specialties, coaching, 288
Speed versus patience, 53
Spock, B., 234
Spontaneity, 258
Stakeholders, of coaching, 271–274
Statements, in coaching conversations, 154–155
Stimulus for change, 218
Strategic perspective, 52
Strengths: focus on, versus weaknesses, 225–229; relating weaknesses to, 172, 227–228, 284
Structures and systems: drives fulfilled by, 15; as leadership practice, 15, 21–23
Subpersonalities: in client, 210–216; in coach, 232–234
Success, honoring and celebrating, 105–106

Survey instruments, 142, 144–145, 288
Systems, organizational, 141, 142, 270–271

T
Talent. See Recruiting talent
Talking: emotional appeal through, 70; impact of, on change, 67–74; integration of experiences and, 72–74; logic and, 69; about motivation to change, 123–124; repetition and, 70–72. See also Questioning
Task-versus-people balance, 40–42
Teaching: client-centered, 175–178; as coach role, 9, 64
Team building: creating meaning and, 48–49; drives fulfilled by, 17; as leadership practice, 17, 38–39
Theory X and Theory Y, 25–26
Thinking: changing, through talking, 67–74; cognitive psychology of, 182–190; as component of behavior, 112–113; decision making and, 44–45; developing empathy through, 246–249; emotion and behavior and, 70–72; examining, in contemplation phase, 95–96; mental models and, 75–83, 183–190; neuroscience of, 70–72, 198; types of, 183; values and, 190, 192–194
Thought partner role, 64
360-degree feedback: balance of positive and negative in, 137–138; in coaching for self-knowledge, 110, 111; conducting interviews for, 135–136; constituent interview, 135–141; for motivation to change, 128–129; negative, 89–90, 138, 236–237; for organizational issues, 141; perception in, 140–141; in precontemplation phase, 88–89; specialists in, 288; summarizing, presenting, and reviewing, 135–141, 233; survey instruments for, 142, 144–145, 288; thematic sorting of, 137. See also Feedback
Time frame: for change, 217–222; for maintenance phase, 107, 218–219; short-term versus long-term coaching and, 282–286
Toughness, 233

Training-coaching model, 282, 283–286
Transformational change, 128–129
Triggers, 112, 147
Trust and trust building: in coaching relationship, 63; delegating and, 25–29; influence and, 31; in intuition, 236; obstacles to, 27–28; organizational culture and, 27–29; in precontemplation phase, 88

U
Uptalk, 262

V
Valliant, G., 199
Value differences: creating meaning and, 48; motivation and, 125; rewards and, 36
Values: beliefs and, 192–194; emotions and, 190, 191; examples of work-related, 190; modifying, 191–194; motivation and, 125–128; perspective of, in coaching, 190–194; role of, in behavior, 114, 190–191

Verbatim quotes, from feedback, 136, 137–138
Vision and vision framing: drives fulfilled by, 15; as leadership practice, 15, 19–21; open-mindedness and, 53; personal ambition and, 54–57
Visual learning and teaching, 177
Voice, 260, 262

W
Way of the Peaceful Warrior (Millman), 120
Weaknesses, relating strengths to, 172, 227–228, 284
Wishes, 71–72, 132, 133
Working hypothesis, 160–162
Writing style improvement, 23–25
Written feedback summary, 137–138

X
Xerox Corporation, 286

Z
Zaleznik, A., 12
Zen Buddhism, 52